The Passion of Our Lord

The Passion of Our Lord

Erich H. Kiehl

BAKER BOOK HOUSE
Grand Rapids, Michigan 49516

Printed in the United States of America

Library of Congress Cataloging-in-Publication Data

Kiehl, Erich H., 1920–
    The Passion of Our Lord / Erich H. Kiehl.
        p.   cm.
    Includes bibliographical references and indexes.
    ISBN 0-8010-5286-6
        1. Jesus Christ—Biography—Passion Week. 2. Bible. N. T. Gospels—Criticism,
interpretation, etc. I. Title.
    BT414.K45   1990
    232.96—dc20   90-37618
                                                              CIP

Unless noted otherwise, the Scripture quotations are the author's personal translation. The versions which have been cited are the New American Standard Bible (NASB), the New International Version (NIV), and the Revised Standard Version (RSV).

Contents

123542

Illustrations

Maps

Photos

Figures

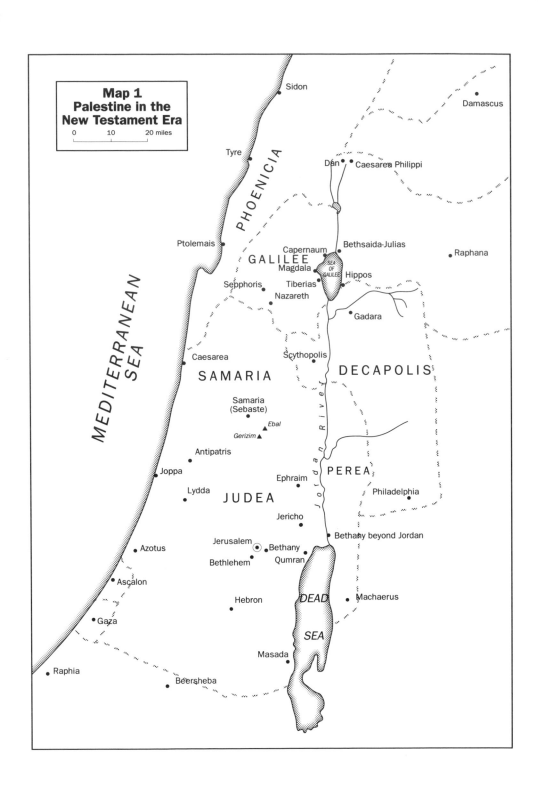

Map 1
Palestine in the
New Testament Era

0   10   20 miles

Preface

Central to the Christian faith is Christ's redemptive work, climaxed in his passion, death, resurrection, and ascension. The apostle Paul carefully stresses this in Galatians 3:13–14; 1 Corinthians 15; Romans 3–8; Ephesians 1:4–7; and Colossians 1:13–20 as well as elsewhere in his writings. To fully understand the true significance of Christ's redemptive work, it is important to be well acquainted with the total context of the decisive events in his life and ministry.

In 1969, Josef Blinzler's monumental work *Der Prozess Jesu* appeared in its fourth revised edition. He died some months later. Also published in 1969 was the English translation of *The Passion and Resurrection of Jesus Christ,* a study by Pierre Benoit of the Ecole Biblique in Jerusalem. This was followed in 1973 by his *Jesus and the Gospel,* volume 1, which contains a number of updated chapters on Jesus' passion.

Recent years have seen the appearance of a number of titles with the emphasis on tradition history as seen from various critical viewpoints. These generally stress the subjective opinions of modern scholars rather than let each of the Gospel writers speak on his own terms within the total context of the events of the passion.

A basic purpose of the present title is to let each of the Gospel writers speak on his own terms regarding Jesus' passion. At the same time careful attention is paid to the total setting, for example, the messianic expectations, both the Jewish and Roman law of that time, the topography of Jerusalem, the historical sites where these events took place, and recent archeological researches, including the 1968 discovery of the bones of a man crucified in the first half of the first century A.D. Thus far these are the only remains to have been found of the many

thousands crucified in the immediate area of Jerusalem prior
to its fall in 70 A.D. We will also note that some of the Dead Sea
Scrolls shed helpful light on the subject of Jesus' crucifixion.
These are a few of the various sources upon which we will
draw as we examine in detail the passion of our Lord.

A word of deep appreciation is due to Mark Schuler, who, as
a doctoral candidate, provided much helpful information, and
also to my wife for her constant encouragement and understanding. My prayer is that the chapters which follow will provide the reader with a clearer understanding of the climactic
role of Jesus as the obedient Suffering and then Victorious
Servant.

1

Messianic Hopes and the Coming of Jesus

God's Covenant with His Chosen People

Crucial for understanding the people's reaction to Jesus' ministry is their misunderstanding of the covenant relationship with God. As Paul so carefully points out in his letter to the Galatians, the covenant relationship was strictly a relationship of grace, of undeserved love rather than merit. To understand this distinction requires a quick summary of the Old Testament.

Before speaking words of judgment after the fall of Adam and Eve, God spoke the word of grace recorded in Genesis 3:15: the woman's Seed would crush the evil one. This promise set the stage for all subsequent events.

God promised Noah that Japheth would dwell in the tents of Shem (Gen. 9:27a). Years later God called Abraham to leave the city of Haran and go to Canaan. He promised, "In you shall all the families of the earth be blessed" (Gen. 12:3). God repeated this promise a number of times (Gen. 17:1–8; 22:18). God also told Abraham that although his descendants would be strangers in a foreign land for four hundred years, they would return to the land of Canaan (Gen. 15:13–16).

The opening chapters of Exodus speak of the status of Abraham's descendants as slaves in Egypt, as chattel to be used for the benefit of the state. But according to Exodus 2:24, "God remembered his covenant with Abraham, Isaac, and Jacob." In keeping with his promise to Abraham, God called Moses to lead Abraham's descendants out of Egypt with a mighty hand.

In the plagues God mocked the gods of Egypt, which were personified powers of nature. For example, the ninth plague of dense darkness showed the impotence of the great Egyptian sun-god, Amon-Re.[1] God destroyed Pharaoh's military might in the Red Sea. Through these actions God made the children of Israel a free people. He provided for them and led them to Mount Sinai, where he formally received them as his covenant people in accordance with his promise in Genesis 12.

The setting and the words spoken underline that this historical event was strictly a matter of grace. Note that God told his people Israel: "You yourselves have seen what I did to the Egyptians, and how I carried you on eagles' wings and brought you to myself" (Exod. 19:4). He also said: "I am the LORD your God, who brought you out of Egypt, out of the land of slavery" (Exod. 20:2 NIV). As the people prepared to cross the Jordan forty years later, God through Moses reminded them, "The LORD did not set his affection on you and choose you because you were more in number than other peoples, for you were the fewest of all peoples" (Deut. 7:7). These passages stress that the special status accorded the people of Israel was due totally to God's grace.

At Mount Sinai God laid down the covenant:

1. The people would have a special status which was due to his grace.
2. God himself would be their King and would guide, provide for, and protect them.
3. The people would live according to the guidelines of the covenant.
4. They would be God's own people, a nation set apart, royal priests.
5. In the strategic central location of Canaan they would witness to the rest of the nations with life and lips.
6. The covenant would involve judgment: how they lived as God's covenant people would determine whether they would be saved or condemned.

God kept his promise to give the descendants of Abraham the land of Canaan as the covenant land. Unfortunately they failed to destroy all the pagans living there. As God had warned them (Deut. 7:1–6), Israel's failure to destroy the Canaanites and their fertility gods, which so intimately reflected the capricious climate and the agricultural vocations of Canaan, ultimately led to the downfall of Israel as a nation.

The great golden era of David and Solomon gave way to a divided nation. The northern kingdom fell into the worship of the fertility gods. Through prophets like Elijah and Elisha, God sought to call the northern kingdom back to covenant living. During the silver era of great prosperity God sent the prophets Amos and Hosea to call Israel back. Amos's urgent message may be summarized, "The kingdom of Israel is not the kingdom of God!"[2]

When Israel failed to listen, its history came to an end in 722 B.C. Its capital Samaria fell, and the people were taken into exile. But Judah also failed to listen to prophets such as Isaiah and Jeremiah. In 587 B.C. the Babylonians destroyed Jerusalem and the temple in accordance with Isaiah's prophecy (Isa. 39:5–7) and the repeated warnings of Jeremiah. The covenant people were deprived of their special status; the covenant land was lost.

Messianic Expectations

Nonetheless, God's covenant of grace remained. The Babylonian exile and the challenging postexilic period had a profound effect on the people. They learned that God alone is God—monotheism. They increasingly became a law-orientated people. They were concerned to gather and preserve the sacred documents of the Scriptures. The institution of the synagog became firmly established. Israel remembered God's promises of the Messiah and, because of their painful experiences, molded and shaped these promises to envision a Messiah whose coming would usher in a glorious and victorious era on earth.

God's promises sustained the people as their political situation again deteriorated. After a century of subjection to the Ptolemies, Palestine fell to the Seleucids in 198 B.C.

Antiochus IV tried to force paganism on the Jews and virtually suspended the practice of their ancestral faith (1 Macc. 1:41–43). His tyranny resulted in the Maccabean revolt (168 B.C.). Warfare against the Seleucids and internecine strife continued for years. Still, at the death of John Hyrcanus in 104

B.C., the Hasmonean (Jewish) realm had reached its greatest extent since Solomon's time.

Hyrcanus's successors were unprincipled characters. Their thirst for personal power and military conquest was marked by family jealousy, intrigue, and murder. As a result, they forfeited the good will of the Jewish nation. After the death of Alexander Jannaeus, his wife, Salome Alexandra, ushered in a brief golden age. Her death in 67 B.C. led to strife between her two sons. In 63 B.C. the Roman general Pompey took over Palestine and made it part of the Roman Empire.

These events are mirrored in the noncanonical Psalms of Solomon, which date from the first century B.C.[3] Psalm 17 is of special importance, for it describes the reaction of the Jews (and, it is thought, especially of the Pharisees) to all that the Jews in Palestine had gone through. This noncanonical psalm reflects the messianic prophecies of the Old Testament and their misinterpretation by the Jews. It is an expression of their hopes and dreams as an oppressed and pious people. These same hopes are also reflected in the reactions of those who heard the words of Jesus and witnessed his deeds.

What are the key points of these Jewish messianic expectations? First of all, in keeping with God's promises his Spirit would return to the covenant land (Isa. 40:3–5; Mal. 3:1; 4:5–6). God would send the Messiah of David's line (2 Sam. 7:12–16; Jer. 23:5–6; Mic. 5:2), who would free his covenant people and land from the hated Roman rule. It was expected that the Messiah would be only a human being and not divine, despite the prophecies of Isaiah (7:14; 9:6–7). He would be chosen by God for this awesome task and filled with his Spirit (Isa. 11). In contrast to the wicked kings that had ruled Israel since before the exile (see 1 Sam. 8:10–18), he would be a just and righteous ruler (see Deut. 17:14–20), serving as God's messianic agent.

The Messiah's coming would initially be marked by judgment. Gentiles and wicked Jews would be destroyed, including tax collectors, prostitutes, and other public sinners. Then God's children would be set free and empowered to live fully as his covenant people.

This activity of the Messiah would usher in an age of heaven on earth. The literature of these messianic expectations uses the imagery of the year of jubilee (Lev. 25:8–55). There would always be an abundance of food with little toil and work—a great blessing to the Jews, for Palestine's climate is very capricious. Hunger and starvation were a constant threat. Heavy taxation and the fact that much of the country had been taken over by rich landowners, both Jews and Gentiles, kept many living at a bare subsistence level.[4] These factors resulted in the dream of a constant abundance of food in the messianic age.

In keeping with the prophecies of Isaiah (29:18; 35:3–6; 42:6–7; 61:1–3), the people also thought that, like hunger, all sorrow, sickness, and death would vanish in the glorious period of the earthly Messiah. Eventually, Gentiles would stream to the light to become part of the earthly messianic bliss as proselytes (Isa. 60). And then, sometime in the indefinite future a new heaven and a new earth would come. Just what that meant and when it would come were matters of debate.[5]

Reactions to Jesus' Words and Deeds

These messianic expectations were bound to color the people's reaction to Jesus. We must look first, however, at John the Baptist, who began his ministry at Bethany beyond Jordan, the strategic international ford of the Jordan River near Jericho. Matthew's account gives this summary of his message: "Repent, for the kingdom of heaven [God] is here" (Matt. 3:2). John's message attracted many from all over the land of Palestine. His popularity induced even the Pharisees and Sadducees to come to his baptism, but to them John spoke words of condemnation (Matt. 3:7–10; Luke 3:7–9).

When the Sanhedrin sent an official committee of inquiry to John, he avoided all identifications loaded with earthly messianic overtones, but simply replied in the words of Isaiah 40:3, "I am the voice of one crying in the desert, 'Prepare the way for the Lord.'" He told his inquirers of one who was much greater than he and who even then stood among them (John 1:19–28). Later, John twice pointed out Jesus as "the Lamb of God who takes away the sins of the world" (John 1:29, 36).

Matthew records that Jesus' message, like that of John, was "Repent; the kingdom of heaven is here!" (4:17). But the people heard something completely different from what Jesus meant. They understood the "kingdom of heaven" to mean the glorious coming of the earthly messianic age which they so anxiously awaited. In their view the kingdom was long overdue. This was what God owed them after so many years of anxious waiting and much suffering. For many the imperative "Repent!" was out of place. Because of their attempt to live as God's faithful people, there was no need for them to repent.

Jesus' words attracted much attention, for he taught as one who had authority and not as the scribes (Matt. 7:29). The many miracles which he did in keeping with his Father's will also caught the people's attention.[6] While at a feast in Jerusalem, Jesus healed an invalid at the Pool of Bethesda on the Sabbath and told the man to take his bed and go home (John 5). This act aroused the enmity of the Jewish leaders. Since the man's life was not in danger, they considered it illegal for Jesus to heal him on the Sabbath.

In the ensuing dialog between Jesus and the Jewish leaders, he stressed the crucial role of this miracle. It witnessed that he was the certified agent of the Father. As A. E. Harvey carefully documents, Jewish law placed heavy emphasis on proper witness and certified agents.[7] After the feeding of the five thousand (John 6) and in healing the young man born blind (John 9) Jesus again stressed that the Father was the source of his authority. But his authoritative teaching and his signs and miracles earned him the enmity of the Jewish leaders.

Especially noteworthy in Jesus' teaching is his use of parables. Although the Greek word *parabolē* has the general meaning of any kind of analogy, Jesus' parables consisted of stories of everyday life which illustrated spiritual principles. In Matthew, Jesus usually begins each parable with a phrase which is properly translated: "It is with the kingdom of God as with . . . ," or "The kingdom of God may be compared to. . . ." With but a few exceptions (the parable of the sower [Matt. 13:3–9, 18–23; Mark 4:3–9, 14–20; Luke 8:5–8, 11–15] and that of the weeds [Matt. 13:24–30, 36–43]), Jesus did not interpret his parables. His purpose was to cause people to ponder what he was saying, so that, through the Spirit's work, they might arrive at the true spiritual meaning of the parable. The problem was that his hearers seemed always to identify any reference to the kingdom of God with a glorious earthly reign of the Messiah for whom they so urgently longed.[8]

A careful reading of the Gospels underlines that Jesus' disciples also shared the common messianic view. Consider, for example, what Peter must have had in mind when he declared that Jesus was the Christ (Matt. 16:13–20; Mark 8:27–30; Luke 9:18–21). Immediately after Peter's noble confession Jesus told his disciples "how he must go to Jerusalem, and suffer many things of the elders and chief priests and scribes, and be killed, and the third day be raised up." Peter rebuked him, "God forbid it, Lord! This shall never happen to you!" Jesus replied, "Get behind me, Satan! You are a stumbling block to me; for you are not setting your mind on the things of God, but of men" (Matt. 16:21–23).

This event took place shortly before Jesus' transfiguration, in the late summer or fall before his passion. It is interesting to note that the disciples continued to misunderstand the true nature of Jesus' mission. Their actions at the Passover meal are a dramatic example. And even after Jesus' resurrection, moments before his ascension, they still asked, "Lord, do you at this time restore the kingdom to Israel?" (Acts 1:6). Note the meaning and implications of their question.

It took the unfolding of God's plan at Pentecost and subsequent events for the disciples to understand more fully the true nature and significance of Jesus' coming, climaxed by his passion, death, resurrection, and ascension. Only then did they begin to understand what their true role was to be in the eternal plan of God.

2

Up to Jerusalem

The Raising of Lazarus and Its Aftermath

In the closing weeks of his ministry, Jesus interrupted his activity in Perea, east of the Jordan, to go to Bethany to raise Lazarus from the dead (John 11:1–44). John underlines the harsh certainty of Lazarus's death. He notes that Jesus ordered the stone to be removed from the entrance to the tomb, and that Martha told Jesus: "Lord, he stinks; he has been dead four days!" (v. 39). John graphically describes how Lazarus came out of the tomb, his body wrapped in graveclothes and his face covered. This moved Jesus to order, "Unwind the graveclothes and let him go!" (v. 44).

John notes the reaction of those present. Some believed on Jesus, but others informed the Pharisees of what Jesus had done. Ever since the healing of the invalid on the Sabbath and the ensuing dialog, the Pharisees, termed "the Jews" in John 5:16, had been angry with Jesus. John notes that "they kept on seeking to execute him, because not only did he keep on breaking the Sabbath, but he kept on saying that God was his Father, making himself equal with God" (v. 18).

The result was that the "chief priests and Pharisees" (John 11:47)—a term here seemingly used for the Jewish council and further identified as the "Sanhedrin"—convened to consider action.[1] The fact that Jesus had raised Lazarus from the dead was beyond dispute. This was a tremendous miracle. The council was concerned about the reaction of the people to Jesus. How would they react now that the Passover was drawing near, a time when messianic expectations could run rampant? And

how would the Romans react, if they suspected an uprising on
the part of the Jewish masses? From the events of 4 B.C. after
Herod's death the council knew how purposefully the Romans
could act in times of crisis. At that time two thousand rebels
were crucified.[2] Accordingly, the council feared the Romans
might now take away both their "place" and "nation" (v. 48). In
this instance "place" refers to the temple (cf. John 4:20; Acts
6:13; 7:7; 21:28; 2 Macc. 5:19) and "nation" to the Jewish people (2 Macc. 1:29).

The leading role at the council meeting was taken by Caiaphas, "who was high priest that year" (John 11:49). (History
informs us that Caiaphas served as high priest from ca. A.D. 18
to 36. "That year" probably refers to the year in which Jesus'
passion took place.[3]) It is important to remember that the
Roman governor could depose the high priest at any time.[4]
The possibility of a popular uprising against Rome in the quest
for an earthly messianic kingdom would threaten not only the
Jewish nation, but above all the privileged position of the council and its members. And so Caiaphas stressed that it was better for one man, namely Jesus, to be executed than for the
nation to face disaster at the hands of the Romans. The tone of
his words is an example of the rudeness which characterized
the Sadducees. Caiaphas contemptuously regarded the other
council members as ignorant. John notes, however, that the
substance of the priest's words was from God.

In verse 50 we find the words *laos* and *ethnos:* "it is better . . .
that one man die for the people *(laos)* than that the whole
nation *(ethnos)* perish" (NIV). In the New Testament, the word
laos is the usual term for God's covenant people. The word *ethnos* is a general term for the Gentiles. However, here Caiaphas
uses *ethnos* for the Jewish nation. Obviously the priest had no
conception of the full import of his words: Christ's victorious
suffering, death, and resurrection would result in the gathering
of "the children of God scattered abroad," both Jews and
Gentiles, to become members of God's family (vv. 51–52; cf.
1 Pet. 1:1).[5]

John proceeds to note that Jesus and his disciples traveled
north around twenty miles to a town called Ephraim, which
was near the wilderness (v. 54). Ephraim has often been identified with a village known today as et-Taiyibeh.[6] However, inas-
much as Jesus went into a quiet retreat with his disciples, there

is another place which better fits the requirements. This site is known today as 'Ain Samniya. It is closer to the edge of the hills bordering the Jordan Valley. It is an ideal place for retreat in early spring. Because of its low altitude, it is warmer than et-Taiyibeh and has plenty of water. Around the sides of the valley of 'Ain Samniya are many shallow caves to provide shelter.[7]

Jesus' Final Journey to Jerusalem

After some time had passed, Jesus and his disciples walked from Ephraim through Samaria to join the Galilean pilgrims on their journey down to Jerusalem for the Passover. Near the border of Samaria and western Perea he healed ten lepers, only one of whom—a Samaritan—returned to thank him (Luke 17:11–19).

Pilgrims going from Galilee to Jerusalem walked down the valley on the east side of the Jordan in order to avoid Samaria. The relations between the Jews and the Samaritans were any-thing but cordial, as an earlier experience of Jesus and his disciples indicates (Luke 9:51–56). In addition, travel was more difficult in the hilly terrain of the area west of the Jordan than in the flat terrain east of the Jordan. The Jordan Valley south of the Sea of Galilee varies from about 700 to 1,000 feet below sea level. The effect on temperature made travel at the time of the Passover much more appealing than travel in summer.

The approach of the Passover was a time of great messianic expectation. In Jewish thought, the best possible time for the Messiah to appear would be at this festival. Several events which took place during Jesus' journey to Jerusalem with the pilgrims on the east side of the Jordan seem to indicate that the coming kingdom was on everyone's mind.

When the disciples rebuked those who brought little children to Jesus, he said: "Permit the little children to come to me, and forbid them not; for of such is the kingdom of God. Truly I say to you, whoever shall not receive the kingdom of God as a little child, shall in no wise enter it" (Luke 18:16–17). This event, together with the episode of the rich young man who asked, "What shall I do to inherit eternal life?" (Matt. 19:16–26; Mark 10:17–27; Luke 18:18–27), refutes the mistaken Jewish view that one could qualify for the messianic kingdom through merit. The same thought is reflected in Peter's question: "We have left all and followed you. What shall we have?" (Matt. 19:27). Jesus' reply stressed that grace, not merit, is decisive (Matt. 19:28–20:16; Mark 10:28–31; Luke 18:28–30).

Soon afterwards Jesus again told his disciples of his coming passion, to be followed by his resurrection on the third day (Matt. 20:17–19; Mark 10:32–34; Luke 18:31–34). Seemingly right after this, Salome, the mother of James and John, asked Jesus to promise that one son would sit at his right and the other at his left in his earthly messianic glory. Jesus responded by correcting their mistaken view of his messianic role. He again stated that his role was "to serve and to give his life as a ransom for many" (Matt. 20:20–28; Mark 10:35–45).

Having crossed the Jordan River, Jesus was greeted in Jericho by blind Bartimaeus and his companion with the cry, "Jesus, Son of David, have mercy on us!" The term "Son of David" goes back to God's promise through his prophet Nathan to David (2 Sam. 7:12–16). In the past, Jesus had discouraged anyone who called him "Son of David," probably because of the messianic misconceptions of the people (see Matt. 9:27–31; 15:22–24). But now he accepted the title and gave sight to both men. Luke notes that the people praised God. For the first time Jesus had accepted this crucial messianic title (Matt. 20:29–34; Mark 10:46–52; Luke 18:35–43).

Jesus went on to suburban Jericho, which lay to the southwest of the site of Old Testament Jericho. It was home for many wealthy. Splendid palaces of the Hasmoneans and of Herod have been excavated. Here Jesus went into the house of Zacchaeus, the director of customs in the lucrative Jericho area (Luke 19:1–10). When the people saw that Jesus went into the house of a tax collector, they murmured. For, as Luke stresses (v. 11), they thought that Jesus was about to usher in a glorious messianic reign on earth. Yet here he was socializing with a tax collector for the Romans, an individual who would undoubtedly be executed at the coming of the Messiah.[8] Jesus answered with the parable of the pounds (vv. 12–27). Then he walked up to Bethany with his disciples; in the process they climbed around 3,000 feet in about 15 miles (John 12:1).

Chronological Framework

John 12:1 provides very important time information. John notes that six days before the Passover Jesus came to Bethany, the home of Lazarus, whom Jesus had raised from the dead. This verse helps to establish a chronological framework for the week of Jesus' passion.

In working with this helpful time reference, it must be kept in mind that the Sabbath began on Friday evening at sunset and continued until sunset on Saturday. It must also be noted that Matthew 26:1–16 and Mark 14:1–11 provide essential time information, namely, that two days before the Passover (Thursday) Jesus was anointed and Judas arranged with the council to betray him. A proper study requires that one always note the interrelationships of events as recorded in the four Gospels.

The phrase "six days before the Passover" indicates that Jesus and his disciples arrived in Bethany sometime on Friday before sunset when the Sabbath began and all travel ceased (John 12:1). The triumphant entry into Jerusalem took place on the second day after Jesus' arrival, namely, on Sunday. The third day, Monday, witnessed Jesus' cleansing of the temple. The fourth day, Tuesday, was a busy day during which members of the council sought to entrap him. Later in the day Jesus privately spoke to his disciples on the Mount of Olives (Matt. 24–25). His anointing at Bethany in the house of Simon took place in the late afternoon or the early evening of Tuesday.

The Gospels do not provide information as to Jesus' activities on Wednesday, the fifth day. It was on Thursday morning, the sixth day, that Jesus' disciples reminded him of the urgent need to make preparations for the Passover to be eaten that evening. All this dovetails with the information provided by John 12:1. Further, all the information provided in the Gospels indicates that Jesus ate the Passover on Thursday, that is, at the same time as did all the residents of Jerusalem and the pilgrims who had come to observe the Passover (see chap. 5). Such were the events of the week preceding the crucifixion and resurrection.

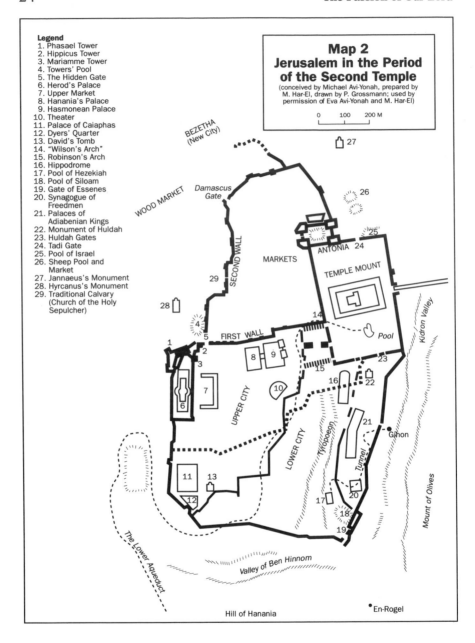

Legend
1. Phasael Tower
2. Hippicus Tower
3. Mariamme Tower
4. Towers' Pool
5. The Hidden Gate
6. Herod's Palace
7. Upper Market
8. Hanania's Palace
9. Hasmonean Palace
10. Theater
11. Palace of Caiaphas
12. Dyers' Quarter
13. David's Tomb
14. "Wilson's Arch"
15. Robinson's Arch
16. Hippodrome
17. Pool of Hezekiah
18. Pool of Siloam
19. Gate of Essenes
20. Synagogue of
    Freedmen
21. Palaces of
    Adiabenian Kings
22. Monument of Huldah
23. Huldah Gates
24. Tadi Gate
25. Pool of Israel
26. Sheep Pool and
    Market
27. Jannaeus's Monument
28. Hyrcanus's Monument
29. Traditional Calvary
    (Church of the Holy
    Sepulcher)

Map 2
Jerusalem in the Period
of the Second Temple
(conceived by Michael Avi-Yonah, prepared by
M. Har-El, drawn by P. Grossmann; used by
permission of Eva Avi-Yonah and M. Har-El)

0   100   200 M

3

The Opening Days
of Holy Week

(Matt. 21:1–22; Mark 11:1–25; Luke 19:28–48;
John 12:12–50)

The Geographical Setting

The Population of First-Century Jerusalem

Joachim Jeremias spent several years early in his life as a
resident of Jerusalem. This experience is evident in his encyclo-
pedic study entitled *Jerusalem in the Time of Jesus*.[1] Knowing
well the geographical setting and also the topography of
Jerusalem, he undertook a study of the possible size of the population of Jerusalem in the first century A.D. He also sought to
discover the number of pilgrims who could have been accommodated within the area of Jerusalem at each of the three great
festivals.

Jeremias notes that the figures given in the works of
Josephus for the number of pilgrims as well as the population
of Jerusalem are unreliable. This is true also of the statistics
given by Tacitus, who probably was indebted for his information to Josephus. Jeremias suggests that the area within the
city walls (excluding, of course, the temple and other public
buildings) permitted a population of about 20,000. The suburban area outside the walls permitted a population of between
5,000 and 10,000. The upper limit for the population of
Jerusalem, then, would have been somewhere between 25,000
and 30,000.

Relevant to our study of the passion of our Lord is the number of pilgrims who could have been accommodated for the Passover. An essential consideration here is the number of lambs which could have been brought to the Court of the Priests to have their throats cut and their blood poured out at the altar of burnt offering during the afternoon in sufficient time to be prepared for the Passover meal. Jeremias regarded figures of 18,000 lambs and 180,000 people as a bit too high.[2] Perhaps figures of 10,000 lambs and 150,000 people are somewhat more realistic.

A basic question follows: How and where could such a large number of pilgrims be accommodated within the metropolitan area of Jerusalem? Some pilgrims may have been able to stay with relatives or friends, or in hostels attached to synagogs. Most of them probably camped out in designated areas outside the walls of Jerusalem.[3] Historical records indicate that burial sites were whitewashed to prevent people from inadvertently stepping on graves, thereby becoming ceremonially unclean for seven days and unable to participate in the festival events.

The Mount of Olives

Pilgrims coming from Galilee and Perea probably camped out on the Mount of Olives, the top of which was not cultivated nor covered with buildings in the New Testament era.[4] The Mount of Olives is a 2½-mile spur of the Central Mountain Range, separated from the immediate area of Jerusalem by the Kidron Valley. Sources differ on the elevations. An official survey map of the Jerusalem area indicates that the highest part, which is in the north and known today as Mount Scopus, has an elevation of almost 2,700 feet above sea level. The next highest part, which is occupied by the Byzantine Church of the Ascension, has an elevation of over 2,600 feet. From there the elevation drops to around 2,400 feet. Bethany (el-'Azariyeh today) lay near the southeastern end of the Mount of Olives. Its elevation was probably a bit over 2,100 feet. The southern part of the Mount of Olives comes to an end where the Kidron Valley winds its way to the east into the Wilderness of Judea.

Presently the road from Jerusalem to Jericho crosses the Kidron Valley at Gethsemane, continues southward along the western slope of the Mount of Olives, turns east through the village of Bethany, and then winds its way through the

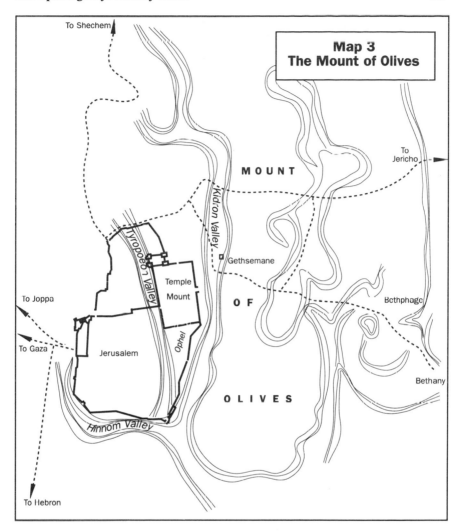

Wilderness of Judea down to Jericho. In Jesus' day a different route was followed. The road to Jericho climbed to the top of the ridge of the central part of the Mount of Olives near where the Lutheran World Federation Hospital is located today. This was also the route of the later Roman road to Jericho.[5]

Sunday: The Triumphal Entry

Scripture sheds no light on Jesus' activity on his last Sabbath day (Saturday). However, on the following day Jesus and his disciples left the area of Bethany, where they had been staying, to go to Jerusalem. (For the journey and entry into Jerusalem see Matt. 21:1–11, 14–17; Mark 11:1–11a; Luke 19:28–44; John 12:12–19.) They climbed the ridge of the Mount of Olives to the area of Bethphage (Matt. 21:1) and then descended on one of the two roads to Jerusalem.

Some overlook the fact that the road from Jericho to Jerusalem in Jesus' day did not pass through Bethany but climbed to the middle part of the Mount of Olives, descended into the upper Kidron Valley, and then went on to Jerusalem. Just where Bethphage lay is somewhat uncertain, but it was apparently a village on the Mount of Olives close to Jerusalem. It was probably located in the area known today as Kefr et-Tur.[6] In rabbinic literature it is described as being within the precincts of Jerusalem, where items were prepared for use in the temple.[7]

When Jesus and his disciples neared Bethphage, he sent two of them ahead to fetch a donkey and her colt. Matthew 21:2 uses the word *onos*. John 12:15 uses the same word, but verse 14 uses the term *onarion*. Both Greek words mean "donkey."[8] When mother and colt had been brought to Jesus (Matt. 21:2, 7), the disciples put their garments on the colt. It is important to note that Jesus rode the colt, which, as both Mark 11:2 and Luke 19:30 record, had not as yet been ridden. Hence, it could be used for sacred purposes (cf. Num. 19:2; Deut. 21:3). In this manner, Jesus made his messianic entrance into Jerusalem.

As Jesus and his company made their way into Jerusalem, they were joined by a multitude of people. Probably these were the Galilean and Perean pilgrims who had come for the Passover and were staying on the Mount of Olives, which figured prominently in their expectations of the Messiah (Ezek. 43:1–4; Zech. 14:3–8). At least some of them had heard Jesus accept the messianic title "Son of David" in Jericho two days before (Matt. 20:29–34; Mark 10:46–52; Luke 18:35–43). Many of the people spread their garments on the road. Others cut branches from trees and spread them on the way. These actions recalled the royal welcome given to Jehu (2 Kings 9:12–13). Plutarch records that Cato of Utica was given a similar reception of great respect.[9]

John records that some members of the crowd met Jesus with palm branches (12:13). Palms have always grown in the area of Jerusalem.[10] Thus, 2 Maccabees 10:7 notes that palm branches were used in the rededication of the temple in 164 B.C. Later, in 141 B.C. when Simon Maccabeus made his triumphal entry into Jerusalem, palms were used as a national symbol of victory (1 Macc. 13:51). Palms later became a national symbol on Jewish coins during the revolts against Roman rule in A.D. 66–70 and 132–135. The joyous reaction of the people to Jesus together with their singing of significant Old Testament passages underlines their intense messianic expectations.[11]

Matthew and John both state that in these events the prophecies of Isaiah 62:11 and Zechariah 9:9 were fulfilled. The opening words of Matthew 21:5, "Tell the daughter of Zion," quote from Isaiah. The balance of verse 5 is a selective quotation of Zechariah. Both the Hebrew and the Septuagint of Zechariah describe the messianic King as being just and bringing salvation; by riding on the colt of a donkey he also shows himself to be humble and peaceful (in the daily life of the ancient world as well as today, the donkey is not an animal of war, but one of toil and abuse). Matthew omits "being just and bringing salvation," seemingly to stress the humility and also the peaceful role of the true messianic King. The note of Jesus' humbleness is also emphasized in Matthew 11:29. In passing, it should be noted that humility was also a characteristic of Moses (Num. 12:3); the Messiah would be in the mold of Moses but greater than he (Deut. 18:15–18).

The description of the anticipated messianic king as found in the noncanonical Psalm of Solomon 17:21–25 stands in stark contrast. The unknown writer of this psalm envisions the messianic king as a great earthly conqueror who would victoriously purge the Gentiles and sinners from Jerusalem and the covenant land.[12]

John 12:16 notes that the disciples, who shared the common view of a conquering earthly Messiah, did not understand the true significance of Jesus' entering Jerusalem as a peaceful Messiah. Only after his death, resurrection, and ascension did they understand Jesus' role in God's eternal plan. The enthusiastic song of the crowds echoed their view of Jesus as the long-awaited earthly conqueror. Joyfully they sang the words of Psalm 118:25–26, the last of the great *Hallel* (or "Praise") Psalms sung antiphonally at the Feast of Tabernacles as well as at the Passover.

The song of the crowds as recorded in Matthew 21:9 reflects the thought of Psalm 118:25. "Hosanna" is a transliteration of the Hebrew *hôšî'â -nnā'*, which means "Save now," or "Save, we pray." But in time it had become a word of joyous acclamation in liturgical usage. The title "Son of David" goes back to the promise God made to David through his prophet Nathan (2 Sam. 7:12–16), namely, that one of his descendants would be the eternal King and establish the eternal house of God.

The words "Blessed is he who comes in the name of the Lord" reflect the key thought of Psalm 118:26. These words seemingly were used by priests to speak a blessing on those who had come to observe a festival at the temple.[13] In time Psalm 118:26 took on messianic significance in Jewish thinking: the Messiah would be sent by God to fulfil the promises he had made through the centuries. An ancient Palestinian recension of the Fourteenth Benediction (the Eighteen Benedictions is the principal supplicatory prayer of the Jewish liturgy), which probably goes back to about 168–165 B.C., echoes this messianic hope:

> Have mercy, O Lord our God, upon thy city Jerusalem,
> And upon Zion, where thy glory dwelleth,
> And upon the kingdom of the house of David thine Anointed.
> Blessed art thou, O Lord, the God of David [who buildest Jerusalem]![14]

This hope is also reflected in the later Babylonian Talmud. The final words of Matthew 21:9 and Mark 11:10 ("Hosanna in the highest!") are an urgent prayer that God in the highest heavens would usher in the long-anticipated earthly messianic age.

Both Luke and John record the reactions of Pharisees who witnessed the event. They feared that the enthusiasm of the people might lead to open rebellion against Rome. The tragic events following Herod's death in 4 B.C. (see p. 20) had not been forgotten. The Roman governor Pilate had probably by this time arrived in Jerusalem together with a large contingent of soldiers to personally assure peace during the potentially explosive Passover festival. In the Pharisaic view, the Roman occupation was part of God's will and could be removed not by insurrection, but only if the people through a more righteous life would prompt God to send the messianic age. Accordingly, as Luke notes (19:39), the Pharisees asked Jesus to rebuke the people. Jesus gave the Pharisees a stern reply.

Luke alone notes Jesus' reaction as he looked down upon Jerusalem. For the Jewish people of that time Jerusalem was the place where God's presence rested. In the messianic age it would be both the spiritual and the earthly power center of the world. Jesus wept bitter tears because the covenant people failed to remember that their special relationship with God was one of grace and not of merit. The misconception of the Pharisees that righteous living could help to bring about the messianic age prevailed.

Jesus foreknew that God's righteous anger would burn against the city. He foresaw the tragic events of A.D. 70 when the Romans would take Jerusalem and destroy it. Many of its people would be crucified, while others would be carried away into slavery. To a degree Luke's description of Jesus' sorrow and bitter tears (19:41–44) recalls the tragic words of Jeremiah 15:1–10.

In describing the reaction of the people of Jerusalem as Jesus and the pilgrims entered the city, Matthew uses a passive form of the verb *seiō*, which means "shake, cause to quake, agitate" (21:10). The related noun *seismos* is used of earthquakes.[15] Thereby, he notes that the crowds were deeply stirred. The Romans could easily have interpreted this flurry of activity as a messianic uprising. The people of Jerusalem remembered the awful events of 4 B.C. when the Roman general Varus brought his legions to Jerusalem to quell the uprising after Herod's death. As a result, two thousand men were crucified, many more were killed or maimed in battle, and still others were sold into slavery.[16]

The reply of the pilgrims to the question, "Who is this?" is noteworthy. Rather than identifying Jesus directly as the long-awaited earthly Messiah, they referred to him as "the prophet" (Matt. 21:11). This is an indirect reference to the messianic prophecy of Deuteronomy 18:15–18.

Mark 11:11 tells us that after entering the city Jesus went to the temple to look around. Matthew 21:14 records that Jesus healed the blind and the lame in the temple. (In Matthew this particular account follows the cleansing of the temple.) This recalls the messianic prophecies of Isaiah 29:18; 35:5–6; and 42:7. Matthew 21:15 notes that *hoi paides* sang to Jesus, "Hosanna to the Son of David." Because Jesus answered the protests of the scribes and chief priests by quoting Psalm 8:2

("From the lips of children . . . you have ordained praise"),
hoi paides is usually translated "children." However, it should
be translated "boys" or "youths."[17] This may well refer to those
who had gone through their bar mitzvah, and had accompanied their fathers to Jerusalem to observe the Passover and the
Feast of Unleavened Bread (Luke 2:41–42).[18]

Monday

The Cursing of the Fig Tree

Matthew 21:18–19 and Mark 11:12–14 record that on the following day Jesus and his disciples left Bethany to go to
Jerusalem. On the way a fig tree with leaves attracted Jesus'
attention, for he was hungry. Now it is important to remember
that most of the people of Palestine of that time were happy to
have two meals a day. Even though their day began at dawn,
the first meal was eaten somewhere between 10 and 11 A.M. It
consisted of some bread and whatever produce was in season.
The second meal was eaten in the late afternoon before sunset;
most people were thankful to have bread and lentil stew (without meat) to eat.

That the tree had leaves is of significance, for Jesus could
legitimately expect that it would have a fig for him to eat. The
leaves might just hide some figs. Fig trees produce two crops a
year (Hos. 9:10; Mic. 7:1). The first, known as winter figs,
ripens in June. Both the Mishnah (ca. A.D. 220) and the later
Talmud report that unripe figs were eaten as soon as they
began to have a reddish color. (While in Palestine in March-
April 1976, I noticed that a fig tree in the compound of the
Albright Institute had leaves and also a few figs with a reddish
color.) The summer figs, the main crop, would ripen in August
or September.[19] On finding that the tree which had looked so
promising was barren, Jesus cursed it.

Some of the prophets had used the image of a fig tree in speaking of God's covenant people Israel (Jer. 8:13; 29:17; Hos. 9:10;
Joel 1:7; Mic. 7:1). The destruction of a fig tree was sometimes
used as a figure of God's wrath being poured out on his unfaithful
covenant people (Isa. 34:4; Hos. 2:12). So then, in cursing the fig
tree, Jesus pointed to God's impending wrath on his unfaithful
covenant people. And not surprisingly, when Peter and the
other disciples expressed amazement that the fig tree had with-

ered, Jesus' reply emphasized the power and importance of exercising faith (Matt. 21:21–22; Mark 11:22–26).

The Cleansing of the Temple

The Gospels record that Jesus twice cleansed the temple. The first episode is reported in John 2:13–22. It took place early in Jesus' ministry and during the first of the three Passovers mentioned in John's Gospel. The second temple cleansing is recorded by the Synoptics, and clearly took place in the closing days of Jesus' ministry.

Following the critical principle of the doublet, namely, that similar narratives in the Scriptures probably recount the same event, some scholars suggest that Jesus cleansed the temple only once. Hence, the account in John is said to have been molded to fit his purpose, whereas the Synoptics did the same, each shaping and embellishing the common account to fit their own specific purpose.[20] A careful comparison, however, establishes that there are two separate events: one taking place early in Jesus' ministry, and the other in the very last days of his

Figure 1
The Southwest Corner of the Temple
(adapted from Yigael Yadin, ed., *Jerusalem Revealed: Archaeology in the Holy City, 1968–1974*
[Jerusalem: Israel Exploration Society, 1975], 26–27; used by permission)

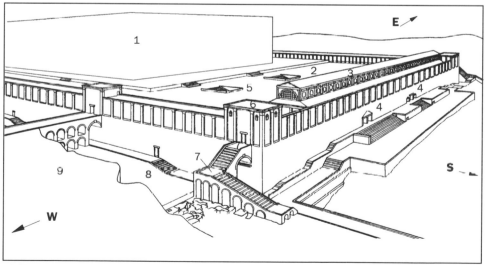

1. The Temple
2. Part of the Court of the Gentiles
3. Royal Colonnade
4. Huldah Gates
5. Entrance to the Stairways to the Huldah Gates
6. "Place of Trumpeting"
7. Stairway to the Portal of the Royal Colonnade
8. Tyropoeon Valley
9. Upper City

Figure 2
The Layout of the Temple as Rebuilt by Herod
(from *The Illustrated Bible Dictionary*, ed. J. D. Douglas, N. Hillyer, et al., rev. ed.
[Leicester, England: Inter-Varsity Press, 1980], 1.327; used by permission)

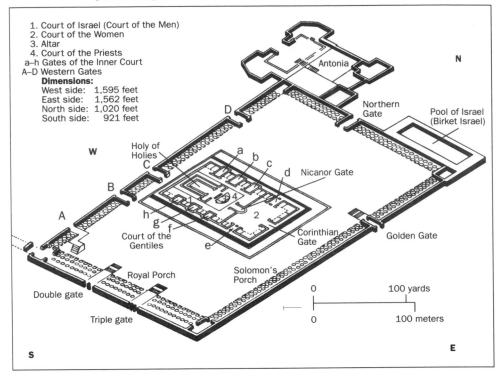

1. Court of Israel (Court of the Men)
2. Court of the Women
3. Altar
4. Court of the Priests
a–h Gates of the Inner Court
A–D Western Gates
Dimensions:
West side: 1,595 feet
East side: 1,562 feet
North side: 1,020 feet
South side: 921 feet

ministry (Matt. 21:12–13; Mark 11:15–18; Luke 19:45–48).

Since the early 1970s, archeological investigation into the architecture and construction of the southern part of the temple area has shed much light on the two episodes of cleansing. In extending the size of the Court of the Gentiles, Herod's architects and engineers had to raise much of the area south of the present Dome of the Rock with stones and earth. Above this rise, stone vaults were built on the west, south, and east slopes of Mount Moriah to provide a level platform.

Herod also built a beautiful three-aisled royal portico or colonnade along the entire length of the south side of the temple.[21] Spacious stairways led up to both the double and the triple Huldah Gates in the south wall, which opened into stairways to the level platform of the Court of the Gentiles. Today the vaulted areas to the east of these stairways are known as Solomon's stables. There are also vaulted areas to the west. It is thought that in these vaulted areas animals were kept for sacrificial purposes, while stalls for moneychangers were located in the royal colonnade above the vaults.[22]

Among the pretexts for the presence of the moneychangers was the temple tax, which was based on Exodus 30:11–16. The tax paid after the Babylonian exile was a third of a shekel (Neh. 10:32–33). Later it was increased to a half shekel, paid by every Jewish male twenty years or older. The poor were not exempt. The tax originally had to be paid in the ancient Hebrew coin and later in Tyrian coin. The latter was considered to be the nearest equivalent to the ancient Hebrew coin. Payment of the tax was due five days before the first of Nisan. Therefore, moneychangers set up to exchange Roman coin into the required Tyrian coin. These were permitted to make a small surcharge.[23]

Jesus' action on Monday was directed against the moneychanging and the sale of sacrificial animals in the temple area, activities which apparently benefited the high-priestly families.[24] In his excavations in what is known today as the Jewish Quarter of the Old City, Nahman Avigad found a weight inscribed with the name "Bar Kathros." This name recalls a folksong attributed to two Jewish sages of the second half of the first century A.D. and preserved in the tradition of the Talmud. This song speaks of the selfishness and injustice of high-priestly families, including those of Kathros and of Annas (see p. 84).[25]

Mark 11:16 notes that Jesus would not permit anyone to carry a vessel through the temple courts. To understand his action one must know the hilly layout of the immediate surroundings of the temple. Mount Ophel, which had been David's Jerusalem, lay to the south and was lower in elevation than the temple area. Mount Ophel was separated from the area to the west by the Tyropoeon Valley, which continued northward along the west wall of the temple, and then ran northwest to the area of the Damascus Gate. Now the easiest way to carry any burden from Mount Ophel to the western part of Jerusalem, known as the Upper City, was to go through one of the Huldah Gates, climb the stairway to the Court of the Gentiles, and then take the bridge leading from one of the western temple gates across the Tyropoeon Valley to the Upper City. Jesus was incensed that many people regarded the sacred area as little more than a convenient shortcut.

As he cleansed the temple, Jesus also taught. His opening words as recorded in Mark 11:17 are a direct quotation from the Septuagint text of Isaiah 56:7: "My house will be called a house of prayer for all nations." In 1 Kings 8:28–30 and elsewhere, the temple is characterized as a house of prayer. The phrase "for all nations" is unique to Isaiah 56:7 and to Mark's account of Jesus' teaching. It needs to be remembered that the area that was within the temple walls and surrounded the temple itself was known as the Court of the Gentiles. The phrase "for all nations" foreshadows what would take place beginning with the day of Pentecost. Each Synoptic account notes that Jesus added to his quotation of Isaiah the words, "But you have made it a den of robbers." He may well have had the high-priestly families in mind.

Mark 11:18 and Luke 19:47–48 record the reaction of the council to Jesus' actions and his teaching. The administration of the temple and its activities was in the hands of the chief priests. Since Jesus' actions and words interfered with what they considered their responsibilities, they were angry with Jesus. His actions only heightened their resolve made after the raising of Lazarus to do away with Jesus. However, since the people looked with great favor on him, the members of the council were afraid to take any public action. Judas's offer on Tuesday evening to betray him at an opportune time gave them the chance they had been waiting for: they could now plot a private arrest (Matt. 26:1–5, 14–16; Mark 14:1–2, 10–11; Luke 22:1–6).

4

Jesus' Final Day of Public Ministry

(Matt. 21:23–26:16; Mark 11:27–14:11; Luke 20:1–22:6; John 12:2–8)

The Day of Controversy

On Tuesday, the final day of his public ministry, Jesus returned to the temple. His actions and words of the previous day had strengthened the council's determination to entrap him. What resulted was a series of confrontations between members of the council and Jesus.

In the first confrontation (Matt. 21:23–22:14; Mark 11:27–12:12; Luke 20:1–19), all parties within the council were represented. Luke is especially careful to note this, identifying the confronters as "the chief priests, the scribes, and the elders" (Luke 20:1). The chief priests represented the high-priestly aristocracy and the Sadducees; the elders, the leading families; and the scribes, the teachers of the Torah and religious legal experts. The scribes were the backbone of the Pharisaic movement, which, as Acts 5:33–40 suggests, may have constituted the majority in the council. At any rate the two principal groups in the council were the Sadducees and Pharisees.[1]

Members of the council confronted Jesus with the demand, "Who authorized you to do these things?" In reply, Jesus used a rabbinical device, answering with a counterquestion: "The baptism of John, was it from heaven or from men?" When they found it expedient not to answer Jesus, he replied with three parables.

The first parable, that of the two sons, is found only in

Matthew 21:28–32. The imagery of the vineyard reflects the people of Israel and God's covenant relationship with them (Isa. 5:1–7). The first son refused to work in his father's vineyard but then changed his mind; the second son promised to work but broke his pledge. When Jesus asked, "Who of the two sons did the will of his father?" the council members answered, "The first." Jesus then proceeded to astound the council members. In their view, tax collectors and harlots were totally unworthy to enter the messianic kingdom. But Jesus said that these public sinners would enter the kingdom of God ahead of the council members, for the tax collectors and harlots would repent and believe! In this way Jesus stressed that salvation, like the covenant with Israel, is by grace, not by works.

Then Jesus spoke a second parable using vineyard imagery, the parable of the wicked lessees (Matt. 21:33–46; Mark 12:1–12; Luke 20:9–19). Jesus set the scene: at harvesttime the lessees refused to render the landowner his due and killed his only son. At the end of the story, Jesus asked, "What will the owner do to those miserable men? He will destroy those wicked men and give the vineyard to others who will observe the terms of the lease." The council members realized that Jesus was speaking of them (Matt. 21:45), and that God's righteous wrath awaited them. This was totally unthinkable, and they blurted out, "God forbid!" (Luke 20:16). But they were afraid to arrest Jesus for fear of the people.

The third parable, that of the man without a wedding garment, is found only in Matthew 22:1–14. The analogy between the kingdom of heaven and a wedding feast (v. 2) evoked the listeners' anticipation of the messianic age. In their thinking, only God's covenant people were worthy to enjoy its blessings and participate in the messianic banquet. Once again, however, Jesus stressed the negative result of unwillingness to live as God's covenant people on his terms: they would experience God's fierce anger and judgment.

The next confrontation (Matt. 22:15–22; Mark 12:13–17; Luke 20:20–26) was between Jesus and the Pharisees along with the Herodians, who questioned him about paying taxes to Caesar, the Gentile overlord. It was a very touchy matter, for in addition to religious objections, the Jews were heavily burdened by the various taxes imposed by Rome.[2] In a graphic reply, Jesus told his questioners that they needed to pay taxes since they enjoyed the benefits of the Roman peace. And they were likewise obligated to bring their offerings to God.

Next the Sadducees, who denied the resurrection, tried to entrap Jesus with a question about marriage at the resurrection (Matt. 22:23–33; Mark 12:18–27; Luke 20:27–40). In his reply, Jesus emphasized the nature of life in the resurrection (there will be no marriage). The people were astonished at his teaching (Matt. 22:33), and the Pharisaic scribes were pleased to hear what Jesus had said (Luke 20:39).

Then once again the Pharisees sought to entrap Jesus, this time with a question about the greatest commandment (Matt. 22:34–40; Mark 12:28–34). Jesus in turn asked the Pharisees about the lineage of the Messiah (Matt. 22:41–46; Mark 12:35–37; Luke 20:41–44). When they replied that the Messiah is "the Son of David," Jesus asked them, "How then does David in the Spirit call him Lord?" After quoting Psalm 110:1, Jesus continued, "If David calls him 'Lord,' how is he his son?" With this the council members' confrontations with Jesus ended, and he seized the opportunity to speak.

The Apocalyptic Discourses of Jesus

To the large crowds present in the temple, Jesus then spoke his final public discourse (Matt. 23; Mark 12:38–40; Luke 20:45–47). It is not known how many of the 150,000 to 180,000 people who may have come to Jerusalem for the Passover festival were there to hear him. But to those who were present, Jesus spoke words of harsh judgment on the scribes and Pharisees. Then after watching rich and poor alike deposit money in the treasury receptacles in the Court of Women (Mark 12:41–44; Luke 21:1–4), Jesus and his disciples left. His public ministry was at an end.

Once outside, the disciples expressed their admiration for the beauty of the temple; using graphic language Jesus bluntly foretold its coming destruction (Matt. 24:1–2; Mark 13:1–2; Luke 21:5–6). The disciples were understandably perplexed. In the messianic age as they envisioned it, the temple would play a central role. To them, its destruction was unthinkable.

Jesus' disciples had questions about the coming destruction.

When they reached the top of the Mount of Olives, Jesus graphically described the end of the world and his second coming (Matt. 24:3–25:46; Mark 13:3–37; Luke 21:7–36). But to the disciples' queries as to when all this would occur, Jesus said, "Watch, for you know not the day when your Lord comes!" (Matt. 24:42).

The words Jesus spoke in Matthew 24 and 25 form his sixth and final discourse as recorded in that Gospel. It was private, heard only by his disciples. Before describing the final judgment, Jesus used a series of illustrations (24:43–51) as well as the parables of the ten virgins (25:1–13) and of the talents (vv. 14–30) to emphasize the importance of faithfully, wisely, and purposefully watching for the Messiah to come. Jesus then gave the authoritative description of what will take place on the last day (vv. 31–46). He began with words which reflect Daniel 7:13–14 and Zechariah 14:5. His image of the Son of man's separating people as a herder separates sheep and goats was very effective in a time when the herding of sheep and goats was an integral part of life. His description of what will happen on the last day echoes what he had said repeatedly in his ministry, and especially in the various discourses of the past three days—relationship with God is a matter solely of grace, not of merit. There is no middle ground.

The Anointing of Jesus

After ending his discourse on Tuesday afternoon, Jesus told his disciples, "You know that after two days comes the Passover, and the Son of man will be handed over to be crucified" (Matt. 26:1–2). Mark states that the Passover and the Feast of Unleavened Bread were two days away (14:1). He then goes on to record, as does Matthew, two events which took place at the same time: the anointment of Jesus and the plot to arrest him secretly (Matt. 26:1–16; Mark 14:1–11; see also Luke 22:1–6; and John 12:2–8).

Probably in the late afternoon or perhaps in the early evening of Tuesday, Jesus and his disciples returned to Bethany, where they were invited to eat in the house of Simon the leper.[3] John notes that Lazarus was one of the guests and that Martha served. While the guests were eating, Mary, the sister of Lazarus and Martha, anointed Jesus with a very precious ointment. John records that she used a *litra*, which is usually translated "pound," but is actually about twelve ounces.[4]

Mark speaks of a long-necked alabaster flask filled with very costly spikenard. Pliny the Elder comments that "the best ointment is preserved in alabaster."[5] To prevent spillage, such a costly flask was sealed; its contents could be used only by breaking off the top. John notes (12:5) that the ointment was worth three hundred denarii—an extraordinary sum since one denarius was a day's pay for the typical hired hand.

What was this costly substance with which Mary anointed Jesus? Matthew uses the Semitic loanword *myron*, which means "ointment" or "perfume."[6] Mark and John use in addition the term *nardos*, which is usually translated "nard" or "spikenard." *Nardos* came from a plant native to Nepal and the Himalaya Mountains, which was later introduced into India. The fragrant oil was extracted from all parts of this plant, especially the roots; then it was mixed with other oils to make spikenard ointment or salve for both cosmetic and medicinal purposes. In the latter case, it was used to treat nervous disorders.[7] John also uses the term *pistikos* to describe the ointment. This can mean "pure, unadulterated," or "liquid," or it may be derived from *pistakia*, "pistachio tree." The last suggestion is the most probable, for the oil of the pistachio nut was used as a base for perfumes.[8]

Matthew and Mark note that Mary anointed Jesus' head. John states that she anointed his feet,[9] and then wiped them with her hair. It seems to have been unthinkable for a respectable Jewish woman to expose her hair publicly.[10] Mary's action demonstrates her great love and respect for Jesus, who had raised her brother Lazarus from the dead.

As the odor filled the house, the disciples were deeply incensed at what they considered a waste of such a precious substance. John focuses on the reaction of Judas, who served as the treasurer for Jesus and his disciples. Judas is characterized as a *kleptēs*, a "sneak thief," who pilfered the contents of the communal moneybag.

In commenting on the disciples' reaction, Jesus again pointed to his coming passion. Concern for the poor was praiseworthy, but Mary, in anointing him before his death, had done "a good work" (Matt. 26:10). Wherever the gospel would be shared in the future, Jesus added, Mary's loving act would be remembered (Matt. 26:13; Mark 14:9).

Judas's Agreement to Betray Jesus

The Synoptics carefully record Judas's agreement to betray Jesus (Matt. 26:14–16; Mark 14:10–11; Luke 22:3–6) and, in so doing, contrast Mary's sacrificial love with Judas's selfish treachery. While Jesus was dining in Bethany, the council was plotting how they could have him furtively arrested and executed.

Judas went to the meeting of the council. There he agreed to betray Jesus secretly into their hands for the price of thirty silver coins. The Greek term used by Matthew (26:15) is *argurion;* each of these coins was worth four drachmas or denarii.[11] The amount involved in the transaction is significant in that it echoes Zechariah 11:12, where the rejected shepherd is paid thirty pieces of silver. Thirty pieces of silver was also the traditional price of a slave (Exod. 21:32). From then on Judas had only to wait for a chance to carry out his commitment to the council.

5

The Passover:
Various Hypotheses

The Chronology of Holy Week

John 12:1 records that six days before the Passover Jesus arrived in Bethany. This means that he and his disciples arrived sometime on Friday before sunset when the Sabbath began. The final and awesome phase of Jesus' redemptive work was about to take place. Jesus knew that "his hour had come for him to leave this world and go to the Father, having loved his own who were in the world; to the end he loved them" (John 13:1).

The Gospels are silent on Jesus' activities on the Sabbath (Saturday), the day after his arrival in the Jerusalem area. However, they carefully note the salient events of Sunday, the second day, on which he rode the colt of a donkey into Jerusalem and was hailed by the Galilean and the Perean pilgrims as the messianic King. Matthew notes that Jesus entered the temple and was hailed by boys *(paides)* as the long-awaited Messiah.

On Monday, the third day, Jesus cursed the fig tree on his way to Jerusalem and later cleansed the temple. John 12:20–50 details the words Jesus spoke in the temple, words that clearly echo Isaiah 53:1 (v. 38) and also Isaiah 6:9–10 (v. 40).

The fourth day, Tuesday, was for Jesus a very busy one. Much of it was spent in the temple in an ongoing dialog with the members of the council as they sought to entrap him (Matt. 21:23–22:46; Mark 11:27–12:37; Luke 20:1–44). Later to his disciples and the crowds at the temple Jesus pronounced woes on the scribes and Pharisees (Matt. 23:1–39). Then privately to his disciples on the Mount of Olives Jesus described the end of the world and his second coming (Matt. 24:3–25:46; Mark 13:3–37; Luke 21:7–36). Late afternoon and evening witnessed the anointing of Jesus and also the agreement of Judas to betray him secretly to the council (Matt. 26:1–16; Mark 14:1–11; Luke 22:1–6; John 12:2–8).

A study of the Gospels indicates that they provide no information as to Jesus' activities on Wednesday. However, on Thursday, the sixth day, the disciples reminded him of the urgent need to prepare for the Passover meal (Matt. 26:17–19; Mark 14:12–16; Luke 22:7–13). The Scriptures provide much information on Jesus' eating the meal with his disciples (Matt. 26:20–29; Mark 14:17–25; Luke 22:14–38; John 13:2–38; 1 Cor. 11:23–26). John 14–17 records the words of comfort and instruction on the Holy Spirit that Jesus spoke at the close of the meal.

The Passover and the Feast of Unleavened Bread

Some debate whether Jesus ate the Passover with his disciples at the usual time (i.e., on Thursday evening) or somewhat earlier. For example, Annie Jaubert insists that Jesus ate the Passover with his disciples several days earlier.[1] Other scholars hold that Jesus ate the Passover meal a day earlier (i.e., on Wednesday) and was crucified and died at the very time the Passover lambs were being slaughtered in the temple on the following day.[2] Another question is whether some other religious meal, such as the *kiddush* or *haburah*, may have been involved.

That there are such diverse views signals the need to study objectively the evidence provided in the Gospels and the customs of the first century A.D. Proper attention must also be given to the requirements of the Passover meal and its role in the religious life and ritual of that time. It is also important in such a study to remember that in the Jewish system of reckoning time a day began at sunset and ended at the following sunset. This is sometimes overlooked in the ongoing debate.

Before describing in detail the various hypotheses, it is necessary to examine the usages of three words that figure in the debate: *pascha* ("Passover"), *azuma* ("Feast of Unleavened

Bread"), and *paraskeuē* ("preparation"). The words *pascha* and *azuma* can be and were used in both a narrow and a wide sense. In its narrow sense the term *pascha* refers to the specific events of the Passover: the removal of all leaven from the house, the preparations for the meal, the slaughter of the Passover lamb, and the eating of the meal itself in the evening in keeping with the first Passover meal. When used in a wide, or general, sense, *pascha* denotes not only the Passover or seder meal, but also the seven-day Feast of Unleavened Bread, which immediately followed the Passover meal. In its narrow sense *azuma* refers specifically to the seven days of the Feast of Unleavened Bread. In its wide sense it includes the day of preparation for the Passover and the Passover meal itself. The meaning of *paraskeuē*, as it figures in the ongoing discussion of the details of the Passover and the trial and crucifixion of our Lord, depends on the context in which it is used. The context helps us determine the specific time and purpose of the "preparation."

The Jaubert Hypothesis

Madame Jaubert espoused a four-day Passover calendar, holding that Jesus ate the Passover with his disciples on Tuesday evening, was arrested during the night, and was taken to be examined by Annas. Peter's denial also took place at this time. On Wednesday morning the council heard witnesses and put Jesus under oath. He was abused and kept overnight in the palace of Caiaphas. Jesus was formally condemned on Thursday morning by the council, taken to Pilate for the first hearing, sent to Herod Antipas, and then kept in detention by Pilate. Early on Friday morning came the second hearing by Pilate, the Barabbas episode, the scourging, and the condemnation. Jesus was taken to Golgotha where he was crucified and died in the late afternoon. The Passover was celebrated by the Jews that evening.

The primary basis for Jaubert's hypothesis is the Syriac *Didascalia* (21), which dates from the third century. Secondary support is found in the writings of Victorinus of Pettau (d. 304) and in a letter of Epiphanius, bishop of Salamis, dating from about A.D. 370.[3] Jaubert's reconstruction of events is based heavily on the noncanonical Book of Jubilees, especially on its lunar calendar. Some hold that the Qumran community followed a calendar very similar (if not identical) to that of the Book of Jubilees.[4]

The sequence of events as reconstructed by Jaubert at first attracted much attention and became rather popular despite decisive objections that were raised. Today the lack of a historical basis for the hypothesis is generally recognized.[5]

Other Hypotheses

It has been urged that the meal recorded in the Gospels strongly resembles the *kiddush,* a ceremony observed at the beginning of the Sabbath and on feast days.[6] What is intriguing is that in the *kiddush* a blessing is spoken over wine; this is followed by the breaking of bread, an act which begins the Sabbath meal. But the differences between the *kiddush* and the Passover of the passion narratives are apparent. At the Passover meal, the bread was broken after the *second* cup of wine. The Sabbath meal is eaten at sunset whereas the Passover meal was eaten somewhat later in the evening. Moreover, Joachim Jeremias has pointed out that the *kiddush* became a custom after the time of Jesus.[7]

Another hypothesis associates the Passover of the Gospels with the *haburah,* which was a meal eaten by a like-minded fellowship. As Jeremias points out, such meals were connected with funerals, weddings, betrothals, and circumcisions. To be a paying guest at such a meal was considered to be meritorious. But the *haburah* does not share characteristics with the Passover meal eaten by Jesus with his disciples.[8]

A few scholars go as far as to maintain that the meal Jesus ate with his disciples the evening before his crucifixion was not the Passover. Judah Benzion Segal, for example, contends that "to the Hebrews the Passover was primarily a New Year festival."[9] Hans Kosmala has made a careful analysis of Segal's view and demonstrated that it is historically untenable.[10]

The Evidence from Scripture

John 12:1 states that Jesus arrived in Bethany six days before the *pascha.* Here the reference is to the Passover in the narrow sense: the day of preparation for and the eating of the Passover meal. This is true of Mark 14:1 as well, which establishes the time of Jesus' anointing—two days before the *pascha.* Verse 2 of Matthew 26 adds that Jesus told his disciples: "You know that after two days comes the Passover, and the Son of man will be handed over to be crucified." All four Gospels state that Jesus was arrested after eating the Passover with his disciples.

Matthew 26:17 and Mark 14:12 record the disciples' rather anxious reminder with reference to the Passover: "On the first day of the Feast of Unleavened Bread, when they sacrificed the Passover, Jesus' disciples said to him, 'Where do you wish that we go and prepare so that we may eat the *pascha*?'" This took place on Thursday, Nisan 14, when all leaven had to be removed from the dwellings, and the Passover lambs and meal had to be prepared.[11] The Gospels of Mark and Luke record what Jesus instructed Peter and John to ask the owner of the house, "Where is the guest chamber, where I may eat the Passover with my disciples?" (Mark 14:14; Luke 22:11). Each of the Synoptics records that the two did as told and prepared the *pascha* (Matt. 26:19; Mark 14:16; Luke 22:13).

Exodus 12:1–20 details God's instructions for the observance of the Passover and the Feast of Unleavened Bread. Note that the Passover lamb was to be killed, properly prepared, and roasted after sunset (vv. 6–8). All yeast (leaven) also had to be removed from the houses on the same day and was not to be brought back until after the seven-day Feast of Unleavened Bread (vv. 15–20), which began immediately after eating the Passover meal.

Leviticus 23:5–8 clearly defines the relationship between the Passover and the seven-day Feast of Unleavened Bread: "In the first month, on the fourteenth day of the month at twilight [lit., between the two evenings] is the LORD's Passover. Then on the fifteenth day of the same month there is the Feast of Unleavened Bread to the LORD; for seven days you shall eat unleavened bread. On the first day you shall have a holy convocation; you shall not do any laborious work. But for seven days you shall present an offering by fire to the LORD" (NASB).

Numbers 28:16–25 provides essentially the same information, but also gives directions regarding the sacrifices for Nisan 15. Deuteronomy 16:1–8 and Ezekiel 45:21–24 likewise record God's instructions for the Passover and the seven-day feast that followed it.

We are told in 2 Chronicles 30 that King Hezekiah invited God's covenant people from Dan to Beersheba (v. 5) to come to

Jerusalem to observe the Passover and the Feast of Unleavened
Bread. Verse 22 states: "So they ate for the appointed seven
days, sacrificing peace offerings and giving thanks to the LORD
God of their fathers" (NASB).[12] The religious meals and sacrifices were prescribed in the Torah and known as the *chagigah*.[13]

Charles Torrey comments on the observance of Nisan 15 and
mentions the *chagigah* in particular:

> This was *the great day* of the feast of unleavened bread, a holiday
> of rejoicing. Plans and preparations for the principal meal on
> *this* day had been made, we may suppose, for days or weeks
> past. . . . If the Jewish householders viewed in John 18:28
> would have been debarred from joining in this festivity with
> their relatives and friends by the act of entering the praetorium,
> it is no wonder that they remained outside! Their thought was
> on the *chagigah* of that day, and the reason for their action could
> hardly have been expressed in any other way than by the words
> of our text.[14]

Jeremias confirms that the *chagigah*, paschal sacrifices, were
eaten during the seven days of the Feast of Unleavened Bread.
In keeping with Deuteronomy 16:2 and 2 Chronicles 35:7,
these were sometimes called *pesah*. By entering the praetorium, members of the Sanhedrin would be rendered unclean
and so prevented from eating such sacrifices, as John notes in
18:28.[15]

It should be pointed out that John never uses the word
azuma ("Feast of Unleavened Bread"), but instead uses *pascha*
("Passover") in the narrow sense and also in the wide sense,
which includes the seven-day feast that followed the Passover
meal. For example, John 19:14 notes that at about the sixth
hour of "the preparation *(paraskeuē)* for the Passover," Pilate
told the Jews, "Behold your King!" Here John clearly has in
view the preparation for the Feast of Unleavened Bread.[16]
When the Jews again called for Jesus' crucifixion, Pilate suc-
cumbed to their demands and sentenced Jesus to die. The
order was carried out at once. Jesus died late in the afternoon
of "the preparation *(paraskeuē)*, the day before the Sabbath
(prosabbaton)" (Mark 15:42). John 19:31 states, "It was the
preparation *(paraskeuē)*, so that the bodies should not remain
on the cross on the Sabbath, for that Sabbath was a high day."
Here John has in view the preparation for the Sabbath. It

should be noted that Josephus likewise used the term "preparation for the Passover" in reference to the seven-day Feast of Unleavened Bread *(Antiquities of the Jews* 17.9.3) and the term "preparation" *(paraskeuē)* by itself to refer to Friday, the day of preparation for the Sabbath (16.6.2).

Through our careful examination of the words *pascha, azuma,* and *paraskeuē* as used in the four Gospels and in light of Jewish practice, it is clear that Jesus ate the Passover meal with his disciples on Thursday evening, was formally condemned by the council early in the morning of the first day of Unleavened Bread (Matt. 27:1; Mark 15:1; Luke 22:66–71), and was tried by Pilate and crucified on Friday, the day of preparation for the solemn Sabbath that followed the Passover.[17]

6

The Passover Meal

(Matt. 26:17–35; Mark 14:12–31; Luke 22:7–38;
John 13:2–17:26)

The Sending of Peter and John to Prepare the Meal

All three Synoptics carefully note that the time had come to prepare for the Passover. Matthew and Mark record that it was "the first day of Unleavened Bread" (Matt. 26:17; Mark 14:12), while Luke states it was "the day of Unleavened Bread" (22:7). Both Matthew and Mark describe it as the day "to prepare to eat the Passover." Luke describes it as the day on which "it was necessary to sacrifice the Passover." It was also the day on which all yeast (leaven) and bread made with yeast had to be removed from the house. All these actions were in keeping with the initial event (Exod. 12) and with the instructions God had given his covenant people (Deut. 16:1–8).

In A.D. 30, the probable year of Jesus' passion, Passover (Nisan 14) fell on Thursday. The disciples must have been wondering where they would eat the Passover. As far as they knew, Jesus had made no arrangements. They knew only that the meal had to be eaten within the confines of the city of Jerusalem. With 120,000 pilgrims in the city in addition to 25,000–30,000 residents,[1] last-minute arrangements would be difficult to make.

Jesus instructed Peter and John to go to Jerusalem (Matt. 26:18; Mark 14:13; Luke 22:8–10). Once there the two would encounter an unusual sight—a man carrying a jar of water. Professional water-carriers in Jesus' time used waterskins for such a task. Fetching water for family needs was the task of the women of the house, and they used water jars (Gen. 24:13; John 4:7).[2] The unusual sight of a man carrying a jar of water has the earmarks of a prearranged signal. It is important to remember that Judas was not to know in advance where Jesus and his disciples would eat the Passover (Luke 22:6).

Jesus' instructions are detailed in Mark and Luke. Peter and John were to follow the water-carrier home and say to the master of the house, the *oikodespotēs*, "The Master says, 'Where is the guest chamber, where I may eat the Passover with my disciples?'" (Mark 14:14; Luke 22:11). Jesus then told the two disciples that the master would show them an *anagaion*, a room upstairs, a big room either under or on the roof, depending on the specific construction of the house.[3] This room, large enough to permit thirteen men to recline while eating the Passover, would also be furnished and ready. The Greek term Mark and Luke use for "furnished" *(estrōmenon)* is also found with "couch" *(klinē)* in the Septuagint of Ezekiel 23:41. They have in view the cushions necessary for reclining to eat the Passover meal. The celebrants were required to recline while eating the Passover to symbolize the rest God gave his covenant people through the exodus and the conquest of the land of Canaan.

Following Jesus' instructions, Peter and John went to Jerusalem. They found the room furnished as Jesus had said, and went on to secure the Passover lamb. They prepared it in accordance with God's instructions to his people (Exod. 12:1–11) so as to be ready for the meal after sunset.

Preparing the Passover Lamb

The Passover lambs were a sacrifice (Exod. 12:27; 34:25; Num. 9:7, 13). The blood of the lambs slain for the first Passover was to be smeared on the doorposts and the lintels of the houses to keep the angel of death from entering (Exod. 12:7, 13). But by the beginning of the last century B.C., if not earlier, the blood was to be poured out at the altar of burnt offering.[4] The proper slaughter of all the lambs within the limited time period would require a carefully planned schedule, for as many as 150,000 persons may have been in Jerusalem for Passover. No fewer than 10 were to be present for a given meal—Josephus notes that the number could range from 10 to 20.[5] Taking 15 as an average yields a total of 10,000 lambs that had to be properly slaughtered in the temple on the afternoon of Nisan 14.

In order for all the Passover lambs to be slaughtered and roasted by sunset, the afternoon was divided into periods. Each of three groups was assigned a specific period to go to the temple area. According to the Masoretic text of Exodus 12:6, "the whole assembly of Israel shall kill [the Passover lambs] between the two evenings." This meant approximately between the hours of 2:30 and 5:30 P.M. However, in Jesus' time, to accommodate the many pilgrims within the limited confines of the Court of the Priests, the first of the three groups was permitted to enter earlier in the afternoon.[6]

The pilgrims entered the Court of the Priests from the north side. Each cut the throat of his lamb. The blood was caught in containers of precious metal, passed down the line of priests, and poured out at the altar of burnt offering. Thereby the lives of the innocent victims were given back to God. Carrying their slaughtered lambs, the pilgrims left the Court of the Priests

Reconstruction of the Temple. A model by Michael Avi-Yonah at the Holyland Hotel. Photo courtesy of Illustrator Photo/Ken Touchton.

The Façade of the Temple. Photo courtesy of the Israeli Government Press Office.

through a gateway on the south side.[7] Then the lambs had to be roasted. This was normally done on pomegranate sticks. When ready, the lambs were served whole, without being cut apart.[8]

Jesus' Arrival

Where was the upper room in which Jesus ate the Passover with his disciples? Today the pilgrim is shown a building in the southwestern section of the Old City, to the south of the extant medieval walls. This is known as the Coenaculum or the Cenacle, but its historical tradition is doubtful. The first attestation that Jesus ate the Passover there goes back to the early part of the fifth century A.D. Seemingly this was the result of an attempt to identify the site as the meeting place of the disciples after Jesus' ascension. The fact is, however, that there is no way to establish where Jesus ate the final Passover with his disciples and instituted the Lord's Supper.[9]

Because the first Passover meal was eaten after sunset (Exod. 12:6–8), every Passover meal thereafter has been eaten after sunset. It is possible that a trumpet blast from the top of the tower at the southwest corner of the temple area was the signal to let people in Jerusalem know that the time to begin the meal had come. It was standard practice to announce the beginning and end of the Sabbath (at sunset on Friday and Saturday respectively) by such a signal. In fact, excavations at this corner have unearthed a large stone with square Hebrew letters identifying the site as the "place of trumpeting."[10]

At sunset Jesus came with the ten disciples to the place where he had arranged to eat the Passover. Luke 22:24 informs us that there arose a dispute among the disciples as to who would be the greatest. To fully understand the situation, bear in mind that the disciples expected that Jesus during this covenant meal commemorating the exodus from Egypt would declare himself to be the great earthly Messiah who would free God's covenant people in Palestine from the hated Roman rule. In fact, there was a Jewish tradition that the Messiah would declare himself and begin the long-expected messianic age at the time of the Passover.[11]

Moreover, Jesus had finally accepted the messianic title "Son of David" at Jericho. He had also accepted the messianic adulation of the people on the previous Sunday. On Monday and Tuesday he had spoken messianic words and performed messianic acts. Surely the Passover meal would be the opportune time for Jesus to declare himself. And whoever reclined next to him would have an excellent chance to be a powerful official in Jesus' earthly messianic kingdom.

In his response, as recorded in Luke 22:25–30, Jesus sought to instruct the disciples regarding his true role as the Messiah. From the time of Peter's confession shortly before the transfiguration, Jesus had reminded them repeatedly that their earthly messianic expectations were all wrong (Matt. 16:21–26; Mark 8:31–37; and Luke 9:22–25; Matt. 18:1–5; Mark 9:33–37; and Luke 9:46–48; Matt. 20:17–28; Mark 10:32–45; and Luke 18:31–34). Note the point Jesus made in Luke 22:27, "I am in the midst of you as he who serves," which he dramatically demonstrated in the footwashing (John 13:2–20).

The Passover Meal

Leonardo da Vinci's well-known masterpiece *The Last Supper* is the image many have of Jesus and his disciples at the Passover meal. But it was a part of the Passover ritual for all to recline while eating in order to symbolize the rest and freedom God had given his covenant people through the mighty act of the exodus. This was observed by all from the richest to the poorest, even though Jews ordinarily sat cross-legged on the floor when they ate their meals.

Jesus and his disciples reclined on couches placed around three sides of the table. What the exact arrangement may have been is impossible to say, for the Gospels do not provide specific information. On the basis of Peter's motioning to John to ask Jesus who would betray him (John 13:23–26), Alfred Edersheim has made the intriguing suggestion that John lay directly across from Peter and next to Jesus.[12]

At the beginning of an everyday meal, the head of the house would say a benediction over the bread. This was not true, however, of the Passover meal. The benediction over the bread came much later on in this leisurely meal marked by vicarious remembrance and earnest messianic expectation. No bread was eaten before this benediction. Drawing on specific information given in the Gospels, 1 Corinthians 10–11, and noncanonical sources makes it possible to reconstruct the order and details of Jesus' final Passover meal.[13]

The First Cup of Wine

Jesus told his disciples, "I have earnestly desired to eat this Passover with you before I suffer. For I say I will not eat it until it is fulfilled in the kingdom of God" (Luke 22:15–16). Then, as the head of the group, Jesus spoke a benediction *(kiddush)* over the first cup of wine (v. 17). The use of wine at Passover is confirmed in the noncanonical Book of Jubilees (49:6, 9). It was customary to mix water with the red wine, but the proportions are not known. Whether during the time of Jesus the participants drank four cups of wine, as they do now, is disputed.[14] It seems probable that the fourth cup was a later addition.

After taking the cup and speaking a blessing, Jesus said, "Take this and divide among yourselves. For I tell you from now on I will not drink of the fruit of the vine until the kingdom of God comes" (vv. 17–18). Some wish to interpret the words in verses 16 and 18 to mean that even though Jesus functioned as the head of the group, he himself did not eat and drink the Passover. Properly understood, however, Jesus' words point forward to the eschatological coming of the kingdom of God, the messianic banquet of eternity. Jesus most certainly did eat this final Passover meal with his disciples.[15]

The Footwashing

Before eating the Passover meal, all participants were to bathe and put on their best clothing. After doing so, Jesus and the ten disciples had walked at least two miles from Bethany, and their sandal-shod feet had become dusty on the way. But Peter and John seemingly had not made the customary provisions to wash the feet of Jesus and the ten disciples. This was a menial task which even a Hebrew slave did not have to do for his master.[16] And this neither Peter nor John was willing to do for the ten disciples.

After the blessing spoken over the first cup came the washing of the right hand. This was done before eating the preliminary dish. At this time Jesus took off his outer garment. He girded himself with a towel and began to wash his disciples' feet. Although a disciple might wash his rabbi's feet, it was unheard of for a rabbi to wash the feet of his disciples.

John's account (13:2–20) singles out Peter's reaction to this unheard-of action. "Lord, you!" he exclaimed, "are you going to wash my feet?" (v. 6). Realizing that Peter did not understand his actions, Jesus replied, "Unless I wash you, you will have no part with me." Peter in his emotional state retorted, "Not only my feet but also my hands and head!" Jesus' response is recorded in verses 10–11: "He who has bathed has no need to wash, except for his feet, but he is totally clean. And you are clean, but not all of you are clean." Jesus knew who would betray him. That is why he said, "Not all of you are clean."

Jesus put on his outer garment and once again reclined with the disciples. The words which he then spoke brought out the deep meaning of his symbolic action of washing their feet. He stressed the importance of true humility (vv. 14–16), and in his closing words characteristically recalled his role as the certified agent of the Father and its implications for them (vv. 18–20).

"One of You Will Betray Me!"

The washing of the right hand was followed by the preliminary dish. It consisted of green herbs, bitter herbs, and a sauce made of a mixture of squeezed and grated fruits, such as apples, dates, figs, and raisins, with spices and vinegar. This dish prompted the celebrants to recall the state slavery and misery which their forebears had experienced in Egypt (Exod. 1–12).[17]

At this point during the Passover meal Jesus became deeply troubled (John 13:21) and solemnly said, "Truly, I tell you that one of you will betray me, one who eats with me!" (Mark 14:18). In his account Luke adds: "For the Son of man goes as it has been determined, but woe be to the man through whom he will be betrayed" (22:22). These words came as a great shock to the disciples. To betray someone with whom one had fellowshiped at table was a gross violation of trust.[18] In Jewish society a disciple would never betray his rabbi! The disciples became extremely distressed, and one by one said to him, "It is not I, is it, Lord?" (Matt. 26:22; Mark 14:19). Jesus replied, "He who dips his hand into the dish with me—he is the one who will betray me. . . . But woe to that man through whom the Son of man will be betrayed. It would be better for that man not to have been born!" (Matt. 26:23–24; note the allusion to Ps. 41:9).

John tells us that at this time the "disciple whom Jesus loved," John's circumlocution for himself, was reclining next to Jesus (13:23). Peter, apparently directly across the table from John and Jesus, motioned to John to ask Jesus who would betray him.[19] John did so, and Jesus replied: "He it is for whom I will dip a morsel of food *(psōmion)* and give it to him" (John 13:26). Then, dipping the morsel, he gave it to Judas. *Psōmion,* the diminutive form of *psōmos,* is used only here in the New Testament; in the present context it refers to the green herbs dipped into the fruit purée or *haroseth* sauce.[20] The Passover Haggadah includes this statement: "Take an olive's bulk of bitter herbs, dip it in the *haroseth,* and say the blessing."[21]

Each of the participants in the Passover was probably lying on his left side, the upper body being supported by the left arm. C. K. Barrett contends that Judas occupied the seat of honor at Jesus' right.[22] But the ease with which John communicated with Jesus would suggest that John had this position. Since Jesus gave Judas the morsel, it is logical to assume that Judas was on Jesus' left.

Matthew records that Judas asked, "Rabbi, is it I?" Jesus

answered, "You have said!" (Matt. 26:25). John notes that Satan entered Judas's heart. "What you do, do quickly," Jesus told Judas (John 13:27). The other disciples did not know what Jesus meant. Some thought that since Judas was the treasurer, Jesus had asked him to purchase the *chagigah* for the next day, the first day of Unleavened Bread.[23] Others thought that Jesus had asked him to give an offering to the poor. Judas left at once. John's closing words, "It was night" (13:30), reflect the awesome spiritual darkness of the betrayer Judas.

"All of You Will Leave Me"

Matthew 26.31–35, Mark 14.27–31, Luke 22.31–38, and John 13:31–38 record the next blow to the emotional state of the disciples. For Jesus to say that one of them would betray him was astounding. But now, quoting Zechariah 13:7b, he told them that all of them would stumble because of him that very night. Whenever in the past Jesus had spoken of his true mission as the obedient Suffering Servant (Isa. 53), the disciples had been offended. In their thinking, he would be the victorious, not the suffering Messiah. And now they were about to face their ultimate test. How would they react to Jesus' arrest and the subsequent events? They would scatter in panic, as sheep flee when their shepherd is struck. (There was a positive note as well, however, for Jesus went on to say, "When I am raised up, I will go before you into Galilee" [Matt. 26:32; Mark 14:28]. The fulfilment of this promise is recorded in John 21.)

Peter reacted to Jesus' words in his typical fashion: "If all shall be offended because of you, I shall never be offended!" (Matt. 26:33; Mark 14:29). Luke records that Peter also said, "Lord, I am ready to go both to prison and to death with you" (22:33). But Jesus replied, "Truly, I tell you that today, on this very night before the cock crows twice, you will deny me three times!" (Mark 14:30). Peter protested, "Even if I must die with you, I will not deny you!" The other disciples said the same (Matt. 26:35; Mark 14:31).

The Main Part of the Passover Meal

After eating the preliminary dish of bitter herbs, the second cup of wine was mixed. The various elements of the main meal had been placed on the table, but were not to be eaten until later. After the mixing of the second cup, the youngest family member would ask, "Why do we eat this meal?" In reply, the head of the family would give a quick summary of the exodus (Exod. 12:26–27) and explain the significance of the various elements of the Passover meal. This was followed by singing the first section of the *Hallel* ("Praise") Psalms (113–14). (These were also sung at the other festivals and by pilgrims making their way down the Jordan Valley to go up to Jerusalem.) Then the second cup, sometimes called the *haggadah* cup, was shared by all. Both hands were then washed before eating the main meal.[24]

The main part of the Passover meal consisted of the Passover lamb, unleavened bread, and bitter herbs (Exod. 12:8) with fruit purée.[25] Ordinarily the head of the family spoke a blessing over the bread at the beginning of every meal. Passover was the only occasion on which this blessing came later. As the head of the group, Jesus took the unleavened bread,[26] spoke a blessing, broke the bread into pieces, and gave it to his disciples (Luke 22:19). This act of Jesus began the main part of the Passover meal. Under normal circumstances, it was a very leisurely meal of pleasant religious fellowship and could go on late into the evening. For many of the poor, this meal provided the rare experience of being able to eat until totally satisfied. Any food still left at midnight had to be destroyed.

The eating of the meal ended when the head of the house spoke a blessing over the third cup, the "cup of blessing" as Paul labels it in 1 Corinthians 10:16. Some scholars maintain that four cups of wine were shared at the Passover, but the evidence is rather late. The first evidence for the fourth cup is found in the Mishnah (*Pesaḥim* 10:1), which is usually dated to A.D. 220.[27]

The Words of Institution

The three Synoptics as well as the apostle Paul record the words of institution (Matt. 26:26–29; Mark 14:22–25; Luke 22:19–20; 1 Cor. 11:23–26). In the past some have questioned whether Luke 22:19b–20 is a valid part of Scripture. The twenty-fifth edition of the Nestle-Aland text and the second edition of the United Bible Societies text enclosed these verses in double brackets, indicating that they were considered to be later additions, though of evident antiquity and importance.[28] The twenty-sixth edition of the Aland text and the third edition (corrected) of the United Bible Societies text have removed the double brackets.[29] These now recognize that the formerly disputed words of Luke 22:19b–20 are a valid part of the text.[30]

At the beginning of the main part of the meal, Jesus took the unleavened bread and spoke a word of blessing, perhaps "Praise be to you, O Lord, Sovereign of the world, who cause bread to come forth from the earth."[31] He broke the bread into pieces and, as was usual, passed these on to the disciples for them to use in eating the Passover lamb and other elements of the main meal. But then Jesus added the following: "Take, eat; this is my body [Matt.], which is being given for you. This do in remembrance of me [Luke and 1 Cor.]."

Jesus' words warrant a close reading. He said, "This [*touto*, referring to the bread] is *(estin)* my body *(to sōma mou)*."[32] He then added a modifying phrase, "which is being given for you." Luke has, literally, "which in behalf of *(hyper)* you is being given [*didomenon*, present passive participle]." Here Jesus refers to his role as the fulfilment of the prophecies of Isaiah 53 and Psalm 22: he will atone vicariously for the sins of the world. The final awesome events of Jesus' role as the Savior of the world were about to begin; in the language of John, Jesus' hour had come.

Both Luke and Paul add the injunction, "This do in remembrance of me" (Paul also repeats the injunction after Jesus' reference to the cup, his blood). The word "remembrance" *(anamnēsis)* has great significance. Deuteronomy 16:3 states that the purpose of the Passover meal and the seven days of the Feast of Unleavened Bread was "that you may remember all the days of your life the day when you came out of the land of Egypt" (NASB).[33] Similarly, Paul, who had earlier spoken of Christ as "our Passover Lamb" (1 Cor. 5:7), states immediately after the words of institution which he had received and faithfully passed on: "For every time you eat this bread and this cup drink, the death of the Lord you announce until he comes" (11:26, following the Greek word order). "Remembrance," then, is more than mere recollection; it is a reliving of the new-covenant meal and its true significance. As Paul says, the bread and cup involve *koinōnia*, fellowship with and participation in the body and blood of Christ, with all which that implies (1 Cor. 10:16–17).[34]

At the end of the meal Jesus spoke a blessing over the third cup, which was called "the cup of blessing" (1 Cor. 10:16), and gave it to all to drink. Matthew and Mark record, "This is the blood of the covenant which is poured out for many," with Matthew adding, "for the forgiveness of sins." Paul in 1 Corinthians 11:25 records, "This cup is the new covenant in my blood." In Luke, Jesus' words are given as, "This cup is the new covenant in my blood, which is poured out in behalf of you."

The phrase "blood of the covenant" recalls the confirmation of the covenant at Mount Sinai, when Moses sacrificed young bulls to the Lord. Half of the blood was sprinkled on the altar, and the other half sprinkled on the people (Exod. 24:1–8). Moses told the people: "Behold, the blood of the covenant, which the LORD has made [lit., cut] with you in accordance with all these words" (v. 8 NASB).

Blood is life itself. Leviticus 17:14 states, "The life of all flesh is its blood." Verse 11 reads, "For the life of the flesh is in the blood, and I have given it to you on the altar to make atonement for your souls; for it is the blood by reason of the life that makes atonement" (NASB). Jesus' blood, his life, was about to be poured out on the cross. The sixth word of the cross, when Jesus called out, "It is finished!" (*tetelestai*, John 19:30), stresses that he voluntarily gave up his life to atone for the sins of all humankind.

The term "covenant" *(diathēkē)* reflects the Hebrew term *bĕrît*, which in its spiritual sense denotes God's relationship of pure grace with his people. Indeed, the Septuagint uses *diathēkē* for the Hebrew *bĕrît*. In classical Greek *diathēkē* usually referred to a last will and testament, but in the New Testament the word is always used in the sense of *bĕrît*, except in Galatians 3:15 and Hebrews 9:16–17.[35] The phrase "new covenant," used by Luke and Paul, recalls God's promise in Jeremiah 31:31–34. The new covenant which God made with his people was made possible only through the innocent suffering, death, and resurrection of Jesus as the obedient Suffering and then Victorious Servant (Isa. 53).[36]

Matthew and Mark note that Jesus said the blood of the covenant is "poured out for many." This phrase recalls the incident when James and John asked that they be granted the privilege of sitting at Jesus' right and left. Jesus told them, "The Son of man did not come to be served, but to serve and give his life as a ransom for many" (Matt. 20:28; Mark 10:45). To understand the meaning of the word "many," it is necessary to realize that although Aramaic and Hebrew have a word for "the whole," they do not have an equivalent of the Greek and English "all." In both instances cited, "many" stands for "the many which one cannot number, the multitude, the whole." A careful reading makes it clear that the Suffering Servant's awesome role is to atone for the sins of the whole world, of all humankind (Isa. 53).[37]

The Passover as the old-covenant meal was a meal of remembrance of and vicarious participation in the events of the exodus. It was also a meal of anticipation for the Jews, who anxiously looked forward to the time when God would send the Messiah to free them from the Roman oppression and usher in the glorious earthly messianic age. The Lord's Supper, the new-covenant meal, is a meal of remembrance of and vicarious participation in Christ's atonement for the sins of the world (Rom. 6:1–11; 2 Cor. 5:18–21; Eph. 2:1–10). The Lord's Supper is also an eschatological meal. Believers look forward to the time when they will share in the joy and bliss of eternal life in grace with the Lord in heaven.[38]

At this point we should look briefly at John 6:25–71, which some scholars believe reflects the words of institution of the Lord's Supper, which are not found elsewhere in John. Jesus is conversing with part of the multitude of five thousand he had fed the previous day. Prior to feeding them, he had healed their sick and had spoken to them of the spiritual kingdom of God. But it was the food that captured their imagination. The crowd had wished to make Jesus the "Bread King," in keeping with their messianic expectations. Jesus had forced them, as well as his disciples, to leave, and then went up the slopes by himself to pray (Matt. 14:22–23; Mark 6:45–46; John 6:14–15).

As a careful literary analysis indicates, the basic point Jesus makes in his discussion with members of the crowd is their need to believe that he is the true Messiah sent by God his Father. Given the miracle of the preceding day, Jesus naturally uses the metaphor of bread and manna. "To eat" serves as a synonym for "believe." The same is true of the verb "drink." When Jesus speaks of eating his flesh (*sarx*, not *sōma* as in the words of institution) and drinking his blood in verses 53–58, he is speaking of believing in him. This is, then, not a reference to the Lord's Supper, but simply one of the many analogies Jesus used and John recorded.[39]

The Discourse in the Upper Room

The disciples had anticipated that the evening of the Passover would be for them the evening of earthly glory. That is why they vied with each other to lie next to Jesus. His washing of their feet and his prediction that he would be betrayed and that all would desert him had a devastating emotional effect on them, as would the events which immediately followed. Probably after drinking the third cup, the cup of blessing, Jesus spoke the comforting and enlightening words of John 14–16.

Note how carefully Jesus speaks to the disciples about the role of the *paraklētos,* the Holy Spirit, "whom the Father will send in my name; he will teach you everything and remind you of everything I told you" (John 14:26). "When the *paraklētos* comes, whom I will send from the Father, the Spirit of truth, who proceeds from the Father, he will witness concerning me" (John 15:26). And again, "When he comes, the Spirit of truth, he will guide you in all truth. For he will not speak of himself, but as many things as he hears he will speak, and what is coming he will tell you. He will glorify me, because he will take from what is mine, and tell it to you. Everything that the Father has is mine. Because of this, I said that he will take from what is mine and will tell it to you" (John 16:13–15). From these verses it is clear that the term *paraklētos* is multi-faceted; "Comforter" covers only part of the meaning.[40]

Jesus ended this discourse with his magnificent high-priestly prayer as recorded in John 17. Matthew 26:30 and Mark 14:26 note that before leaving the upper room Jesus and the disciples sang a hymn. This most likely refers to the singing of the final *Hallel* Psalms (115–18), as was customary at the close of the Passover meal.[41]

Various scenarios have been constructed to elucidate the final words of John 14:31, "Arise, let us go": (1) Jesus delivered the discourse of John 15–17 while on the way to Gethsemane; (2) Jesus went with his disciples to the temple and there spoke the words of John 15–17; (3) the hypothetical final editor added chapters 15–17.[42] But the words, "Arise, let us go," may well be nothing more than a pause before Jesus developed the themes found in John 15–17—the relationship between himself and the church, and the crucial, ongoing role of the Holy Spirit. As C. H. Dodd expressed it, the words of John 14:31 conclude the first part of the dialog without physical movement from the upper room.[43] Leon Morris notes that anyone who has tried to get a fellowship group to disperse will readily understand that the words of John 14:31 must signal an ending of a stage in Jesus' teaching and the beginning of another in the upper room.[44]

Indeed, any other setting for Jesus' discourse is difficult to entertain. The solemn words of John 15–16 and especially the high-priestly prayer as recorded in John 17 would have made little impression if Jesus and his disciples had left the upper room to go to Gethsemane. Passover evening was a time of great joy. The narrow streets were probably filled with people who had eaten the Passover meal in Jerusalem on this night of fervent remembrance and eager anticipation. Josephus records that the temple was regularly opened at midnight and lit up to permit people to celebrate their joy in God's presence.[45] And given all the events which had taken place in the year of Jesus' passion, the crowds would have been especially fired up by messianic expectations. The streets of Jerusalem were surely not conducive to a discussion of ultimate issues.

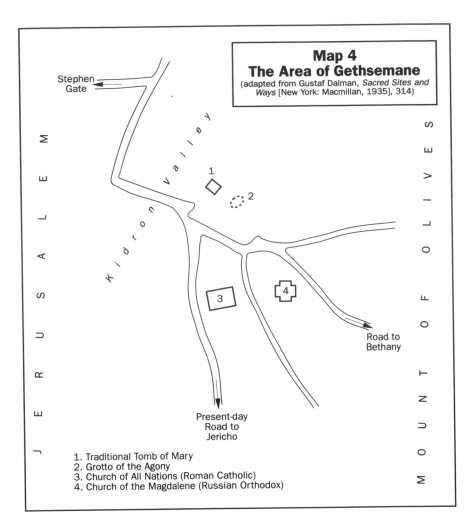

Map 4
The Area of Gethsemane
(adapted from Gustaf Dalman, *Sacred Sites and Ways* [New York: Macmillan, 1935], 314)

Stephen Gate

Kidron valley

1

2

3

4

Road to Bethany

Present-day Road to Jericho

1. Traditional Tomb of Mary
2. Grotto of the Agony
3. Church of All Nations (Roman Catholic)
4. Church of the Magdalene (Russian Orthodox)

JERUSALEM

MOUNT OF OLIVES

7

Jesus in Gethsemane

(Matt. 26:30, 36–46; Mark 14:26, 32–42; Luke 22:39–46; John 18:1)

The Site

After singing the final *Hallel* Psalms, Jesus and his disciples left the upper room. Because it was the night of the Passover, they could not return to wherever they had been staying in the area of Bethany (see Deut. 16:5–7). The Synoptics record that Jesus and the Eleven went out to the Mount of Olives. Since the location of the upper room is not known, it is impossible to specify the route they followed. John does inform us that they walked across the *cheimarros*, a valley through which water runs during the rainy season. This wadi is known as the Kidron Valley.

The Kidron lies several hundred feet below the area that in Jesus' time was the outer court of the temple. Beginning as a wide depression perhaps half a mile to the north, the Kidron narrows as it descends southward, separating the central hills on which Jerusalem is built from the 2½-mile-long spur known as the Mount of Olives. To the south the Kidron is joined by the Hinnom Valley, turns east, and then winds its way southeast through the Wilderness of Judea to the Dead Sea.

Upon crossing the Kidron, Jesus and his disciples entered a place that John terms a garden. It may have been surrounded by a wall. Matthew and Mark use the term *chōrion*, which means "a piece of land" or "a field." Both Synoptics also provide the name "Gethsemane," which in Hebrew is *gat šěmānē*, "olive-oil press." Gustaf Dalman notes that olive-oil presses were often built in caves because of their warmth. In the first century A.D. olive trees were found, as they are today, on the western slopes of the Mount of Olives.[1]

Where was the place identified as Gethsemane? It cannot be ascertained with certainty because of numerous changes in the area in the past two thousand years. For instance, all trees on each side of Jerusalem were cut down by the Romans during the siege of A.D. 70.[2] Several different places have been suggested as possible sites. The site with the longest tradition is the Grotto of the Agony, which lies just east of the traditional tomb of the Virgin Mary and is accessible only through a narrow passage. The cave itself is 55¾ feet long and 29½ feet wide.[3] In 1681, the Franciscans acquired a nearby plot of ground on which still stand eight very old olive trees. Next to this plot is the edifice known as the Church of All Nations. Built in 1924, it covers most of the site of an older church, which may date back to the time of the Crusades. Underneath are the remains of a Byzantine church, which in turn may date back to A.D. 380. In front of the altar in the Church of All Nations is an outcrop of rock which tourists are told is the very site of Jesus' agony.[4]

The Historical Background

Matthew and Mark record that Jesus left eight of the disciples near the entrance to the garden, and took James, John, and Peter with him (Matt. 26:36–37; Mark 14:32–33). The choice of these three disciples is not surprising. They had witnessed Jesus' raising the daughter of Jairus from the dead (Mark 5:37; Luke 8:51), and also his transfiguration (Matt. 17:1–8; Mark 9:2–8; Luke 9:28–36). And during Jesus' last journey to Jerusalem, James and John had boasted they could drink the cup Jesus would be drinking and undergo the baptism he would experience (Mark 10:35–39).

To best understand Jesus' agony in the garden, it must be seen against a backdrop of Satan's activities, human misunderstandings, and Jesus' foreknowledge of his death. It is important to remember that the temptation of Jesus in the wilderness had resulted in defeat for Satan (Matt. 4:1–11; Mark 1:12–13; Luke 4:1–13). Thereafter, Satan avoided direct confrontation but used Jesus' great popularity with the people to tempt him. Recall how often after a busy day Jesus spent the night in prayer. For example, after Jesus had fed the crowd of more than five thousand, he had to send both the people and his disciples away since they wanted to make him their "Bread King." Then he went up the slope to pray to his heavenly Father (Matt. 14:13–23; Mark 6:30–46; Luke 9:10–17; John 6:1–15).

In addition, Jesus had to contend with the people's, and even the disciples', misunderstanding of his messianic role. Indeed, right after Peter's confession the disciples betrayed their ignorance of the true nature of Jesus' role (Matt. 16:21–26; Mark 8:31–37; Luke 9:22–25). Their misunderstanding showed itself again in the events that followed (Matt. 17:22–23; 18:1–5; Mark 9:30–37; Luke 9:43–48). Note also the reaction of the Galilean and Perean pilgrims on the Sunday before Jesus' passion (Matt. 21:1–11, 14–17; Mark 11:1–11; Luke 19:29–44; John 12:12–19).

John 11:45–54 records the negative reaction of the council after Jesus had raised Lazarus from the dead. And on Tuesday of Holy Week, when Jesus told members of the council the parable of the wicked lessees of the vineyard, they realized he was speaking words of judgment against them. As a result, they wanted to arrest Jesus but were afraid to do so because of the people (Matt. 21:23–46; Mark 11:27–12:12; Luke 20:1–19). That evening, the council rejoiced when Judas arranged to betray Jesus to them secretly (Matt. 26:14–16; Mark 14:10–11; Luke 22:3–6). Luke 22:3 specifically records that Satan had filled Judas's heart.

Yet another element of the backdrop, one that was sure to intensify the drama and tension, was Jesus' foreknowledge of his death. Jesus had already foretold his passion to the disciples right after Peter's confession (Matt. 16:21; Mark 8:31; Luke 9:22) and on the way back to Capernaum (Matt. 17:22–23; Mark 9:30–32; Luke 9:43–45), probably in late summer of A.D. 29. At the first cup of the Passover meal, Jesus once again reminded the disciples of his suffering (Luke 22:15–16). Later, as recorded in all four Gospels, he told them that one of them would betray him, and in the words of institution he foretold that his blood would be shed for the forgiveness of sins (Matt. 26:28; Mark 14:24; Luke 22:20).

All of this—Satan's activities, the misunderstandings, and the foreknowledge of death—must be kept in mind to appreciate what happened to Jesus when he and the three disciples walked farther into Gethsemane. Jesus was now confronted decisively, irrevocably, with his role as the obedient Suffering Servant. The time for God's prophecy spoken in the Garden of Eden to be fulfilled had come (Gen. 3:15).

Jesus' Agony

Matthew and Mark use graphic verbs to describe the shuddering horror that overtook Jesus. C. E. B. Cranfield states that the Greek verb *ekthambeisthai* (Mark 14:33) "denotes a being in the grip of a shuddering horror in the face of the dreadful prospect before him," and that *adēmonein* (Matt. 26:37; Mark 14:33) denotes "an anxiety from which there was no escaping and in which he saw no help and no comfort."[5] Pierre Benoit writes that "it is used of a man who is rendered helpless, disorientated, who is agitated and anguished by the threat of some approaching event."[6] Mark's portrait of the "shocking horror, awe and dismay" that overtook Jesus is even more graphic than that drawn by Matthew.[7]

Both Matthew and Mark note that Jesus told the three, "My soul is exceedingly sorrowful, even unto death. Stay here and be on the alert!" (Matt. 26:38; Mark 14:34). Jesus' lament recalls the words of Psalms 42:5–6, 11; 43:5; and 116:3, one of the *Hallel* Psalms. Some suggest that the phrase "unto death" is reminiscent of feelings experienced by Jonah (4:3, 9), Samson (Judg. 16:16), Elijah (1 Kings 19:4), and the son of Sirach (Sirach 37:2; 51:6). J. Warren Holleran suggests that the phrase might well be translated "'so sad I want to die,' and means a sorrow that brings with it the desire for death."[8] Vincent Taylor describes it as "a sorrow which threatens life itself."[9] And William Lane comments that the horror Jesus felt anticipates his awesome cry, "My God, my God, why have you forsaken me?" The graphic description of sorrow in Mark 14:33–34 prepares for Jesus' words in verse 36.[10]

The admonition to be on the alert calls to mind Exodus 12:42—the Passover night "was a night of watching by the LORD" (RSV) and hence a night of watching by all Israel. Luke notes that Jesus also advised, "Pray that you enter not into temptation" (22:40). Immediately thereafter Jesus went forward a little, in Luke's words "about a stone's throw" (22:41).

The variations in the Synoptics' descriptions of the ensuing horror are telling. Luke records that Jesus knelt down (22:41). Matthew says that Jesus fell (aorist) on his face (26:39). But Mark, by using the imperfect, very vividly notes that in the agony of his soul Jesus kept falling on the ground (14:35).

Jesus then prayed to the Father (Matt. 26:39; Mark 14:35; Luke 22:41). In his analysis of the prayer as found in the Synoptics, David Daube demonstrates that Jesus followed an ancient Jewish prayer pattern: (1) acknowledgment ("Father"), (2) wish ("remove this cup"), and (3) surrender ("not as I will").[11] Looking at the acknowledgments in the three accounts, we find notable variations. Luke records that Jesus addressed the prayer to "Father," whereas Matthew portrays Jesus as saying, "My Father." Mark notes that Jesus began his prayer with "Abba," a term which one would expect Matthew, who wrote specifically for a Jewish audience, to use, since "Abba" was an intimate Jewish expression for "father." Joachim Jeremias, in his study of references to God that occur in prayers, points out that in ancient Palestinian Judaism such intimate terms as "Abba" and "my Father" were never used in personal address to God.[12] Only Jesus uses these expressions—an indication of his intimate relationship with his Father.

After acknowledging in his opening words that "all things are possible" for his Father, Jesus expresses his wish, "Take this cup from me" (Mark 14:36; Luke 22:42 NIV). The reference to the cup recalls the words of Isaiah 51:17–23, especially verses 17 and 22. Verse 17 speaks of "the cup of his [God's] wrath," and verse 22 of "the cup of staggering" (RSV). In these verses "cup" refers to God's righteous wrath, his punishment for sin. A similar use of the word is found in Jeremiah 25:15–29 and 49:12, where the Lord says, "Those who do not deserve to drink the cup must drink it" (NIV). As the sinless God-man (Heb. 4:15) and obedient Servant, Jesus was facing the awesome prospect of drinking the cup, of paying the ultimate penalty for our sin. He would have to become the obedient Suffering Servant before becoming the Victorious Servant (Isa. 52:13–53:12).[13] Jesus saw himself confronted by the judgment of a righteous God. He was nearing the climax of his role as the one who, through his vicarious suffering and death for the sins of the world, was to crush the power of the evil one.[14]

Jesus concludes his prayer with the words, "Not as I will, but as you will" (Matt. 26:39 NIV). In this part of his prayer, Jesus underlines his firm resolve to submit to the will of his heavenly Father, to fulfil the mission for which he had come to earth as the Word made flesh. There was a complete surrender to his Father's will, total submission despite the horrifying events that would soon follow.[15]

What were these events? Jesus would be sought like a common thug and arrested through betrayal by Judas, one of the Twelve. Jesus would endure the hypocritical questioning of Annas and, for speaking the truth, would be condemned by members of the council as a blasphemer. They would abuse him and view his silence as confirming his guilt. At dawn, after a hurried rerun of the nighttime proceedings, the council members would take Jesus to Pilate and force him to condemn Jesus to be crucified, even though Pilate would declare several times that Jesus was innocent. Jesus would then experience the ignominious death of the cross. These events must be kept in mind if we are to have any understanding at all of Jesus' agony, especially the scene recorded in Luke 22:43–44.

Both the twenty-sixth edition of Kurt Aland's *Novum Testamentum Graece* and various editions of the United Bible Societies text of *The Greek New Testament* place Luke 22:43–44 in double brackets, indicating that they were not part of the original text but are of evident antiquity and importance. Joseph Fitzmyer notes that Roman Catholics view these verses as part of the canonical text.[16] After summarizing the external witnesses, however, he rejects the two verses. As Fitzmyer sees it, omitting the verses is in keeping with the rule of textual criticism that the shorter and more difficult reading is to be preferred. He also notes that these verses have no parallel in Matthew and Mark. Though Fitzmyer does admit that the tradition about Jesus' agony in Gethsemane as found in verses 43–44 is ancient, he feels that their emotional aspects militate against the more sober Markan text and betray a later hortatory concern. Bart Ehrman and Mark Plunkett believe these verses were inserted early in the second century.[17]

In his analysis of the textual difficulties, Holleran cites the view of Marie-Joseph Lagrange that "while interpolation is not absolutely impossible, it remains highly improbable since the author would have to have lived before the middle of the second century and to have composed the verses in Luke's style. Thus the addition of the verses could really be explained only on the grounds of authentic tradition. Suppression, on the other hand, could be explained on doctrinal grounds."[18] Verses 43–44 may have figured in the Docetic and Arian controversies, and their omission may well be due to "an orthodox copyist's desire to remove narrative details which detract from an understanding of Jesus as fully divine."[19]

A careful analysis of Luke 22:43–44 supports the inclusion of these verses in the canon. The vocabulary is in keeping with Lukan style, as is the medical interest (see Col. 4:14). These verses are also in accord with Luke's purpose to present Jesus' reactions to the events leading to his death on the cross. I. Howard Marshall concludes that even though "the original form of the tradition is obscure, the tradition of Jesus' prayer is no doubt historical."[20]

Luke begins verse 43 with *ōphthē*, a passive form of the verb *horaō*. This typical Lukan word means "to see with the human eye," an inappropriate term if the angel from heaven had been an invisible spiritual presence.[21] In response to Jesus' prayer, the angel is sent to strengthen (*enischyōn*) him; the Greek word is a present participle indicating Jesus' ongoing need. The extent of his agony at this time is graphically stated in Hebrews 5:7–8. It has been suggested that helpful parallel uses of the Greek verb *enischyōn* can be found in the Septuagint version of Daniel 10:18–19 and Isaiah 41:10 and 42:6. The effect of the angel's presence seems to have been that Jesus prayed more earnestly and fervently to remain faithful to his heavenly Father's will.

Luke also notes that Jesus' sweat became like drops of blood falling on the ground. Is Luke using figurative language, or did Jesus actually sweat blood? Alfred Plummer cites the case of Charles IX of France.[22] William Hobart provides examples from Greek medical literature,[23] as does W. W. Keen from nineteenth-century medical literature.[24] Benoit tells us of a man who sweat blood as he was about to be executed during World War I.[25]

In medical terminology the phenomenon of blood mixing with sweat is known as hematidrosis. Bloody sweat is a very rare phenomenon, but it may occur in someone who has a blood disorder or is in a highly emotional state. Extreme men-

tal agony can cause the blood vessels that supply the sweat
glands to enlarge. These vessels rupture, and blood mixes with
sweat. The skin in the immediate area may become so sensitive
that clothing chafes it. When someone experiences hematidrosis, as Jesus did, the blood loss is minimal.[26]

After praying and receiving strength, Jesus returned to find
his disciples sleeping. He asked Peter, "Could you not watch
with me one hour?" (Matt. 26:40; Mark 14:37). The question is
all the more pointed since earlier in the evening Peter had
emphatically said that he would die with Jesus even if all the
other disciples deserted (Matt. 26:33–35; Mark 14:29–31; Luke
22:33; John 13:37). Jesus went on to admonish Peter, James,
and John to keep on the alert, lest they fall into temptation. He
noted that by nature humans are weak, but through the work
of God's Spirit they can strive against the weakness of the sin-
ful flesh. Then, as Matthew 26:42 records, Jesus prayed the
same prayer a second time.

When Jesus returned to the three, he again found them
sleeping. He went back to pray yet a third time, repeating the
thoughts of his previous prayer (Matt. 26:44).

Jesus' words on finding his disciples sleeping a third time
can be taken as a statement ("You are still sleeping and taking
your rest"), a command ("Sleep on, then, and take your rest"),
or a reproachful question ("Why are you sleeping and taking
your rest?"). The Greek word *apechei* (Mark 14:41) is probably
best translated, "Enough of this!" or "It is settled!"[27] Jesus then
explains what he means. Satan's hour has come. The Son of
man will be betrayed and handed over to sinners. Having finished his explanation, he rouses the three from their slumber,
"Get up. Let us go to meet the betrayer who is approaching!"
(Matt. 26:46; Mark 14:42).

8

Jesus' Arrest

(Matt. 26:47–56; Mark 14:43–52; Luke 22:47–53;
John 18:2–12)

The Arresting Group

Matthew 26:46 and Mark 14:42 record that Jesus said to his disciples, "Get up. Let us go to meet the betrayer who is approaching!" All four Gospels provide information on the composition of the arresting group. Luke uses the terms "chief priests" and "elders" (22:52), which indicate that members of the council were present. Also on the scene, according to Luke, were officers of the temple police.[1] Joachim Jeremias notes that the temple official next in rank to the high priest was the captain of the temple, a member of the Annas-Caiaphas family. The captain had charge of the temple police.[2] Because of the importance of Jesus' arrest, it is possible that this official may have been present.

All three Synoptics use the general term *ochlos* ("crowd") in the first verse of their accounts of Jesus' arrest. Matthew and Mark note that the crowd was sent by the chief priests, scribes, and elders (Matt. 26:47; Mark 14:43), that is, by the council. Josef Blinzler explains that the council had under its jurisdiction auxiliary police who were in charge of maintaining public order outside the immediate area of the temple. They had the power to arrest, to guard prisoners and bring them to court, and to carry out sentences as ordered by the court.[3]

John reports that members of the Roman military were also involved. He uses the technical term *speira* ("cohort") and also mentions the captain in charge, the *chiliarchos* (John 18:3, 12).

Some scholars contend that the Jewish forces mentioned above are in view, thereby excluding any reference to the Roman military.[4] However, Raymond Brown and others point out that in the New Testament the term *speira* always denotes Roman soldiers.[5] For example, Acts 21:31–32 refers to the Roman commander *(chiliarchos)* and his troops *(speira)* who rescued Paul from the attacking mob in the temple. The *chiliarchos* was the Roman commander in chief except when the governor was personally present during the three great Jewish festivals (Unleavened Bread, Pentecost, and Tabernacles) to discourage messianic nationalism from erupting into violence.[6]

Josephus notes that a cohort of Roman soldiers was regularly stationed in Jerusalem at the Castle Antonia.[7] The location of this fortress at the northwestern corner of the temple was of strategic importance. As Acts 21:34–35 indicates, a stairway connected the fortress with the temple, which was under constant surveillance to prevent an uprising. Soldiers kept watch from the flat roofs of the colonnades of the east, north, and west walls of the temple.[8] But the southeast tower of the fortress, which was somewhat higher than the other three, was the best observation post for the Romans. It is probable that an alert from this tower resulted in Paul's being rescued from the mob (Acts 21:30–36).

To return to Jesus' arrest, we are told in John 18:12 that the Roman cohort took an active part.[9] Use of the term *speira* does not necessarily mean that an entire cohort, consisting of six hundred men, was involved. It implies only that a sufficient number of Roman soldiers was present to assure that whatever situation might arise would be properly handled.

It is likely that the Jewish leaders had arranged for the soldiers. The messianic events of Palm Sunday and Jesus' popularity with the people, evident as well during his dialogs with members of the council on Tuesday, made it clear that any action taken against Jesus might have serious negative consequences for the Jewish leaders. The Synoptics note that while the council desired to apprehend Jesus, they were afraid to do so (Matt. 21:46; Mark 12:12; Luke 20:19), and that Judas agreed to betray Jesus "apart from the crowd" (Luke 22:6). Accordingly, the Jewish leaders arranged for a military escort to accompany them. It is very probable that the Roman escort was authorized by Pilate himself. That he knew of Jesus' arrest beforehand can be inferred from the governor's initial conversation with the council members (John 18:29–32). The message to Pilate from his wife may well be further evidence (Matt. 27:19).[10]

John records that the arresting group came with *phanoi* and *lampades*. The Greek grammarian Phrynichus suggests that these terms were originally synonyms, but by the New Testament era had acquired separate meanings. *Phanos* meant "lantern," *lampas* usually meant "lamp." However, in this instance it seems to have meant "torch."[11] The Jewish police also carried clubs and what Luke calls *machairai* (22:52). The latter were probably weapons with a short blade, more akin to a dagger than a sword.[12]

The Initial Contact

John notes that Jesus asked the arresting group, "For whom are you looking?" (18:4). When they answered, "Jesus of Nazareth," he replied, "*Egō eimi*." When he said this, they stepped back and fell on the ground. In normal circumstances *egō eimi* would mean merely "I am the one you are looking for." But the situation was far from normal, as is clear from the arresters' falling to the ground. To understand the full import of Jesus' reply, it is necessary to review John's use of *egō eimi* throughout his Gospel account (see, e.g., John 8:24, 28, 58).[13]

Then Jesus asked the arresters a second time, "For whom are you looking?" Upon their reply, he said, "If you seek me, then let these men go their way." John notes that this fulfilled what Jesus had said earlier: "Of those whom you gave me, I have lost none" (John 18:7–9; cf. 6:39; 10:27–30; 17:12).

The Arrest

Judas had prearranged a signal with the arresting group; the person he would kiss was to be arrested (Matt. 26:48; Mark 14:44). Judas approached Jesus and said, "Greetings, Teacher!" Then he kissed Jesus, the customary sign of respect a disciple gave his teacher. Jesus replied, "Friend, do what you came for!" (Matt. 26:50). The Greek word for friend, *hetairos*, is used three times in the New Testament, always as a polite but firm rebuke. In the parable of the laborers in the vineyard, Jesus used *hetairos* to refer to the leader of those grumbling about the owner's generosity in paying all the same wage (Matt. 20:13). Jesus also used it in the parable of the wedding feast to refer to the man who was not wearing a wedding garment (Matt. 22:12). Then in his rebuke of Judas, Jesus used *hetairos* again.

While the arresting group took Jesus into custody, Peter drew his *machaira*, a daggerlike weapon, and cut off the right ear of Malchus, a servant of the high priest. Jesus firmly told Peter to sheath his dagger (Matt. 26:52; John 18:11). Jesus' words as recorded in Matthew 26:53–54 underscore his decision to remain faithful to the will of his Father. If it were Jesus' will, the Father could send more than twelve legions of angels. But Jesus' role was to be the obedient Suffering Servant foretold in the Scriptures.

The Synoptics record that Jesus then addressed the Jewish members of the arresting crowd, pointedly asking why they came out to arrest him as a common robber (*lēstēs*) or thug (Matt. 26:55–56; Mark 14:48–49; Luke 22:52–53). He reminded them that he had daily taught in the temple, where they could easily have arrested him. Then Jesus explained that what was happening was in fulfilment of the Scriptures (e.g., Isa. 53). But this was their hour of darkness (Luke 22:53). Then the disciples fled, in keeping with words Jesus spoke at the Passover meal (e.g., Mark 14:27; cf. Zech. 13:7).

Mark is unique in recording the incident of a young man who was following Jesus (14:51–52). There are no clues as to the identity of the young man. The fact that he wore a garment of very fine linen, *sindōn*, suggests some wealth. When a member of the arresting group grabbed the garment, the young man ran away *gymnos*, naked. As several commentators suggest, *gymnos* here probably means that only a short tunic or undergarment *(chitōn)* continued to cover his otherwise naked body.[14] Perhaps under his tunic the young man had on a *subligaculum*, a band of cloth that was wound around the thighs and loins and worn at all times.[15]

9

Jesus' Trial before the Council

(Matt. 26:57–27:1; Mark 14:53–15:1; Luke 22:54–71;
John 18:12–27)

Contemporary Issues

The Gospel accounts of the Jewish council's proceedings against Jesus, beginning with the hearing before Annas and ending with the events of the trial at dawn, have undergone much scrutiny. There are ongoing debates as to which of the Gospels has priority, and who is indebted to whom. And questions are raised regarding the nature of the oral tradition(s) underlying the Gospel accounts of Jesus' trial.

In his *Trial of Jesus*, David R. Catchpole provides a very helpful survey of both Christian and Jewish interpretations of the trial narratives; he covers scholarship from about 1770 into the 1960s.[1] In addition, numerous studies analyzing the trial from a variety of viewpoints have appeared.[2] The dominant view of current critical scholarship holds that the Synoptic and Johannine accounts cannot be reconciled. The reader will recall that John makes it clear that both Jewish and Roman authorities were involved in Jesus' arrest. And John alone notes that the Sanhedrin did not have capital powers (18:31). Accordingly, he emphasizes the Roman trial and responsibility. The Synoptics, on the other hand, place a heavier emphasis on the role of the Jewish leaders. Some critics feel that these accounts are colored by anti-Semitism.[3] With regard to the various critical viewpoints Herbert Danby states: "The moment we begin to criticize or harmonize these different forms of the proceedings, or attempt to revise or restate what happened, or prefer one of the Gospels' evidence to the detriment of the others, we are in the realms of mere conjecture, and any conclusions arrived at must be to a marked extent subjective and precarious. We can only be guided by probabilities."[4]

Another area of interest is whether Jesus' trial was conducted in accordance with the regulations in the Mishnah. Various scholars point out that the regulations of the Mishnah are essentially theoretical and reflect at least in part a time (A.D. 220) when the council no longer existed. Josef Blinzler contends that the more humane provisions of the Mishnah were not operative in Jesus' day.[5] George Moore notes, "The inquiry whether the trial of Jesus was 'legal,' i.e. whether it conformed to the rules in the Mishnah, is futile because it assumes that those rules represent the judicial procedure of the old Sanhedrin."[6] And Danby, who translated the Mishnah, stressed that its legal provisions reflect Pharisaic views, whereas Sadducean principles dominated in Jesus' day.[7] Since the Pharisees were well represented on the council, however, this point should not be overstressed.

The High-Priestly Families

Some understanding of the high-priestly office is necessary to our study of the trial narratives. From the beginning this office was hereditary. The high priest had to be descended from Aaron and later on from Zadok, the priest of David and Solomon (2 Sam. 15:24–37; 1 Kings 2:35; 4:2; 2 Chron. 31:10). During the Maccabean revolt against the tumultuous rule of Palestine by the Seleucids, Jonathan became the first Hasmonean high priest (152 B.C.). Upon his death, his brother Simon became not only ethnarch but also high priest (1 Macc. 10:1–21; 14:38–49). His descendants were high priests after him. When Herod the Great came to power (37 B.C.), he abolished the hereditary high priesthood. He appointed and deposed high priests at will, a practice continued by the Romans.

Even though the high priesthood was no longer hereditary, it was still considered to be the prerogative of a few families. This is borne out by a listing of the high priests from the time of Herod the Great to the destruction of Jerusalem in A.D. 70:

from the Boëthus family, six were appointed to the office; from the Annas (Ananus) family, eight; from the Phiabi family, three; and from the Camithus family, three.[8] Not only the high priests themselves, including those who had been deposed, but also members of their privileged families were classified as "chief priests." As such, they had the right to a seat and a vote in the Jewish council, the Sanhedrin.[9]

Joachim Jeremias describes the responsibilities and privileges of the high priest. Aside from serving as the chairman or president of the council, the high priest played the key role in the rites on the Day of Atonement, entering the Holy of Holies to sprinkle the sacrificial blood at the place where until 587 B.C. the ark of the covenant had stood. He could take part in any sacrifice he wanted and had first choice whenever consecrated objects were distributed. Josephus informs us that he also officiated on the Sabbath, at the Feast of the New Moon, and during the three great festivals (Unleavened Bread, Pentecost, and Tabernacles). He also represented his fellow Jews in dealings with Rome.[10]

The high priest had firm control of the temple organization and hierarchy. Ranking next to the high priest was the captain of the temple, who substituted for the high priest whenever he was unable to fulfil his responsibilities, for example, on the

---

Figure 3
The Temple Hierarchy

High priest

Captain of the temple guard

The Cultus	Administration	Finance
Leaders of the twenty-four weekly courses	Overseers (7)	Treasurers (3)
Leaders of the daily courses		
Ordinary priests		

The priests served for two weeks each year and at the three great festivals. When not in temple service at Jerusalem, they taught the covenant people in their hometowns and villages. The captain of the temple and at least one of the treasurers were customarily members of the high-priestly family in power.

Figure 4
Isometric Plan of a Mansion in the Upper City

Overlooking the Mount of Olives and the southwest corner of the temple, this mansion covered an area of almost 6,500 square feet. The large reception hall was 36 feet long and 21 feet wide. The mansion was destroyed in A.D. 70 (Nahman Avigad, *Discovering Jerusalem* [Nashville: Thomas Nelson, 1983], 99; used by permission).

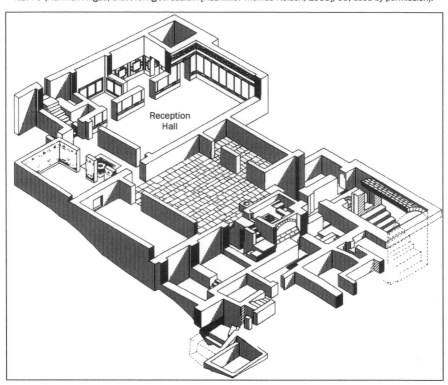

Figure 5
An Artist's Reconstruction of the Reception Hall

This magnificent room was highly ornamented in white stucco. The trial of Jesus in the high priest's palace may have taken place in a hall much like this one (Avigad, *Discovering Jerusalem,* 102; used by permission).

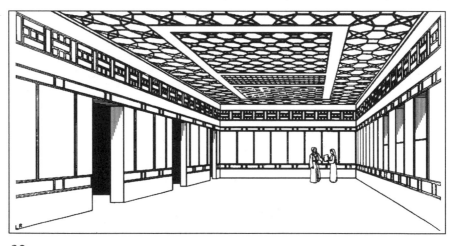

Day of Atonement. It seems that a person could not become high priest without having previously held the position of captain. The captain was in charge of all worship at the temple and of the officiating priests. He also served as head of the temple police. All these responsibilities made him a very powerful person. It is thought that the captain of the temple usually belonged to the same family as the high priest.[11]

Another high-ranking post was that of the temple overseers, who were entrusted with the keys and supervision of the temple. Next in line came the three treasurers, who were in charge of the financial affairs of the temple. Like the high priest and captain, they were members of the council and were included among the "chief priests." At least some of them may well have been part of the family of the incumbent high priest.[12]

In addition to the status accorded high priests and their families, it is likely that they lived in sumptuous residences. Josephus records that Annas the high priest lived in the Upper City.[13] A wall separated this area from the slopes of the Lower City, which descended into the Tyropoeon Valley. Another wall extending from the temple to the praetorium, the fortress-palace of Herod, separated the Upper City from the area to the north. A map of Jerusalem in the second-temple period, prepared under the direction of Michael Avi-Yonah, suggests that the high priest's palace lay a short distance south of the praetorium near the west wall of Jerusalem (see p. 24). It is impossible to be more precise in locating the site.

In 1969 Nahman Avigad began excavations in what is known today as the Jewish Quarter of the Old City, which in Jesus' day was part of the Upper City. Avigad's work has brought to light some large dwellings which were destroyed by the Romans in A.D. 70. One house, built in the first century B.C. and destroyed very early in the first century A.D., covered an area of 2,144 square feet. Its rooms were arranged around a central courtyard.[14] A palatial mansion was found near the scarp of the Tyropoeon Valley, south-southwest of the temple. It covered an area of almost 6,500 square feet. Its main floor was arranged around a square courtyard paved with stone. A doorway from the courtyard led to a vestibule which opened into a large hall 36 feet long and 21 feet wide. There were also several baths. Discovered in this mansion were beautiful mosaics, delicate ceramics, and costly glassware and stone tables.[15] These and other finds provide some idea as to the size and nature of the palatial mansions in which the high-priestly families lived. By contrast the ordinary citizens of Jerusalem lived in very cramped quarters.

Because of misuse of their status and position, the high-priestly families were not held in high regard. This is evident from a folksong preserved in the Talmud. It reflects the pain of people suffering from the injustice of the high-priestly families, who misused their power and status to further their own ends (see p. 35 for evidence from Avigad's excavations):

> Woe is me because of the house of Boëthus,
>   woe is me because of their slaves.
> Woe is me because of the house of Hanan [i.e., Annas],
>   woe is me because of their incantations.
> Woe is me because of the house of Kathros,
>   woe is me because of their pens.
> Woe is me because of the house of Ishmael, son of Phiabi,
>   woe is me because of their fists.
> For they are the high priests, and their sons are treasurers,
>   and their sons-in-law are trustees,
>   and their servants beat the people with staves.[16]

The Interrogation before Annas

Jesus was taken for a private hearing before Annas, the father-in-law of Caiaphas and head of the powerful Annas family, known for its power, wealth, and greed (John 18:12–14, 19–23).[17] Annas himself had been high priest in the years A.D. 6 to 15. As Pierre Benoit notes, Annas after his retirement used his influence and power to fill the office with "his own creatures so that he could continue to direct affairs."[18] In fact, five of Annas's sons and one grandson served as high priests.[19] And now Caiaphas was high priest. John says he was high priest "that year" (18:13) since the Roman governor could depose him at will. The note that Caiaphas had advised the Jews that it would be good if one man died for the people (18:14) recalls the brash comment found in John 11:49–50.

Even though Annas was well informed on Jesus' activity, he pretended to be uninformed. He asked Jesus about his disciples and the substance of his teaching (18:19). Cleverly Annas implied that Jesus' activity had been secret. The priest was laying the groundwork for a charge of subversive action and speech.

Jesus replied that all he had said and done had been public: he had spoken to the world (v. 20). Here, as in John 7:4 and 12:19, the term "world" means "everybody." He stressed his public activity in the synagogs, where his fellow Jews came to worship, as well as in the temple. John's Gospel records Jesus' earlier activities and words in the temple, which was the focal point of Jewish interest and worship, especially during the Passover period. The four Gospels underscore the public nature of Jesus' activities and words from Palm Sunday through Tuesday.

Jesus continued, "Why do you question me? You should be questioning those who heard me." The key consideration here is that under Jewish law a man was considered innocent, and could not be put on trial, until substantial evidence of guilt had been provided by witnesses. Only then could a trial take place. Only then, as Israel Abrahams has shown, could Annas begin interrogating Jesus. When Jesus tells Annas to question the many people who have heard him speak publicly, Jesus is emphasizing this crucial legal point.[20]

Jesus' straightforward reply, evidence of his knowledge of the law, was embarrassing for Annas and his retainers. In response, one of them slapped Jesus, probably on the face. Jesus rebuked him, challenging the official to specify what had been improper about the reply. The attempt to secure incriminating information having failed, Annas sent Jesus to Caiaphas for the council proceedings.

Aside from trying to secure evidence against Jesus, what purpose did the interrogation before Annas serve? It must be remembered that even though the arrest of Jesus was expected, members of the council had to be notified that he was in custody and that they had to come for an emergency meeting late in the night. This meant that messengers had to be sent out to inform the council members to come at once. But this was the evening of Passover, an occasion for celebrating with one's family. It would take time for council members to disengage themselves from their family festivities and come to the high-priestly palace. The interrogation before Annas succeeded in taking up some of this time, though it did fail to achieve its major purpose—securing damaging evidence against Jesus.

The Night Proceedings of the Council

Matthew (26:57, 59–68) and Mark (14:53, 55–65) record the night proceedings of the council against Jesus. Both note that chief priests, elders, and scribes were present. The elders were the heads of leading families.[21] The scribes were the professional Bible scholars, experts in the Torah and its interpretation. Included in their number were various social classes and occupations. The Pharisaic members of the council were scribes.[22] In general, the council was divided between Pharisees and Sadducees, who were represented by the chief priests. The incident involving Gamaliel in Acts 5:33–40 seems to suggest that the Pharisees were in the majority, but this is a matter of ongoing debate.

The Mishnah, though not always reflective of first-century conditions, is helpful in determining the makeup and organization of the council in Jesus' day. The plenary council consisted of seventy members and the high priest, who served as the president. In the official chamber the members sat on elevated tiers in a semicircle so that they could see each other. In trial situations a secretary for the defense sat on one side and a secretary for the prosecution on the other. The defendant and the witnesses were placed in the center. Twenty-three members constituted a quorum.[23]

Matthew and Mark record that the purpose of the night meeting was to find a valid reason to sentence Jesus to death. Matthew states specifically that the council was seeking false witness against Jesus (26:59). Many came forward, but no two of them agreed with each other in every detail, as was required by law. Bear in mind that in Jewish legal practice witnesses were not allowed to hear each other's evidence,[24] and that in capital cases the unanimous testimony of two was required for conviction (Num. 35:30; Deut. 17:6; 19:15).[25]

After much false witness there was testimony about Jesus' cleansing the temple when he came to Jerusalem for the Passover in the first year of his ministry (John 2:13–22). When challenged to give a sign that would validate his right to cleanse the temple, Jesus had said: "Destroy this temple, and in three days I will raise it" (v. 19). Though in verses 21–22 John informs us that Jesus' reference to the temple was typological, the response recorded in verse 20 indicates that the Jews took Jesus' words literally.

To speak against a temple was a very serious offense in the time of Jesus. To desecrate a temple in any way was regarded as sacrilege, a crime carrying the death sentence. In fact, the authorities of a temple could execute anyone guilty of desecration. This was the one exception to the rule restricting to the emperor and his designated governors the right to impose capital punishment. The exception held for the temple at Jerusalem: signs warning Gentiles not to enter the sacred area explicitly stated that doing so would subject the transgressor to execution.[26] Jeremiah's experience clearly demonstrates that speaking against the temple was also considered a crime worthy of death (Jer. 26:1–19).

Two witnesses came forward to testify concerning Jesus' remarks about the temple (Matt. 26:60–61), but even their statements did not agree (Mark 14:59). It is possible that Matthew reflects the words of one witness, "This one said, 'I am able to destroy the temple of God and in three days rebuild it'" (26:61), and that Mark records the words of the other, "We heard this one say, 'I will destroy this temple made with hands, and in three days I will build another not made with hands'" (14:58). While the main thrust was the same, there was variation in detail: "I am able to destroy" versus "I will destroy"; "the temple of God" versus "this temple made with hands" and "another not made with hands." Because of these discrepancies, the testimonies had to be disallowed.[27]

"Are You the Messiah, the Son of God?"

The night proceedings had gone totally against the council. The testimony of all the witnesses resulted in utter failure for the prosecution. Caiaphas, as the high priest, then stepped forward and asked Jesus, "Do you not answer? What is it that these witnesses are saying against you?" (Matt. 26:62; Mark 14:60). Jesus' failure to reply to the various false witnesses had frustrated Caiaphas. But Jesus remained silent.

Matthew 26:63 records that Caiaphas then put Jesus under oath and questioned him. According to Abrahams, this maneuvering by the high priest violated Jewish legal procedure.[28]

Caiaphas said, "I adjure you under oath by the living God, that you tell us if you are the Messiah, the Son of God!" Mark uses the expression "Son of the Blessed," "Blessed" being a Jewish circumlocution for God.

To better understand Caiaphas's action, it is important to remember the events of the past week. On Sunday Jesus had received the messianic adulation of the Galilean and Perean pilgrims as well as that of the older boys in the temple. He had performed a messianic act in cleansing the temple. And much of what he said on Tuesday had messianic implications.

Caiaphas's reference to "the Messiah, the Son of God" (Matthew) and "the Son of the Blessed" (Mark) has its roots in 2 Samuel 7:12–16, where God through Nathan told David that his would be a stable dynasty. David's descendants would sit on the throne as long as the kingship would last. But God also promised that one of David's descendants would sit on the eternal throne and build the eternal house of God. This descendant would be the Son of God. The Qumran documents interpret both 2 Samuel 7:14 and Psalm 2 messianically, and stress that the Messiah would be both a son of David and the Son of God (1QSa 2:1ff.; 4QFlor 10f.). Moreover, a number of other Old Testament passages reveal that the Messiah would be a descendant of David (Isa. 11:1; Jer. 23:5; Mic. 5:2). Incidentally, the term "Messiah" comes from the Hebrew verb "to anoint." Every king was anointed with olive oil. In time "Messiah" gained the specific meaning of "The Anointed," namely, the eternal King promised long ago. To prove that Jesus was the fulfilment of this promise, the New Testament lays stress on his descent from David (Matt. 1; Luke 1:26–38, 69; 2:4, 11).

But what precisely did Caiaphas have in mind when he asked whether Jesus was the Messiah, the Son of God? The Jews of that time interpreted the term "Messiah" in the light of Psalm of Solomon 17 and similar passages in noncanonical Jewish apocalyptic literature. The Messiah would be an earthly conqueror. He would be an ordinary human being, but as the one chosen for the messianic task, he would also be the "Son of God," just as a king in the Old Testament period, having been chosen for the royal task, was to represent God and carry out his will (Deut. 17:14–20).[29]

Jesus' reply is essentially the same in Matthew (26:64) and Mark (14:62). But in Matthew's account, written for Jewish readers, Jesus makes an important point by using legal phraseology which his hearers should have understood: "You have said [it], but I say to you. . . ." Basically Jesus told them that he was not the victorious messiah of Caiaphas's expectations, the earthly conqueror the Jews were so fervently awaiting. Rather, he was the Messiah in the true biblical sense, the son of David and Son of God foretold through the centuries.[30]

In his answer Jesus quotes from Daniel 7:13 and Psalm 110:1. Instead of calling himself Messiah, he borrows the term "Son of man" from Daniel. Throughout his ministry "Son of man" had been Jesus' favorite self-designation. As a study of the Jewish Pseudepigrapha indicates, "Son of man" was not a term used at that time for the Messiah. Hence it was a revealing yet concealing term into which Jesus could build proper meaning through his words and deeds.[31] Borrowing from Psalm 110:1, Jesus also said that he would be "sitting at the right hand of power." The term "power" was a Jewish circumlocution for God. Hence Jesus was saying that he would be sitting at God's right hand, with all which that implies. This will be visibly fulfilled at Christ's final coming, when he will return in all his heavenly glory (Matt. 25:31–46). In using these important texts Jesus said in essence, "Today you will condemn me as a blasphemer, but in the future you will see me coming on the clouds of heaven on the last day. Then you will know that what I said was true, but it will be too late."[32]

Caiaphas's reaction was dramatic: he tore his clothes (Matt. 26:65; Mark 14:63). These were not his ceremonial high-priestly garments, which were normally kept in the custody of the Roman governor and released only for special occasions. Tearing one's clothes was a gesture of indignation or of sorrow (2 Kings 18:37; 19:1; Judith 14:19). In this specific instance it was probably also a signal that the council's purpose had been achieved. When Caiaphas asked the council members for their verdict, they were unanimous that Jesus was guilty of blasphemy and deserved to die.

Some scholars suggest that the mishnaic interpretation of blasphemy was already current at this time. This interpretation, which is based on Leviticus 24:10–16, is found in *Sanhedrin* 7:5a, which specifically states: "'The blasphemer' is not culpable unless he pronounces the Name itself,"[33] that is, unless he utters the sacred tetragrammaton YHWH. But

Blinzler and others argue convincingly that this interpretation of the Leviticus passage did not arise until after the time of Jesus.[34]

Jesus' answer to Caiaphas in a sense typified what had aroused the anger of the Jews and members of the council as early as Jesus' first cleansing of the temple. Jesus had claimed to be the certified agent of God, the one sent by the Father. The Father had given him the power to raise the dead and to judge the world (John 5:16–47; 7:16–18, 28–29). Jesus had said, "I and the Father are one!" (John 10:30). The signs and miracles Jesus had performed proved that what he said about himself was and is true; in the Johannine usage of the word, "true" always means "eternally true."[35] Indeed, John in his prologue clearly asserts that Jesus is the eternal Word made flesh. His role is to "exegete the Father" (John 1:1–18). Under the guidance of the Spirit, this theme is developed throughout the entire Gospel. John 20:30–31 carefully notes how the total life and ministry of Jesus, his words and his deeds, fulfilled the emphasis of the prologue: he had been sent to reveal the Father. In the eyes of the council, this claim of Jesus was blasphemy. Therefore, the members agreed that he was to be condemned.

The Abuse of Jesus

The Synoptics include an incident that took place immediately after the council rendered its verdict. Though the accounts differ in some details, they basically record that the council members covered Jesus' face with a cloth, spat on him, and hit him (Matt. 26:67–68; Mark 14:65; Luke 22:63–65). Historically, such actions were gestures rejecting those guilty of certain sins (Num. 12:14; Deut. 25:9; Job 30:10). What Jesus suffered at the hands of the council members brings to mind the torment of the Suffering Servant as recorded in Isaiah 53 and 50:6—"I gave my back to the smiters, and my cheeks to those who pulled out the beard; I hid not my face from shame and spitting" (RSV).

Medical specialists note that the physical suffering that results from such abuse is immense. Remember, too, that Jesus' extreme mental anguish in Gethsemane had already led to his sweating blood, a rare phenomenon known as hematidrosis. Since this condition leaves the skin very sensitive and tender, the blows Jesus experienced at the hands of the council members must have been very painful.[36]

Matthew, Mark, and Luke record that in addition to the physical abuse, the council members bade the blindfolded Jesus to prophesy and identify his attackers. This is an indication that their actions entailed more than rejection and judgment. Pertinent here is Isaiah 11:3: "His delight is in the fear of the LORD. He will not judge by what he sees with his eyes, or decide by what he hears with his ears." Now the Hebrew word Isaiah used for "delight" is literally "smell." Hence the first part of this verse could read: "His smell is through the fear of the LORD." Those who subscribed to this reading of the verse interpreted it to mean that the true Messiah could and would judge through the sense of smell. He would not need to use his eyes nor his ears. That Jesus remained silent and did not identify those who struck him confirmed to the council that their verdict was correct and just. Jesus was not what he had said he was. He was a blasphemer!

Similar treatment was accorded Simon Bar Kochba (also known as Bar Koziba), who as a messianic pretender led an unsuccessful revolt against Roman rule in Palestine in A.D. 132–135. The highly regarded Rabbi Akiba ben Joseph had acclaimed him as the Messiah. Simon and his forces were disastrously defeated. When Simon was unable to identify those who were abusing him, he was condemned to death and executed as a false messiah. The justification for this sentence was Isaiah 11:3—through his sense of smell the true Messiah should be able to identify his abusers.[37]

Peter's Denials

Each of the four Gospels records the denials of Peter (Matt. 26:58, 69–75; Mark 14:54, 66–72; Luke 22:54–62; John 18:15–18, 25–27). All note that Peter followed the arresting group from a distance. Only the Johannine account mentions that "another disciple who was known to the high priest" preceded Peter into the high-priestly palace (v. 15). B. F. Westcott comments, "The reader cannot fail to identify the disciple with St. John."[38] Leon Morris notes that there was a heavy trade in salted fish between people of Galilee and Jerusalem. Since John's father, Zebedee, was in the fishing business and had hired servants (Mark 1:20), he may well have had trade relations with the high-priestly house of Annas and Caiaphas.[39]

Though the precise details of Peter's three denials are difficult to establish with certainty, the following summation repre-
sents the essential elements of the Gospel accounts. The first
denial occurred when Peter was warming himself at a fire in
the courtyard. The maid who served as the doorkeeper asked
Peter, "You aren't one of this man's disciples, are you?" (John
18:17). The presence of the Greek particle *mē* is taken by some
to imply that a negative answer was expected. Others hold that
by the first century A.D., the particle *mē* had lost this implication. The maid's query is to be taken as a simple question.[40] In
John's account, Peter's reply is a simple "I am not."

Matthew (26:69–70) and Mark (14:66–68) provide more-
detailed information than does John. Instead of referring to
Jesus as "this man," in Matthew the maid speaks of "Jesus the
Galilean," and in Mark of "the Nazarene, Jesus." Both accounts
include a Jewish legal phrase Peter used in his denial. Matthew
has, "I know not what you are saying," while Mark records, "I
neither know nor understand what you are saying." In the noncanonical Testament of Joseph, written sometime in the second
century B.C., a trader accused of stealing people from Canaan
and selling them as slaves replies, "I pray you, my lord, I do not
know what you are saying."[41] The same formula is found in the
Mishnah (*Šebu'ot* 8:3). Peter, then, used a legal formula to deny
what he had earlier affirmed (Mark 8:29; 14:29, 31; and parallels in the other Gospels).

After the first denial Peter retreated to a less public place
under the colonnade of the courtyard. Mark notes, "And the
cock crowed" (v. 68b). In the third corrected edition of the
United Bible Societies text, these words are enclosed in brackets, indicating that their validity is disputed. Among others,
C. E. B. Cranfield suggests that they should probably be retained.
Their omission seems to be due to harmonizing by copyists
(none of the other Gospels includes this important time
notice).[42] We should also note that these words recall Jesus'
statement in Mark 14:30.

While seeking safety in the shadows of the colonnade, Peter
was confronted by the same maid (Mark 14:69) and at least one
other person (Matt. 26:71; Luke 22:58) who said, "This one was
with Jesus the Nazarene." Matthew is most complete in recording that Peter denied with an oath: "I know not the man!" Note
the implications of the verb "to know."

Luke tells us that after the second denial Peter stayed in the safety of the shadows of the colonnade for about an hour. In the ancient world, the term "hour" referred to an indefinite period of time. Then Peter apparently drifted back to those standing around the fire in the courtyard. He was again challenged by them. "Surely," they said, "you are one of them; your speech betrays you" (Matt. 26:73). Both Mark and Luke note that those confronting Peter stressed his Galilean accent. In John's account a relative of Malchus, whose ear Peter had cut off in Gethsemane (John 18:10), asked, "Did I not see you in the garden with him?" (v. 26).

In reply to the challenge, Peter began to invoke a curse on himself and swear, "I know not the man of whom you speak!" (Mark 14:71). The essence of the curse must have been something like, "May I be accursed if what I say is untrue" (cf. 1 Sam. 20:13; 2 Sam. 3:9; Acts 23:12). At that moment, the rooster crowed for the second time. And then Peter recalled, as J. Neville Birdsall stresses, not only what Jesus had said earlier that evening, but also his own boast that had prompted Jesus' remark (John 13:37–38).[43] As Luke notes, at that very moment Jesus looked at Peter. What the specific circumstance was we are not told.

The reference to the cock's crowing has received much scholarly attention. Hans Kosmala, who spent many years in Jerusalem, supplies helpful information. He recorded the times when, under normal circumstances, he heard roosters crowing during the night. His data indicate that the first cycle of crowing began at about 12:30 A.M., the second at about 1:30, and the third at about 2:30. The crowing in each of the three cycles lasted from three to five minutes. Kosmala also notes that Mark 13:35 mentions four night watches: evening, midnight, cockcrow, and dawn; the third, that of the cockcrow, lasts from midnight to around 3 A.M. Drawing on classical literature, he points out that this system of dividing the night into watches was fairly standard throughout the Mediterranean world at that time.[44]

Mark alone records a first (14:68) and then a second cockcrow (v. 72). The other three Gospel accounts mention only the cockcrow after Peter's third denial. This has given rise to a number of textual variants for both of the Markan verses. But Mark's report of the words Jesus spoke to Peter at the Passover meal (v. 30) illuminates the Evangelist's careful attention to the second cockcrow after the third denial. Many copyists apparently omitted the reference to the second cockcrow in Mark 14:30 and 72 in an effort to harmonize these verses with the other Gospels.

When Jesus looked at him, Peter remembered what had been foretold (Luke 22:61); the disciple then left the high-priestly palace and shed bitter tears. The use of *epibalōn* in Mark 14:72 is somewhat puzzling. Since it is followed by the imperfect verb *eklaien*, perhaps *epibalōn* is best translated "began"; that is, "he began and kept on crying." Matthew and Luke add the adverb *pikrōs* ("bitterly"), which points to deep remorse for having denied Jesus.[45]

Jesus' Trial at Dawn

The night proceedings had to be ratified by a legal meeting of the council.[46] Matthew 27:1 records that it took place at dawn *(prōia);* Mark 15:1 adds the word *euthys*—it took place "immediately at dawn." Keep in mind here that Roman trials began at dawn. Luke merely states that the council convened "when it was day."

Whereas Matthew and Mark only mention the morning trial, Luke 22:66–71 provides essential detail. He notes the three groups that were represented in the council and uses the technical legal term *synedrion* (Sanhedrin).[47] Jesus was again asked the crucial question that had been asked at the climax of the night proceedings, "Are you the Christ? Tell us." Jesus replied, "If I tell you, you will not believe. If I ask, you will not answer." Thereby he conveyed the pointlessness of giving them an answer, however truthful it might be. He then reiterated what he had said in the night proceedings, "From now on the Son of man will be seated at the right hand of the power of God!"

The council members responded by asking Jesus, "You, are you the Son of God?" Luke notes that Jesus again used a Jewish legal formula, "You say that I am." The implication is the same as that of Jesus' declaration in the night proceedings: "I am more than you think I am."[48] The council's verdict came quickly: "What need do we have for further witness? We ourselves have heard it from his own mouth!"

10

The Death of Judas

(Matt. 27:3–10; Acts 1:18–19)

Judas and the Chief Priests

Only Matthew 27:3–10 and Acts 1:18–19 tell us what happened to Judas after his betrayal of Jesus. In taking up these texts, it is important to remember that Matthew as one of Jesus' disciples was well acquainted with Judas's betrayal and death. The account in Acts occurs as a parenthetical insertion into Peter's postascension, pre-Pentecost speech urging the disciples to elect a properly qualified person to fill the vacancy left by Judas.

Upon seeing that Jesus had been condemned by the council, Judas was filled with remorse *(metamelomai)* for what he had done (Matt. 27:3). His subsequent actions suggest, however, that in this instance the Greek verb does not have its usual biblical meaning of "repent."[1] Judas went to the council, specifically identified as the "chief priests" and "elders," and told them, "I have sinned in betraying innocent blood." The variant reading which adds "of the righteous one" *(tou dikaiou)* is patently a later interpolation by copyists.

Judas's attempt to return the thirty pieces of silver was rebuffed. The council's laconic refusal, "What is that to us? You see to it!" is both a classical and a Semitic idiom.[2] It implies that each party in the agreement has kept its commitment, so the matter is closed. The problem was Judas's, not theirs! They refused to acknowledge that as Judas had betrayed innocent blood, they too had unjustly condemned an innocent man.

95

Through the words of Judas, Matthew again emphasizes the innocence of Jesus.

Matthew notes that Judas took the thirty pieces of silver and threw them into the temple. Just where in the temple *(naos)* we are not told. The Greek word can refer to the precincts of the temple or the sanctuary itself, including the Holy of Holies. Otto Michel suggests that in this instance Matthew is referring to the temple precincts.[3] D. A. Carson, on the other hand, states that the meaning here is probably the sanctuary itself, into which only priests were permitted to enter.[4] Joachim Jeremias, on the basis of a mishnaic reference to an ordinance of Hillel the Elder ('*Arakin* 9:4), posits that Judas did this to revoke, as it were, the sale of Jesus, thereby making the chief priests responsible for the use of the money.[5] Some commentators do not share his view, feeling that it reflects the thought of a later period.

Judas then went and hanged himself (Matt. 27:5). Although the verb *(apanchomai)* is not used anywhere else in the New Testament, the Septuagint uses it in 2 Samuel 17:23 of Ahithophel's suicide. Giuseppe Ricciotti suggests that Acts 1:18b records what happened after Judas's suicide: his body fell to the ground and was torn open.[6] F. F. Bruce notes that the Greek word *prēnēs* can mean that Judas's body "swelled up," a suggestion already made by Papias, a second-century bishop.[7] Other interpretations of this event by the early church fathers were equally gruesome and macabre.[8]

Acts 1:19 notes that the site of Judas's tragic end was Akeldama, an Aramaic name for "the field of blood."[9] Verse 20 conflates two passages from psalms ascribed to David—Psalm 69:25 and 109:8. Both psalms speak of sufferings that enemies inflicted on David, the ancestor of the Messiah (2 Sam. 7:12–16). In a sense these enemies are a type of Judas. "May their habitation be deserted," importuned David in a foreshadowing of the accursed field bought with Judas's thirty pieces of silver. (Matthew 27:7 states that the site became a cemetery for strangers who died in Jerusalem.) And then in Psalm 109, amid a series of curses against his enemy, the psalmist urges, "May another take his place of leadership" (v. 8), a prefiguring of Peter's suggestion that a qualified person be chosen to fill the vacancy left by Judas.[10]

The Purchase of the Potter's Field

Matthew records the sensitivity of the chief priests to ceremonial correctness (27:6). On the basis of Deuteronomy 23:18, they decided that money such as Judas's thirty pieces of silver could not be deposited in the temple treasury *(korbanas)*, a term used only here in the New Testament. After all, it was blood money. And so the chief priests used the money to purchase the potter's field to serve as a burial place for pilgrims who died in Jerusalem.

The reference to the potter in Matthew 27:7 has aroused much discussion, especially in view of the Old Testament texts reflected in verses 9–10. Some suggest that the Hebrew word for "potter" *(yāṣar)* was somehow confused with the word for "treasury" *('ôṣār)*. And this accounts for Matthew's reference to Zechariah 11:12–13 and Jeremiah 18:1–17; 19; and 32:6–15.[11] Charles Torrey proposed that in some cases the Hebrew term for "potter" can be interpreted as "founder," that is, a person who molded precious objects out of the various metals offered to the temple treasury.[12] But careful study of the Old Testament passages Matthew conflates in 27:9–10 indicates that the reference is indeed to the potter and the potter's field.[13] Matthew mentions Jeremiah specifically since he had served before Zechariah and was probably better known. Jeremiah served as God's spokesman during the tragic years leading up to Jerusalem's destruction in 587 B.C. Zechariah served at the same time as Haggai (ca. 520) and was probably the next to the last prophet of God's covenant people.

Let us look briefly at the Old Testament texts Matthew uses in verses 9–10. Zechariah 11:4–17 draws on the imagery of shepherd life. The shepherds and the buyers (vv. 5, 8, 17) were the leaders of Israel; they slaughtered the sheep (Israel). Zechariah was told by God to shepherd the sheep, even though they were marked for slaughter (vv. 4, 7). When he realized that both the shepherds and the sheep detested him, he decided to resign. He received thirty pieces of silver as his pay, which God told him to throw to the potter. So Zechariah went to the temple and threw it to the potter, who may have been one of the workers who supplied the temple with pottery. Zechariah's action was a graphic image of the judgment that awaited God's unfaithful covenant people.

The image of the potter and his work is dominant in

Jeremiah 18. Jeremiah is told to go to the potter's house and watch him at work. When a jar being formed on the wheel is marred, the potter reshapes it as he thinks best. In verses 5–17 God points out that he is himself the potter, the Lord of history, and that he is using Jeremiah to call the clay, the faithless covenant people, to repentance.

In Jeremiah 19 God tells the prophet to buy a pottery jar and take some of the elders and priests to the Valley of Hinnom, near the Potsherd Gate. There he is to tell them of God's impending righteous judgment on Judah. In this valley they had offered their own sons as sacrifices to Baal and Molech. In consequence God would send destruction on Jerusalem, and this valley would become a cemetery and henceforth be called "the Valley of Slaughter." After delivering this message Jeremiah is to smash the jar beyond repair to symbolize God's impending wrath on his faithless people.

In Jeremiah 32:6–15, the last of the Old Testament passages reflected in Matthew 27:9–10, Jeremiah is imprisoned because of his prophecies. In obedience to God, he buys his cousin's field in Anathoth for seventeen shekels of silver. Here we have a foreshadowing of the purchase of the potter's field with the money paid to Judas.

The Location of Akeldama

Where was Akeldama? The traditional site lies on the south side of the Hinnom Valley where the Tyropoeon, Hinnom, and Kidron valleys meet. This area served as an industrial quarter for Jerusalem.[14] It had two crucial elements for various trades, namely water and fire. Nearby in the Kidron Valley was the spring of En-rogel. The area was also supplied by a conduit from the spring of Gihon, located to the north near the foot of the western slope of the Kidron Valley. The air currents that pass through the three valleys were very helpful in fanning the fires of pottery kilns and the furnaces of the metalworkers. The Hinnom Valley was also used for burning trash. Hence all the connotations that attach to the name "Gehenna" (lit., "valley of Hinnom").

It is significant for our purposes that the Potsherd Gate lay near where the three valleys met. The clay needed by potters was once found in significant amounts in this area. It is not surprising, then, that a burial ground on the site was known as the potter's field. Further evidence of the location of Akeldama is that many caves on the steep south slopes of the Hinnom were used for burial purposes. Eusebius and Jerome among other church fathers record that in their time the area of the potter's field was still used as a burial ground for strangers who died in Jerusalem. Later the Crusaders built the Church of Saint Mary on the site.[15]

11

Jesus before Pilate and Herod

(Matt. 27:2, 11–14; Mark 15:1–5; Luke 23:1–12;
John 18:28–38)

The council had reached its verdict, namely, that Jesus was guilty of blasphemy. According to the Old Testament, blasphemy was punishable by stoning (Lev. 24:10–16). But this was a verdict the council could not carry out. Except for sacrilege, the council had lost its power of capital punishment. The only one who could order an execution was the Roman governor.[1]

We know from the writings of Matthew and Mark that the morning proceedings of the council took place at the crack of dawn. This was in keeping with Roman practice. Seneca, the Roman philosopher and tutor of Nero, complains, "All these thousands hurrying to the forum at the break of day—how base their cases, and how much baser are their advocates!"[2] Pliny the Elder, while serving as the prefect of the Roman navy, completed his working day by the end of the fourth or fifth hour. The Roman time system, like ours, began at midnight. The emperor Vespasian began his official duties before dawn, so that he could later in the morning take care of the many demands the public made on his time.[3]

The Praetorium

As the ruling representative of the Roman emperor in the province of Judea, Pilate was technically a prefect. This was confirmed by the exciting find of a fragmentary inscription in the excavations at Caesarea. Written in Latin in the time of Tiberius, it includes the words "Pontius Pilate, Prefect of Judea."[4] Later the title "prefect" gave way to "procurator." Both

Josephus and Tacitus speak of Pilate as a procurator.[5] As the emperor's appointed ruler of Judea, he stayed at the praetorium whenever he visited Jerusalem. His presence was especially necessary at the time of the three great pilgrim festivals.[6]

The traveler in Jerusalem today who is looking for the site of Jesus' trial before Pilate is usually shown the spot once occupied by the Castle Antonia at the northwest corner of the temple area. As we mentioned before (p. 76), the Roman soldiers watched over the temple from this fortress.[7] For a time it also served as the Jerusalem residence of Herod the Great. However, he found living within the austere confines of this fortress very unpleasant. So he built a beautiful residence for himself along the west wall of the city. At present this area is part of the grounds of the Armenian patriarchate and of the Citadel.

Herod built his new palace-fortress along the west wall for several reasons. The site itself is about a hundred feet higher than the temple area. This fact made it desirable for defensive reasons. At the north end of the palace, he built a fortress with three towers named Hippicus, Phasael, and Mariamme. The Hippicus tower was over 120 feet high and contained a reservoir for rainwater. It probably stood where the northwest tower of the Citadel stands today. The tallest tower, Phasael, was a square structure, each side being about 60 feet long. Its height has been estimated at 135 feet. Phasael contained beautiful apartments and even a Roman bath. Today it is popularly but erroneously called "David's Tower." The third tower, Mariamme, stood to the south of the other towers and apparently dominated the royal apartments as well as the nearby forum (market) of the Upper City and the surrounding residential area. It was over 83 feet high.[8]

Josephus waxes eloquent in describing the beauty and splendor of Herod's palace.[9] It covered an area about 1,000 feet long and more than 200 feet wide. The entire palace was surrounded by a decorative wall 45 feet high. Two large buildings, located at the respective ends of the palace area, each contained elegantly furnished rooms, including a large banquet hall. These two buildings were connected by a semicircular colonnade, inside of which were courtyards and gardens with exotic plants and trees, pools, and statues from which water flowed.[10]

Reconstruction of Herod's Palace-Fortress. A model by Michael Avi-Yonah at the Holyland Hotel. Photos courtesy of the Israeli Government Press Office.

(A) The entrance to the complex is the arched gateway on the right. The fortress with its three towers (Phasael, Hippicus, and Mariamme) is at the upper left. The trial before Pilate probably took place in the building next to the wall separating the fortress from the palace area.

(B) Reconstruction of the praetorium looking south-southeast from the fortress. Beyond the palace wall to the left was a market area.

Even though some scholars place Jesus' Roman trial at the Castle Antonia, history is clear that Herod's palace was the praetorium, the seat of the prefect or governor. When Archelaus, the son of Herod the Great, was deposed in A.D. 6, his possessions were confiscated by the Roman government. His residence in Jerusalem, formerly his father's palace, became the residence of the Roman governor whenever he visited the city. The fortress at the north end of the palace was occupied by Roman soldiers. These together with the garrison at the Castle Antonia controlled and guarded Jerusalem.

Various writings confirm our identification of the praetorium. Philo termed Herod's palace "the house of the governor." He also noted that Pilate brought to Herod's former palace golden shields that bore a dedication to the emperor (see p. 119).[11] From writings by Josephus we know that when Gessius Florus (ca. A.D. 64–66) was governor, a conflict broke out at Herod's palace. The Jewish historian also recorded that the governor Cumanus (48–52) sent reinforcements from this palace to the Antonia fortress.[12] In secular literature the Greek word *aulē* is used for Herod's palace (Josephus so uses this term a number of times), but never for the Antonia. Mark 15:16 records that "the soldiers led Jesus away into the palace *(aulē)*, that is, the praetorium."[13]

Jesus before Pilate

Each of the four Gospels records that immediately after the early morning trial before the council, Jesus was taken to Pilate (Matt. 27:2, 11–14; Mark 15:1–5; Luke 23:1–5; John 18:28–38). Maps of Jerusalem in the first century A.D. show that Herod's palace was but a short distance away, probably no more than four blocks. The entrance was on the east side, opposite the forum of the Upper City. Jesus was brought to the official area of the praetorium, which was in the large northern building. However, the Jews refused to enter lest they become unclean and consequently be unable to eat the special religious meals, the *chagigah*, of the first day of Unleavened Bread (John 18:28). In this passage John uses the term "Passover" in the wide sense, that is, for the seven days of the Feast of Unleavened Bread.

What precisely was it about the Gentiles that the Jews considered to be ceremonially unclean? First, Jews thought that

Gentiles buried corpses, especially of aborted or premature infants, beneath their houses; hence Gentile homes were considered to be permanently unclean (Num. 19:16; 31:19). In addition, Gentile women ignored the regulations laid down in Leviticus 15:19–24 regarding the menstrual cycle, and their impurity was thought to affect their husbands as well. Then, too, Gentiles did not remove all leaven from their houses at the time of the Passover and the Feast of Unleavened Bread, as Deuteronomy 16:4 directed.[14]

The model of Herod's palace constructed under the direction of Michael and Eva Avi-Yonah shows that there was a colonnade which led from the entrance on the east side to the official area at the north end of the complex. The Jews could walk under this colonnade since there were no walls. However, to walk into the official building would have left them ceremonially unclean, and hence unable to participate in the many special services at the temple and in the special religious meals. Knowing their ceremonial scruples, Pilate went outside to meet them, a detail related only by John (18:29). As a matter of fact, John's description of the trial is far more complete than that of the Synoptics, leaving the impression that he may have been present.

As a Roman governor, Pilate was not bound to try non-Roman citizens according to a set procedure, but it seems that he may have often done so. A. N. Sherwin-White, the Oxford classicist, sums up the elements of a typical Roman trial, which Pilate apparently followed:

1. The trial was public, with the governor sitting on the judgment seat (*bēma;* see John 19:13).
2. Two or three accusers, serving as private prosecutors, stood face to face with the accused and stated the charges (this was the role of Tertullus before Felix—Acts 24:1–2).
3. The accused had the right to defend himself. If he remained silent, he was given three opportunities to change his mind and reply to the charges.
4. Under certain circumstances there could be conversation between the governor, who served as the judge, and the people. However, a first-century papyrus warns against this to assure justice.
5. The governor could seek counsel from a committee (see Acts 25:12). This committee was not a jury.

    6. While sitting on the *bēma*, the governor formally pro-
nounced the sentence (John 19:13).[15]

It is likely that, to accommodate the Jews and yet follow
Roman judicial practice, Pilate had the judgment seat brought
outside. In his opening words Pilate basically asked the Jews
for their formal charge against Jesus. Their reply reflects their
contemptuous attitude toward him: "If this fellow were not a
criminal, we would not have brought him to you!" (John
18:30). Pilate retorted, "You [emphatic in the Greek] take him
and judge him according to your law!" (v. 31). These words
suggest that Pilate was well informed about Jesus and the Jews'
religiously motivated hatred of him. The council was then
forced to confess that they had brought Jesus to Pilate because
they did not have capital powers. The word order in the Greek
of verse 31 conveys this well: "To us it is not permitted to execute anyone!" John 18:32 recalls Jesus' various statements to
the disciples concerning his role as the obedient Servant.

    Luke carefully records the various charges the council
brought against Jesus (23:2). They charged him with perverting
the people, that is, with treasonous activity arousing the mobs
against their Roman overlord. Then they charged Jesus with
forbidding the payment of taxes to Caesar. This second charge
misrepresented what Jesus had told some Pharisees and others
three days earlier about their obligation to pay taxes to Caesar
(Matt. 22:15–22; Mark 12:13–17; Luke 20:20–26). At that time
Jesus argued that since they enjoyed the benefits that the pax
Romana had brought them, they had an obligation to pay their
taxes to Rome.[16] It is possible that Pilate through his own
sources was well informed about what Jesus had actually said.
The third charge was one that Pilate could not ignore. In
essence, the council accused Jesus of saying that he was the
earthly messianic king. Such a claim was treason against
Rome, since only Caesar himself could appoint someone to be
a king.

    Pilate then had Jesus taken into the judgment hall to exam-
ine the third charge. The Greek text of John 18:33b conveys the
emphatic nature of Pilate's question: "You, are you the king of
the Jews?" The Synoptics record Jesus' emphatic reply: "You,
you are saying [it]." Jesus had used the same formula in reply-
ing to Caiaphas (Matt. 26:64). The exchange between the pre-

fect and Jesus suggests that Pilate's understanding of the accusation and Jesus' spiritual conception of it did not correspond.

Pilate reminded Jesus that he stood accused by his own people, the council. The prefect pointedly asked, "What have you
done?" (John 18:35). In his reply Jesus stressed that he was not
a threat to Rome because his kingdom is not earthly but spiritual. Verse 37 expresses a point that is emphasized throughout
John's Gospel, namely, that Jesus' role is to witness to the truth,
which in John's account always refers to eternal truth.[17] Then
Jesus restated what he had said many times to his Jewish hearers: "Everyone who is of the truth hears my voice!"[18]

For Pilate truth at best was relative. He then had Jesus
brought outside and declared him innocent of the charges
brought against him by the council. Both Luke (23:4) and John
(18:38) record this first declaration of Jesus' innocence.
Matthew (27:12–13) and Mark (15:3–4) note the council's reaction—they kept on accusing Jesus of many things; but he did
not reply. In keeping with Roman trial procedure, Pilate
reminded Jesus of his right to defend himself. When Jesus continued to be silent, Pilate was amazed. Jesus' reaction was so
different from any the prefect had dealt with in the past. Technically, after declaring Jesus innocent, Pilate should have
released him.

Jesus before Herod Antipas

Luke records that the council then accused Jesus of "stirring
up the people, teaching throughout all Judea, beginning from
Galilee even to this place" (23:5). "Judea" here seems to refer to
all of Jewish Palestine.[19] This accusation was intended to con-
vince Pilate that Jesus was guilty of treason and dangerous to
Roman interests. But Pilate heard the charge differently; he
focused on Jesus' beginning in Galilee. Pilate knew that Herod
Antipas, the tetrarch of Galilee and Perea, had come to
Jerusalem for the Passover and the Feast of Unleavened Bread.
So, as Luke alone records, he sent Jesus to Herod (23:6–12).

Why was Jesus sent to Herod? Sherwin-White takes up the
question whether someone in Roman society who was accused
of a crime was customarily tried in the province where that
crime took place or sent back to one's home province. Gallio,
the proconsul of Achaia, did not question whether Paul was

from the province of Achaia (Acts 18:12–16), nor did Felix hesitate to try the case of Paul when the Roman commander at Jerusalem sent the apostle to Caesarea (Acts 24). It seems that the accused was usually tried in the province in which the alleged crime took place. One question for which there is no answer remains: Did the special extradition rights that had been accorded to Herod the Great apply to Herod Antipas also? If so, as Sherwin-White suggests, therein would lie the reason for Pilate's action. Others suggest that Pilate simply wished to secure Herod's advice regarding the case.[20]

Since the palace of his father had been taken over by the Romans, Herod Antipas stayed at the Hasmonean Palace, which was located in the Upper City on the heights of the western slopes of the Tyropoeon Valley.[21] This beautiful palace, which faced the temple, was but a short distance from the praetorium.[22] Jesus was taken there under guard of Roman soldiers.

Luke notes that Herod Antipas was very happy to see Jesus (23:8). He hoped that Jesus would perform some miracle or wonder for him. Herod questioned Jesus at length, but Jesus did not answer him. Members of the council vehemently accused Jesus, but failed to get a judgment from Herod against him. Then Herod and his bodyguards (or retainers) mocked Jesus; the Greek says they ridiculed and despised him. Finally, Herod put a bright, shining garment on Jesus and sent him back to Pilate. As Pilate told the council members, Herod had found in Jesus no guilt worthy of death (Luke 23:15).[23]

12

Jesus' Final Trial before Pilate

(Matt. 27:15–30; Mark 15:6–19; Luke 23:13–25;
John 18:39–19:16)

Following his appearance before Herod Antipas, Jesus was returned to Pilate. Though the exact order of subsequent events is difficult to establish with certainty, it seems probable that Pilate's meeting with the council, as recorded in Luke 23:13–16, took place next. Pilate reported that neither he nor Herod had found Jesus guilty of the charges brought against him. Jesus was in no way guilty of anything that required the death penalty. Seemingly Pilate's pronouncement triggered the Barabbas episode.

The Paschal Amnesty

The "Barabbas or Jesus" episode draws on a custom known as the paschal amnesty. The biblical texts speak of the release of one prisoner as a tradition (Matt. 27:15; Mark 15:6; John 18:39), but its source is uncertain. Scholars have found possible parallels in Rome, Egypt, and Assyria. Some of them point to the Roman Feast of the Lectisternium, which first took place in 399 B.C.[1] However, a comparison of the prisoner release described by the Roman historian Livy and that described in the Gospels demonstrates that the two are not parallel.[2]

Other scholars are intrigued by an Egyptian papyrus that dates from around A.D. 85 and speaks of a scoundrel who had locked up not only one of his creditors, but some women of the creditor's household as well. The magistrate Vegetus decreed that the scoundrel was worthy of being scourged, but that the people should decide his fate.³ A detailed comparison with the Barabbas episode shows that this interesting papyrus has no connection with the paschal amnesty, though it does indicate that the Roman governor had the right to free someone guilty of a misdeed or crime.⁴

Still others suggest that the paschal amnesty has its source in Assyrian history. Rubrics in the Babylonian-Assyrian calendar mention the release of a prisoner. However, the month for such a release was Marcheshvan, which occurred in autumn rather than spring.⁵ Whether the memory of this custom was the source of the paschal amnesty is difficult to determine.

Ernst Bammel suggests that the paschal amnesty had a Jewish origin.⁶ In speaking of the Passover lamb, the Mishnah states, "They may slaughter for one . . . whom they promised to bring out of prison" *(Pesaḥim* 8:6). Charles Chavel has researched whatever historical evidence could be found and concluded that even though the Mishnah itself dates from about A.D. 220, the reference here is to a custom which goes back several centuries. Seemingly it began with the Hasmonean kings, who released a political prisoner at the time of the Passover to assure people that it was safe to come to Jerusalem. Josef Blinzler suggests that this procedure probably happened often and most likely became a regular occurrence. Apparently the Romans accommodated themselves to this Jewish custom whenever it was advantageous for them to do so.⁷

Matthew records that Pilate had a notable—one might even say notorious—Jewish prisoner in custody (27:16). Mark records that he had been involved in an uprising during which he had committed murder (15:7). John 18:40 describes him as a *lēstēs.* As John uses the term, it means not merely "robber" and "brigand," but more specifically "guerilla" or "insurgent against Rome." Josephus regularly uses the term in the same way.⁸

Richard Husband argues that the use of the Greek phrase *desmios episēmos* ("a notable prisoner") in Matthew 27:16 and the verb *deō* in Mark 15:1 (Jesus was "bound" before being led to Pilate for trial) suggest that Barabbas had not as yet been tried. Husband notes that Herod Antipas had arrested, bound *(edēsen),* and put John the Baptist into prison (Matt. 14:3), but had not sentenced him. By analogy with the cases of John and

Jesus, Husband concludes that Barabbas had been accused and imprisoned, but not yet tried. If he had already been found guilty of insurrection, he would have been sentenced to death, a verdict that was usually carried out at once.[9]

The name "Barabbas" is the Greek form of an Aramaic name, *Bar 'Abba'*, a patronymic that means "son of Abba," that is, "son of the father." Some assert that the name means "son of the teacher," but this would necessitate that it be spelled "Barrabbas."[10] Various Greek manuscripts insert in Matthew 27:16 the name "Jesus" before the name "Barabbas," or in verse 17 *Iēsoun ton* before "Barabbas," resulting in "Jesus the Barabbas." Consequently, some hold that Barabbas was known as "Jesus Barabbas," or even that Jesus and Barabbas were actually one and the same person. But if we follow the usual principles of textual criticism, it becomes clear that these are later insertions and not part of the original text.[11]

The People's Choice

Accounts of the "Barabbas or Jesus" episode in the Gospels differ in some details (Matt. 27:15–21; Mark 15:6–11; Luke 23:13–19; John 18:39–40). Mark suggests that the crowd *(ochlos)* present with the council members asked that the paschal amnesty be observed. Matthew records that Pilate asked them whom they wanted him to release: Jesus or Barabbas. Matthew and Mark both note that Pilate was aware that Jesus had been handed over to him because of envy. According to Mark and John, Pilate asked whether he should release "the king of the Jews," echoing the term the council had apparently used in their charges against Jesus. In both Matthew and Mark we are told that members of the council urged the people to ask for Barabbas.

The question arises, Of whom did the crowd that was present with the council consist? It has at times been said that those who sang praises to Jesus as the messianic King on the previous Sunday now chose Barabbas and demanded Jesus' crucifixion. It must be remembered, however, that the people singing messianic praises to Jesus on Palm Sunday were Galilean and Perean pilgrims. Most of them had probably camped out on the Mount of Olives since there was not enough room in Jerusalem for the many pilgrims who had come for the Passover and the Feast of Unleavened Bread. It is also important to remember that the Passover was a joyous festival. The temple was opened at midnight for the pious to enter, and at dawn came the special sacrifices of the first day of the Feast of Unleavened Bread. Many of the pilgrims would have been at the temple, since participation in these important religious rites was their basic purpose for making the journey to Jerusalem. And consider, too, the agreement of Judas with the council to betray Jesus secretly in such a way and at such a time that no one would know what was happening (Luke 22:6). Is it likely that the pilgrims would have heard about Jesus' arrest and arrived at the praetorium so early in the morning?

Some scholars, after carefully noting these facts, have plausibly suggested that the crowd present with the council at the praetorium were Jerusalemites. They were probably common people who lived in the area known as the Lower City, which was south and east of the walls separating the wealthy Upper City from the crowded slopes of the Tyropoeon Valley.[12] It is also possible that at least some of the crowd were retainers of the high-priestly families who had been alerted to be on hand to impress on Pilate the importance of yielding to the council's demands. Furthermore, unemployment in Jerusalem was always very high. Since the good will of the powerful families was an important factor in securing employment, it would not have been difficult for the council to assemble a crowd.[13]

Matthew alone records that Pilate's wife sent him a message while he was awaiting the people's choice (27:19). She warned her husband not to have anything to do with "that just man" (here *dikaios* probably means "innocent"). She explained that because of Jesus she had been deeply disturbed by a dream. Beyond this brief reference nothing is known about her.

Questions have been raised about this episode involving Pilate's wife. Her knowledge of Jesus' arrest and even her presence in Jerusalem have been matters of debate. Some have suggested that the wife of the prefect could not accompany her husband to his seat of government. The year A.D. 21 saw such a proposal come before the Roman senate, but it was defeated, as Tacitus records.[14] With regard to Jesus' arrest, we have already noted (p. 76) that Roman troops were involved. The permission for these troops to escort the council had most likely been given by Pilate himself, who had come to Jerusalem to make certain that no uprising would take place during the highly emotional observance of the Passover with its remembrance of the exodus and earnest desire to be set free from the Roman overlord. Hence Pilate's wife could well have known about the arrest of Jesus.

When Pilate asked for the decision of the people, they emphatically demanded the freedom of Barabbas—a common thug, murderer, and insurgent. To Pilate's question, "What shall I do with Jesus who is called Christ?" (or, "whom you call the king of the Jews?"), they kept on shouting, "Crucify, crucify him!" When, as the Synoptics record, Pilate asked, "What evil has he done?" they shouted louder than ever, "Crucify him!" Luke notes that Pilate asked for the third time, "What evil has he done? I have found no cause for execution in him! So I will flog him and release him" (23:22).

The Flogging and Mockery

The subject of the flogging Jesus endured is extremely complex. Luke informs us that after Herod sent Jesus back to the praetorium, Pilate told the council and the people with them, "I will chastise him and let him go" (23:16). After they demanded Barabbas and asked for Jesus' crucifixion, Pilate repeated this statement (v. 22). In each case, Luke uses the Greek term *paideuō*, which in contexts referring to physical discipline can mean anything from whipping, a lesser punishment, to scourging, a severe punishment.[15]

Luke is silent as to whether Pilate acted on his intention to flog Jesus. But John (19:1–3) records that immediately after the crowd chose Barabbas, Pilate had Jesus led into the fortress to be beaten by the soldiers, who also mocked and made sport of him. Then Pilate presented Jesus to the crowd again, at which time there were further exchanges between the governor and the Jews. Finally, he handed Jesus over to be crucified. Matthew (27:26–30) and Mark (15:15–19) also speak of the beating, but they place it *after* Pilate had formally sentenced Jesus to be crucified. Do these accounts refer to a single event? And if so, when did the beating take place?

Pierre Benoit contends that the mockery came in what he terms "the middle of the trial," but the scourging took place after Pilate sentenced Jesus to be crucified.[16] John Robinson focuses on the fact that both Matthew and Mark end their accounts of the final hearing before Pilate with the scourging and mockery, placing them just prior to Jesus' being led out for crucifixion.[17] After careful analysis Josef Blinzler, on the other hand, came to the conclusion that John's account provides the most detailed and complete picture of the closing part of Jesus' trial before Pilate. Hence it is best to follow John's sequence of the events that led to Jesus' formal sentencing.[18]

Before we examine what the biblical witness says about the beating and mockery of Jesus, we should briefly consider the kinds of beatings inflicted by the Romans. Basically there were three different kinds, distinguished by degree and purpose. The lightest, known as *fustigatio*, served as a warning for those convicted of petty crimes such as might be committed by youthful offenders. A more severe type of beating was known as *flagellatio*. The severest form, which was known as *verberatio* and often preceded crucifixion, was scourging. When it preceded crucifixion, care was taken that it not cause death, its sole purpose being to increase the agony of crucifixion.[19]

As recorded in John's Gospel, after the people chose Barabbas, Pilate ordered his soldiers to take Jesus into the fortress, which was located at the north end of Herod's palace. John uses the Greek word *mastigoō* to indicate the beating that Jesus received. James Moulton and George Milligan call this verb "the regular term for punishment by scourging."[20] Its meaning is not necessarily so restricted, however; depending upon the context, it can mean "whip," "flog," or "scourge."[21] In speaking of the beating, Matthew 27:26 and Mark 15:15 use the verb *phragelloō*, which means "to flog or scourge"—the punishment inflicted after a sentence of death had been pronounced.[22] We would, of course, expect Matthew and Mark to use this verb, since they place the beating after Pilate had spoken sentence on Jesus. But Pilate's words in Luke 23:16 and 22 ("I will chastise him and then release him") and the sequence of events in John 19 indicate that the purpose of the beating was to satisfy Jesus' accusers and persuade them not to ask for the death sentence. Hence Jesus' beating was not the severe form of punishment that normally preceded crucifixion. Pierre Barbet supports this view,[23] which in no way diminishes Jesus' agony. For the hematidrosis that Jesus suffered in Gethsemane had left the skin particularly sensitive to any form of flogging.[24]

Matthew, Mark, and John describe the crude mockery that Jesus endured at the hands of the soldiers in the fortress (Matt. 27:27–30; Mark 15:16–19; John 19:2–3). Mark and John record that the soldiers put a "purple" garment on Jesus. The Greek term used here *(porphyrous)* usually refers to a garment treated with a very expensive purple dye. Matthew, however, speaks of a "red" *(kokkinos)* robe; this may refer to the ordinary red cloak worn by Roman soldiers.[25]

Matthew, Mark, and John also record that the soldiers, mocking the claim that Jesus was a king, twisted a crown of thorns to place on his head. All three use a Greek word *(akantha)* that can refer to any kind of thorny plant.[26] At least a dozen different species of spiny plants, including a variety of thistles, abound in Jerusalem. Michael Zohary suggests that the very common thorny burnet may have been used by the soldiers to form the crown. He also states that according to Christian tradition the materials for the crown came from a stately evergreen known as "Christ's thorn."[27] Others suggest that the crown was made from the long thorns that grow at the base of the axis of date-palm fronds *(Phoenix dactylifera)*. In fact, coins ranging from the time of Ptolemy III Euergetes (246–221 B.C.) to Augustus (27 B.C.–14 A.D.) depict sovereigns wearing such crowns. Although this suggestion has some appeal, it is doubtful that palm thorns were available to soldiers on such short notice.[28]

To symbolize a scepter, the soldiers put a reed into Jesus' hand (Matt. 27:29). Reeds, as Zohary explains, grew extensively in the biblical period and were used for many purposes, including the making of flutes and walking sticks.[29] The soldiers used the reed to hit Jesus on the head as well (Matt. 27:30; Mark 15:19); they also hit him with their hands (John 19:3). These acts, coupled with the crown of thorns that lacerated his scalp, caused him much pain. Bear in mind that the aftereffects of hematidrosis continued to make his skin very sensitive.[30] In addition, Matthew and Mark record that the soldiers spit on Jesus. They kneeled before him and mockingly said, "Hail, king of the Jews!"

Before bringing Jesus out to the council members and people, Pilate told them, "I bring him out to you so you may know that I find him not guilty of any crime" (John 19:4). In other words, Pilate was yet again declaring Jesus' innocence. When

Jesus came out of the praetorium, Pilate said, "Behold the man!"—in Latin, *"Ecce homo!"* Just what he meant is difficult to ascertain.[31]

"Crucify Him!"

A careful reading of John's account of Jesus' Roman trial suggests that the disciple may have been present in the praetorium and witnessed Pilate's deep disappointment that his ploy to both satisfy the council and free Jesus had failed. The chief priests together with the temple police loudly cried out, "Crucify, crucify him" (John 19:6). In John 19:6b–16 is recorded Pilate's final futile attempt to release Jesus. His reply to the crowd reads, literally, "Take him *you* and crucify [him], for *I* do not find in him any crime." The Greek clearly contrasts "you" *(hymeis)* and "I" *(egō)*. Earlier the council members had acknowledged that they did not have capital powers (18:31), a fact that Pilate as the Roman governor knew well. His retort demonstrates his exasperation with the council's unyielding effort to force him to sentence Jesus to death.

The Jews replied, "We have a law, and according to the law he must die, for he has made himself the Son of God!" (John 19:7). This statement reminds us that John's Gospel stresses the role of witness and of the certified agent in the Jewish legal system.[32] Jesus' signs and miracles authenticated his role as the Father's agent. But, in the council's view, by pretending to speak and act for God, Jesus was guilty of blasphemy and hence had to be executed (Lev. 24:16; Deut. 13). They had already come to this conclusion after Jesus healed the sick man at the pool of Bethesda. Indeed, the Jews were all the more eager to execute Jesus not only because he was abolishing the Sabbath, but also because he even called God his Father, making himself equal with God (John 5:18). The raising of Lazarus was the final straw; the council resolved to condemn Jesus to death (John 11:47–50).[33] Their conviction that they were obeying God's law calls to mind Jesus' words to his disciples in the upper room: "The hour is coming when the man who puts you to death will think that he is serving God" (John 16:2).

Upon hearing the council's reasoning for the death sentence, Pilate had Jesus brought into the audience hall of the praetorium (John 19:9). John records that Pilate was very much afraid. Jesus' behavior during the proceedings had left a deep impression on Pilate. Jesus, in his quiet dignity, was a most unusual prisoner. When Pilate inquired, "Where are you from?" he was asking whether Jesus' origin was human or divine. But Jesus did not answer. As foretold by the prophet Isaiah, the obedient Suffering Servant would not open his mouth (53:7).

Pilate sharply reminded Jesus where his fate lay: Pilate could release him or have him executed. Jesus stunned Pilate with his reply: these proceedings were not in the hands of the governor, but in the hands of God ("from above"; see John 3:3, 7, 31). All that was happening was part of God's gracious plan of salvation as expressed through Old Testament prophecies and Jesus' prior words. Then Jesus added, "He [masculine singular] who handed me over to you has the greater sin" (19:11b). To whom was Jesus referring? Although opinions vary, the reference is very likely to Caiaphas, who as head of the council had handed Jesus over to Pilate.[34] John then notes that Pilate kept on trying to release Jesus (v. 12).

"Not a Friend of Caesar"

Pilate's determination to release Jesus caused the Jews to cry out, "If you release this man, you are not a friend of Caesar. Everyone who makes himself a king speaks against Caesar!" (John 19:12). Before exploring what effect this cry had on Pilate, we must examine what it meant to be a friend of Caesar. The use of "friend" in political contexts goes back to Ptolemaic Egypt as well as to the Seleucids. Though it has been suggested that the term "friend of Caesar" was not used as an official title before the time of Vespasian (A.D. 69–79),[35] the term "friend" with political implications was already used in the latter period of the Roman Republic, and both Augustus and Tiberius used the term "friend of Caesar" for those who in their estimation were worthy of special recognition and status. Anyone of senatorial or equestrian rank could under proper conditions qualify to be declared a friend of Caesar. Some suggest that Pilate was granted this special status through the influence of Sejanus, who, before his execution in A.D. 31, had been for some years a powerful confidant of Tiberius.[36]

For Pilate the words, "If you release this man, you are not a friend of Caesar," contained a fearsome threat. Pilate knew the dour, suspicious nature of the emperor Tiberius (A.D. 14–37). History records that Tiberius had grave emotional problems. And a recent study suggests that some of the Roman emperors suffered from the effects of lead poisoning. Their food was cooked in utensils coated with lead, and the wine they drank was supplemented by a grape syrup that had been boiled in leaden containers. This syrup, which prevented further fermentation and added color and fragrance, made drinking wine the major source of lead poisoning.[37] All indications are that Tiberius was affected. He spent the final years of his reign (A.D. 27–37) in seclusion on the isle of Capri. His death was hailed with a sigh of relief.

Pilate was well aware of the consequences of not being a friend of Caesar. History records that Tiberius regularly deprived suspected enemies of the right to make a will. This usually meant confiscation of one's property and loss of Roman citizenship as well. He could be deported to a small and undesirable island, though execution was much more likely.[38] Pilate's judgment was surely affected by the threat to his property and life. It should also be remembered that the Jews and the Herodian family had powerful lobbies in Rome, and that a number of Pilate's previous actions had given them great cause for offense.

Since Roman military standards bore images of the emperor and other symbols that reflected pagan worship patterns, it was customary for Roman soldiers not to bring them to Jerusalem, where they would offend the Jews. But Pilate had ordered soldiers to enter Jerusalem at night, carrying their standards as evidence of his loyalty to the emperor, who had appointed him to be the governor of Judea. Josephus records that when the people of Jerusalem vigorously protested at Caesarea, Pilate was forced to have the standards removed.[39]

Another source of friction involved Jerusalem's inadequate water supply, which was partly due to the tremendous need for water in the temple. To alleviate the situation, Pilate had used temple funds to build an aqueduct to bring in water from a spring located about halfway between Bethlehem and Hebron. Even though the additional water was appreciated, Pilate's right to use temple funds was protested. To quell the demonstration, Pilate ordered plainclothesmen to bludgeon the protesters.[40] Some suggest that this episode may be reflected in

Luke 13:1. But since no further detail is given, the suggestion must remain hypothetical.

In a third incident, which would take place a few years after Jesus' crucifixion, Pilate placed in his palace in Jerusalem some golden shields honoring Tiberius. Incensed, the Jewish leaders petitioned the emperor, and Pilate was forced to back down. This incident was recorded by Philo, the Jewish philosopher-theologian from Alexandria.[41] It needs to be remembered that neither he nor Josephus was favorable toward Pilate. Given the fact that Tiberius with his concern for the welfare of the provinces permitted Pilate to serve as governor from 26 to 36, we should view the negative reports with a measure of restraint.[42]

The Jews' questioning of Pilate's loyalty to Tiberius proved too much for the governor. He brought Jesus out before the people and then sat down on the judge's bench. Pilate told them, "See your king!" The crowd responded with, "Crucify him!" Pilate's query, "Shall I crucify your king?" elicited the chief priests' reply, "We have no king but Caesar!"

Pilate recognized that his attempts to free Jesus, whom he had repeatedly declared innocent, were fruitless, and that he was exposing himself to grave danger. So, as Matthew records, Pilate publicly washed his hands (27:24), in keeping with what seems to have been a Jewish custom (Deut. 21:6–9). He told the people, "I am innocent of the blood of this man!" The crowd answered, "His blood be on us and our children!" The council had condemned Jesus according to their understanding of the law. When they and the people with them accepted responsibility for Jesus' blood, they spoke only for themselves, not for all of the Jewish nation.[43] Then, sitting on the official seat of judgment, Pilate ordered Barabbas to be released in accordance with the demands of the crowd (Matt. 27:26; Mark 15:15; Luke 23:25). He ordered Jesus to be crucified. In Latin the official words were *Ibis in crucem*—"you will go to the cross!"[44]

John specifies the time at which Pilate declared judgment: "it was the preparation of the Passover; it was about the sixth hour" (19:14). As we explained earlier (p. 48), John never uses the term "the Feast of Unleavened Bread"; rather, he sometimes uses the term "Passover" in its wide sense for the Passover itself and the seven-day Feast of Unleavened Bread that immediately followed it. The phrase "preparation of the Passover" refers to the many rites and sacrifices that were part of the first day of the Feast of Unleavened Bread. Jesus, then, was condemned and crucified on Friday. This interpretation is supported by John's use of the term "preparation" in verse 31. Here the preparation is for the Sabbath, which began at sunset on Friday.[45]

How are we to understand John's reference to the time of day—"it was about the sixth hour"? A careful study suggests that John used the Roman system of reckoning time from midnight. Although this suggestion is often disputed, it makes sense in each of the contexts where John gives a time reference. For example, the "tenth hour" of John 1:39, when the two disciples of John the Baptist came to Jesus, was likely around 10 A.M. In the hot climate of the Jordan Valley near Jericho, which lies about 900 feet below sea level, midmorning is a good time to find shelter from the heat of the sun.[46] By the same reckoning, the "sixth hour," the moment of Pilate's decision, would have been around 6 A.M. History informs us that trials began at the crack of dawn in the first century A.D. and were conducted with much more dispatch than in our age. So, sometime after sunrise, the trial before Pilate ended with Jesus' being formally sentenced to be crucified.

The Roman Elements of the Trial

Before we leave the subject of the trial before Pilate, it should be noted that while Roman governors were not required to follow any set procedures in trying non-Romans, many of the elements of a Roman trial can be found in the Gospels' record of Jesus' trial (see pp. 105–6):

1. The trial was public, with the governor sitting on the judgment seat (*bēma*). Since the council members would not enter the courtroom because of their fear of becoming ceremonially unclean, Pilate conducted part of the trial outside and part inside the judgment hall. It is probable that Pilate sat on the judgment seat when he was presiding inside. We know for sure that he sat on the judgment seat when he spoke the formal sentence outside the judgment hall (John 19:13).

2. The accusers served also as the prosecutors. Members of the council accused Jesus again and again, probably through Caiaphas or a formal spokesman.
3. The accused had the right to defend himself. If he failed to do so, he was given three opportunities to change his mind and reply to the charges. The Gospel records note that Pilate conversed with Jesus inside the judgment hall. Twice Pilate reminded Jesus of his right to defend himself (Matt. 27:13–14 [= Mark 15:4–5]; John 19:10).
4. Under certain circumstances there could be conversation between the governor and the people. Consider here the verbal exchanges in the Barabbas episode, which led to the final word of the people: "His blood be on us and our children."
5. The governor could seek counsel from one or more advisers. Herod Antipas served Pilate in this capacity.
6. Sentence was formally pronounced while the governor sat on the official judgment seat (John 19:13–16).[47]

13

Jesus' Crucifixion

(Matt. 27:31–50; Mark 15:20–37; Luke 23:26–46;
John 19.16–30)

Crucifixion in the Ancient World

Crucifixion has been described as a most barbaric and incredibly cruel form of execution.[1] This has become evident from a variety of medical studies and analyses as well as from the remains of a young man who was crucified in the first half of the first century A.D.

The precursor to crucifixion seems to have been impalement, which dates back to the Assyrians. Known for their cold-blooded, wanton brutality, the Assyrians would take a man from his house in the middle of the night, remove a doorpost from the house, sharpen it, and plant it in the ground. Then they would throw the man on the pointed post so it would catch him under the rib cage. He would be left to hang until he died.

Evidence of impalement is found in works of art from Assyria. A relief from the royal palace of Sennacherib depicts several Jews who were impaled for defending Lachish against his onslaught in 701 B.C. A similar relief, going back to the military campaigns of Shalmaneser III (858–824 B.C.), is found in the British Museum.[2] Impalement is even mentioned in Scripture. When Darius learned in 520 B.C. that Cyrus's nearly twenty-year-old decree to rebuild the temple at Jerusalem had not been carried out, he reissued the order and added, "Furthermore, I decree that if anyone changes this edict, a beam is to be pulled from his house and he is to be lifted up and impaled on it" (Ezra 6:11).

We know from Herodotus that crucifixion was practiced already by the Persians. Darius, for example, had three thousand citizens of Babylon crucified.[3] Martin Hengel points out that this barbaric form of execution was practiced also by the Scythians, Taurians, and Celts, and to some degree by Alexander the Great and his successors.[4]

Josef Blinzler notes that Jewish law does not include crucifixion as a form of execution; however, the Jews did carry out some crucifixions. Alcimus, a Hellenistic Jew whom Demetrius I Soter in 162 B.C. appointed to serve as high priest, had sixty of his Hasidic opponents crucified. And in 88 B.C. Alexander Jannaeus had eight hundred Pharisees who were his opponents crucified in Jerusalem; as they were hanging on their crosses, he had their families slaughtered before their eyes.[5]

The Romans may have learned about crucifixion from their enemies the Carthaginians. Crucifixion eventually became a common punishment for slaves, non-Romans, and, as Hengel points out, Roman citizens who committed certain crimes. Spartacus led a revolt of slaves in 73–71 B.C. When he was defeated, Crassus had six thousand slaves crucified on the Via Appia between Rome and Capua.[6] This barbarous form of execution was intended to discourage future slave rebellions. Tacitus records that a special place in Rome—the Campus Esquilinus, a short distance beyond the present church of Santa Maria Maggiore—was reserved for the punishment of slaves.[7]

Non-Romans who lived within the confines of the empire, including Palestine, were subject to crucifixion. When a rebellion broke out soon after Herod's death in 4 B.C., the Roman legate, Quintilius Varus, crucified two thousand Jews.[8] During his term as governor of Judea (A.D. 52–60), Felix had a large number of Jews who resisted Roman overlordship crucified.[9] In A.D. 66 Gessius Florus even had a number of Jews who were Roman citizens of equestrian rank crucified for their resistance to Roman rule.[10] During the siege of Jerusalem in A.D. 70, Roman soldiers caught Jews trying to flee. As Josephus records, they were whipped, tormented in various ways, and then crucified outside the walls of the city. For several months, as many as five hundred a day were crucified. As soon as one Jew died, his place was filled by another. Although Titus, the Roman commander, pitied those experiencing such a gruesome death, conditions forced him to allow the practice to continue.[11]

It has been a common perception that Roman citizens were never crucified. History reveals that this is not true. On rare occasions crucifixion was imposed on Roman citizens for serious crimes, especially high treason. Suetonius records that Galba condemned a Roman citizen who had poisoned his ward in order to gain the legacy. When this man protested that he was a Roman citizen, he was crucified on a high cross that had been painted white.[12]

Archeological Evidence

Despite the thousands of crucifixions that took place in the immediate area of Jerusalem, until recently no remains of those crucified had ever been found. Then, in 1968, while footings and foundations for an apartment complex were being laid, burial caves were found at Giv'at ha-Mivtar, a little north of where the road from the Mount of Olives ends at the Nablus Road. In keeping with Israeli law, archeologists had a limited time to excavate and study the discoveries.

The tomb complex was on two levels. Burial niches extended 5 to 6 feet into the rock from the burial chamber on each level. These niches, technically termed loculi, were 12 to 18 inches wide. This tomb complex proved to be part of a huge Jewish cemetery dating from the second century B.C. to A.D. 70. It extended from Mount Scopus, the northern part of the Mount of Olives, to the Sanhedrin tombs in the northwestern part of Jerusalem.

Three of the loculi contained small stone boxes, known as ossuaries, in which skeletal remains were deposited. In one were found the remains of a young man who, according to the osteologists, was between twenty-four and twenty-eight when he died. He was about 5½ feet tall and of slender build. The bones of his limbs were fine. He had engaged in only moderate muscular activity. The skull showed that he had a slightly asymmetrical face and a cleft palate. Of special interest was the fact that the right and left heel bones had been fastened together by a 5½-inch nail. Under the head of the nail were fragments of a block of either acacia or pistacio wood. The point of the nail was bent over and had granulated fragments of olive wood attached to it.

This spectacular find has elicited various theories as to the manner in which the young man was crucified.[13] Clearly, his body was supported by a small seat *(sedile)* under his buttocks. But were his knees kept far apart, or were they bent and folded together on one side? On the basis of the manner in which the heels were nailed together, Yigael Yadin suggested that the knees were kept far apart. In support of this view he pointed to an undecipherable word on the inscription of the ossuary and proposed the reading *h'qwl*, "the one hanged with knees apart." Vilhelm Möller-Christensen essentially agreed with Yadin, though he differed as to how the heels were nailed together. Joseph Zias and Eliezer Sekeles made the improbable suggestion that the right foot was nailed to the right side of the upright and the left foot to the left. The angle of a fracture of the left calf, however, seems to indicate that the knees had been folded together on one side.

Also found were the arm bones of the victim. They had been nailed to the horizontal crossbeam. A scratch on the right forearm indicates that the nail had penetrated just above the wrist between the radius and the ulna. This is noteworthy, for artists typically make the mistake of placing the nails in the palms, which, as a matter of fact, are not strong enough to support the weight of a body.

It is likely that, in keeping with Jewish religious custom, the body was taken down and buried before sunset. Hence the victim's legs were broken to hasten death. The tip having bent over, it was impossible to pull the nail out. And so, to remove the body from the cross, the feet had to be amputated by heavy blows. The feet were then buried with the rest of the body, and the remains later placed in the ossuary.

The Method

Hengel points out that there were a number of methods of crucifixion. Seneca wrote, "I see crosses there, not just of one kind but made in many different ways: some have their victims with head down to the ground; some impale their private parts; others stretch out their arms on the gibbet."[14] Josephus records that in their rage against the defenders of Jerusalem, Titus's troops whipped and tortured those whom they caught, and then crucified them in many different positions.[15]

There were two main types of crosses: one was shaped like a

T, with the top of the upright being level with the crossbeam; in the other, the upright extended above the crossbeam. The latter was known as the *crux immissa* or *capitata,* and the former as the *crux commissa.* The X-shaped cross, which is called the Saint Andrew cross, seems to have been unknown in Jesus' day. A low cross was technically termed *crux humilis,* and a high cross *crux sublimis.* The former was more common.[16]

The upright *(stipes)* of the cross was left in position at the place of execution. The crossbeam *(patibulum),* which weighed about 100 pounds, was carried by the condemned against the nape of his neck to the site of the crucifixion. During the procession his arms were probably tied to the crossbeam, which after the crucifixion was returned for its next victim.

A superscription *(titulus)* giving the reason for the crucifixion was either fastened around the neck of the victim or carried ahead of him by a soldier.[17] The superscription was written in black or red on a whitewashed piece of wood. It was placed above the head after the victim had been nailed to the cross.[18] Once death occurred, the board was removed, whitewashed, and used again, for wood is a precious commodity in Palestine.[19]

A wooden seat *(sedile)* was often positioned about midway on the upright so that the buttocks of the condemned would have some support. This device served to lengthen the agony. Although artists frequently depict a footrest *(suppedaneum)* under the feet of the condemned, this feature did not appear until the sixth century. The feet were usually nailed to the upright, one on top of the other.[20]

Those who were crucified customarily had all of their garments removed. But because of Jewish sensibilities the Romans permitted the wearing of a loincloth. A Roman captain was in charge of the execution detail. Four soldiers were assigned to carry out the actual crucifixion and then guard the cross until death occurred. For their troubles they were permitted to divide the victim's clothing amongst themselves.

When the crucifixion procession reached the place of execution, the condemned was laid on the ground with his arms stretched out on the crossbeam. Although various methods were used, in most cases the wrists were nailed to the crossbeam with spikes 5 to 7 inches long and about .4 across. The victim would then be lifted up, and the crossbeam would be fastened to the upright.[21] In the case of the T-shaped cross, there was a mortise in the middle of the crossbeam. In the case of the *crux immissa*, the crossbeam was placed against a specially shaped area of the upright where it could be securely fastened.[22]

The Agony

Much has been written by medical specialists concerning the agony of crucifixion.[23] A person sentenced to die on the cross was usually scourged first. Women, Roman senators, and soldiers, however, were exempt from scourging except in extreme cases. The scourge (*flagrum* or *flagellum*) had a short handle and several long leather thongs, which were either single or braided together. Small metal balls or sharp pieces of bone were attached to the end of these thongs. The person being flogged was stripped of his clothing, tied to an upright post, and beaten on his back, buttocks, and legs. Whereas God had forbidden his covenant people to inflict more than forty lashes, the Romans had no such limitation.[24] Scourging cut into the skin and the subcutaneous tissue. It cut into the muscles and tore ribbons of flesh loose. The extreme pain and loss of blood could cause the victim to go into shock. While the purpose was not to kill the victim, but to intensify the agony of carrying the crossbeam and hanging on the cross, severe flogging could result in an early death on the cross.[25]

Carrying the heavy crossbeam afterward involved much pain. After arriving at the place of crucifixion, the victim was laid on the rough ground, with both arms still tied to the crossbeam. An iron spike was driven through the middle part of each wrist between the carpal bones. The loss of blood was moderate since the spike did not penetrate a major artery. However, the trunk of the median nerve was seriously injured in the process; the result was great pain.[26]

The execution detail then raised the victim from the ground and securely fastened the crossbeam to the upright. This in itself entailed incredible anguish. The feet were then nailed to the upright, one on top of the other, through the metatarsus. Injury to the nerves in this area caused intense pain.[27]

The wooden seat that was constructed on most crosses provided the victim some support, but also lengthened the agony before death set in. If there were no seat and the feet were not

Figure 6
Crucifixion: The Nailing of the Wrists
(from William D. Edwards, Wesley J. Gabel, and Floyd E. Hosmer, "On the Physical Death of Jesus Christ," *JAMA* 25 [March 25, 1986]: 1455–63; used by permission of the Mayo Foundation)

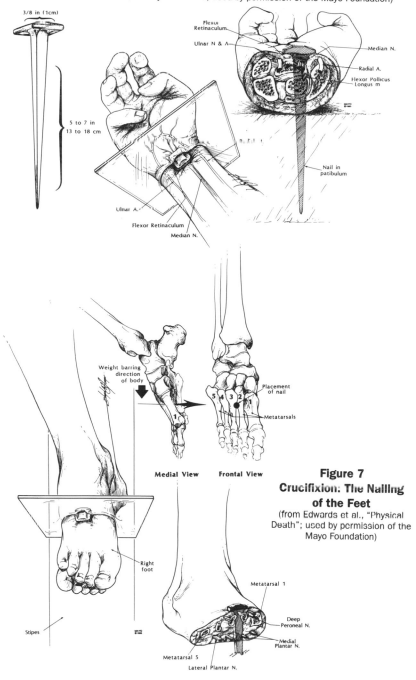

Figure 7
Crucifixion: The Nailing of the Feet
(from Edwards et al., "Physical Death"; used by permission of the Mayo Foundation)

nailed, the victim would hang by his arms. His body would soon experience a tetanic spasm, which would prevent exhalation and lead to suffocation. But with the seat the victim might live as long as two days.[28]

Crucifixion seriously interfered with the breathing process. Because of the weight of the body and muscular contractions caused by the arms' being nailed to the cross, air inhaled into the lungs could not be properly exhaled. The victim soon learned that he could exhale by using his feet to push his body up and by flexing his elbows and shoulders. But this would result in muscle cramps and searing pain in the wrists and feet. Each effort to inhale and to exhale caused agony and increasing weariness. The victim would be soaked with perspiration and experience great thirst. The pain and shock often led to mental impairment. The actual cause of death varied from one victim to another. The two main causes, however, were shock and suffocation, both of which brought on asphyxia—too little oxygen and too much carbon dioxide in the blood.[29]

Because in Jewish Palestine the victims had to be off the cross and buried by sunset, the Romans customarily hastened

Figure 8
Crucifixion: Difficulties in Breathing
(from Edwards et al., "Physical Death"; used by permission of the Mayo Foundation)

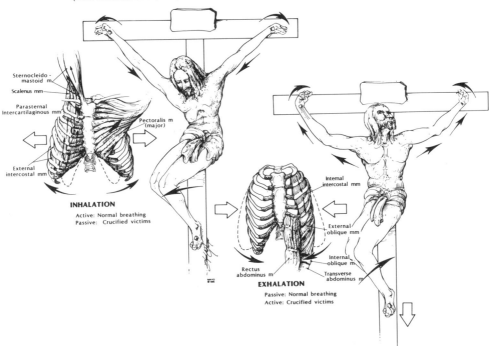

death by breaking their legs *(crurifragium)*. Excruciating pain was experienced as the legs and then, if necessary, the thigh bones were broken with heavy metal bars, but asphyxia and death came within minutes.

The Crucifixion of Jesus

All four Gospels include accounts of the crucifixion, the climactic event of Jesus' role as the obedient Suffering Servant (Matt. 27:31–50; Mark 15:20–37; Luke 23:26–46; John 19:16–30). After Pilate had pronounced sentence, Jesus was taken back into the fortress at the north end of the praetorium to be prepared for execution. We have already seen that Jesus had been flogged earlier (p. 114), so he was probably not scourged at this time. It is possible, however, that the soldiers mocked him again as they prepared him for execution. They took off the purple robe they had used to ridicule him earlier, and reclothed him with his own garments. It is reasonable to assume that they also had to prepare the two evildoers who were to be crucified with Jesus (Luke 23:32).

The crucifixion detail proceeded to a site outside the city walls (Heb. 13:12). Although not expressly stated, it appears that Jesus was unable in his weakened condition to carry the heavy crossbeam. So a passerby, namely, Simon of Cyrene, who was coming from the country area outside Jerusalem, was forced to carry the cross (Matt. 27:32; Mark 15:21; Luke 23:26). That he was coming from the country does not mean that he had been working in his field, for this was the first day of the Feast of Unleavened Bread. The term *agros* is used here in the sense of "the country as opposed to city or village."[30]

What else do we know about the man who carried Jesus' cross? In view of the names of his two sons (Mark 15:21) and an ossuary found in a burial cave of Cyrenian Jews and bearing the inscription "Alexander son of Simon," some believe that he was a Jew of the Diaspora who now resided in the Jerusalem area.[31] However, the names Simon, Alexander, and Rufus were common in Jesus' time, and so do not constitute absolute proof. Simon may well have come from Cyrene to participate in the religious observances of the Passover and the Feast of Unleavened Bread. He may have been staying somewhere in the immediate area of Jerusalem for this festival period.

Cyrene was a city on the North African shoreline west of

Alexandria. Josephus records that Ptolemy I Soter (323–285 B.C.) founded a Jewish colony there to ensure the area's loyalty.[32] Josephus also notes that Jews were one of four groups composing the city's population.[33] Furthermore, Cyrene is represented in the list of those present for the Feast of First Fruits, during which the Pentecost event took place (Acts 2:10).[34] These facts taken together do offer some support for the theory that Simon was a Jew.

While Jesus was being led out to the place of execution, he was followed by a large crowd. Only Luke records the reaction of the women of Jerusalem (23:27–31).[35] In traditional manner they lamented Jesus' fate by beating their breasts. Jesus turned and spoke to them. To be barren was normally considered a reproach (Isa. 54:1–10; Luke 1:25), but Jesus said it would be considered a blessing in the coming days. In alluding to the future destruction of Jerusalem (Luke 23:30–31), Jesus used words recalling Hosea 10:8 and Ezekiel 17:24. And the whole episode recalls his own bitter tears because of the cruel fate that awaited Jerusalem in A.D. 70.

The place of execution was near Jerusalem (John 19:20), outside the walls of the city (Heb. 13:12), and close to a busy street (Mark 15:29).[36] It was known as Golgotha, "the place of the skull." "Golgotha" is the Greek form of the Aramaic *gulgultā'*; the Hebrew form is *gulgōlet*. The Latin for "skull" is *calvaria*, from which comes the term "Calvary." Some suggest that the topographical features of the site resembled a skull. Others propose that Golgotha is simply a figurative name for the place of execution. The latter is probably the better suggestion since uprights were always in place, awaiting the next victims.[37]

Where were Golgotha and the nearby garden tomb in which Jesus was buried? In all honesty, no certain answer can be given. Two sites, however, do have their proponents. One is Gordon's Calvary, a rock outcropping located a little east of the Damascus Gate and bearing some resemblance to a skull.[38] However, the most striking points of resemblance were not present in Jesus' day, but are due to later construction activity.

The second site, which is located within the medieval walls of Jerusalem, is on the grounds of what is known as the Church of the Holy Sepulchre. Near the main entrance a narrow, steep stairway leads upward to the so-called Chapel of the Cross, where presumably Jesus was crucified. Not far away on ground level under a large rotunda is the site that some regard as the location of Jesus' tomb. Although much has been written to support the claim that the Church of the Holy Sepulchre is the site of Golgotha and Jesus' tomb, many questions about the claim, for which there are no adequate answers, remain. Such a claim must be firmly grounded in history.[39]

When the execution detail arrived at the site of Golgotha, Jesus and the two evildoers were crucified. Matthew (27:38) and Mark (15:27) use the term *lēstai,* which usually means "robbers," but can, as in the case of Barabbas, also mean "zealots" or "rebels." The fact that Jesus was crucified between the two fulfils the prophecy of Isaiah 53:12, "He was numbered with the transgressors."

Both Matthew and Mark mention the custom of offering those about to be crucified a narcotic drink to lessen the awesome pain. Tradition holds that it was provided by the respected women of Jerusalem.[40] Matthew (27:34) speaks of wine mixed with gall; Mark (15:23) notes that it was mixed with myrrh. Dioscorides Pedanius, an army doctor who studied almost six hundred plants and a thousand drugs, notes the narcotic qualities of myrrh.[41] Pliny also mentions a narcotic drink of this nature.[42]

John 19:23–24 records that the soldiers assigned to Jesus' crucifixion divided his garments. Jesus' tunic or undergarment *(chitōn)* was a single piece of material. Rather than divide it, they decided to cast lots for it. John notes that this fulfilled Psalm 22:18, which he quotes from the Septuagint: "They divided my garments among them and cast lots for my clothing."

Mark notes that the crucifixion had taken place by the third hour (15:25). Since he followed the Jewish system of reckoning time from sunrise, this would have been somewhere around 9 A.M. It is important to remember, however, that such references are always approximate. (Clocks were, of course, a much later invention.)

The First Three Words on the Cross

Luke records that after Jesus had been nailed to the cross, with an evildoer on either side of him, he cried out, "Father, forgive them; for they know not what they do!" (23:34). Both the United Bible Societies text (3d ed. [corrected]) and the

Aland text (26th ed.) put this saying of Jesus in double brackets, indicating that in their view it was a later addition, though of evident antiquity and importance. Many scholars agree that this saying has no place within the text. Others feel that it is an authentic word of Jesus and must be included. I. Howard Marshall sums up the arguments on both sides and comes down in favor of inclusion.[43] Pierre Benoit notes that even though B, D, and some other uncials omit it, from the beginning of the second century such church fathers as Tatian, Irenaeus, and Origen regarded this word as authentic.[44] Inclusion is also in keeping with Luke's accent on forgiveness.

Jesus asks for the forgiveness of all who were involved in crucifying him, including the soldiers who carried out Pilate's order.[45] David Daube discusses this word of Jesus in some detail. He notes a number of similar statements: Peter's remark in Acts 3:17, Stephen in Acts 7:60, and Paul in Acts 13:27. Daube also calls attention to the Book of Jonah and the Day of Atonement, which lay particular emphasis on sins committed in ignorance.[46]

Some manuscripts of Luke (23:38) proceed to tell us, as does John 19:20, that the superscription was written in Hebrew (or Aramaic), Greek, and Latin. Such multilingual inscriptions were not uncommon at that time.[47] John gives the most complete rendering: JESUS OF NAZARETH, KING OF THE JEWS. In Latin the superscription reads: IESUS NAZARENUS REX IUDAEORUM. Note that the first letters of these four words form the acronym *INRI*, which is often used liturgically. Since the place of crucifixion was near the city, many passed by and read the superscription. The council protested to Pilate and told him to change it to read: "He said, 'I am the king of the Jews.'" Pilate's firm reply was, "What I have written, I have written!" (John 19:21–22).

The Synoptics record the mockery of the council and others who passed the place of execution, wagging their heads (Matt. 27:39–43; Mark 15:29–32; Luke 23:35–37). This recalls Psalm 22:7 and Lamentations 2:15. The first words of mockery recorded by Matthew and Mark repeat the accusation of the false witnesses that Jesus was seeking to destroy the temple (Matt. 26:61; Mark 14:57–58). To speak against the temple was a crime worthy of death. Jesus' taunters then challenged him to come down from the cross and save himself. Their challenge was a mockery of the response Jesus had given Caiaphas: "In the future you will see the Son of man coming on the clouds of heaven" (Matt. 26:64; Mark 14:62). In effect they said, "Prove that you are what you said you are!" The temptation for Jesus to come down and demonstrate the truth of his words must have been tremendous. But he needed to carry out his voluntary role as the Suffering Servant, obedient to the will of his heavenly Father.

Other words of mockery coming from the chief priests, scribes, and elders referred to Jesus' healing ministry, including his raising some from the dead. In essence, they were deriding Jesus as a false prophet who was now being punished by God (see Deut. 13). Matthew 27:43 records a mocking reference to Psalm 22:8: "He trusts in the LORD; let the LORD rescue him. Let him deliver him, since he delights in him" (NIV).

The two crucified with Jesus joined in the mockery (Matt. 27:44; Mark 15:32; cf. Luke 23:39–43). One said to Jesus, "Are you not the Christ [the Messiah]? Save yourself and us!" But the second evildoer then rebuked the first. Alfred Plummer paraphrases the rebuke: "You and he will soon have to appear before God. Does not even fear restrain you from adding to your sins; whereas he has nothing to answer for!"[48] The repentant evildoer then turned to Jesus and said, "Remember me when you come as King." He believed that Jesus was the Messiah and as such would have a kingdom. Joachim Jeremias notes that the Greek phrase *en tē basileia sou* is correctly translated "as King." The textual variant *eis tēn basileian sou* ("into your kingdom") "arose when the Semitism was no longer understood and *basileia* was mistakenly regarded as a spatial kingdom."[49]

Jesus replied with a solemn asseveration, "Truly I say to you, today with me you will be in paradise." He gave the penitent evildoer the blessed assurance of being with him after death. That is, the malefactor was promised eternal fellowship with Jesus in heaven. The word "paradise" is a Persian loanword, originally referring to the private gardens of Persian kings and nobility. It was used in the Septuagint for the Garden of Eden (Gen. 2–3; 13:10; Isa. 51:3; Ezek. 28:13; 31:8). In the New Testament it occurs here and in 2 Corinthians 12:4 and Revelation 2:7 for heaven.[50]

John 19:26–27 records Jesus' third word on the cross. Jesus

saw his mother, some other women, and John standing near the cross.[51] As usual, John does not mention his own name but refers to himself as "the disciple whom Jesus loved." As the eldest son of Mary, Jesus was responsible for her welfare. (The eldest son normally took over the leadership of the family at the death of the father and received a greater percentage of the inheritance.) Jesus in his third word assured Mary that John would take care of her. He then told John, "See your mother!" John records that from this time on he assumed the responsibility Jesus had given him.

There is a tradition that John took Mary with him to Ephesus. Some scholars hold that this tradition stems from the fact that the third ecumenical council, which in A.D. 431 declared that Mary was the "mother of God," met at Ephesus, probably in the so-called Church of the Virgin Mary. Others claim that Mary did indeed live out the later years of her life and die here. They even point to a specific house on the southern ridge of what was once the glittering city of Ephesus.[52]

Jesus' Final Hours

The Synoptics record that an unnatural darkness covered the land ($g\bar{e}$) from around noon until three o'clock in the afternoon (Matt. 27:45; Mark 15:33; Luke 23:44). The Greek word refers most likely to the land of Palestine. Among relevant Old Testament texts, Exodus 10:21–23 and Amos 8:9–10 portray darkness as a sign of God's judgment. Strikingly, Amos speaks of darkness beginning at noon and turning religious festivals into a time of sorrow and mourning. The darkness during the crucifixion obviously was a sign of judgment on the land and the covenant people. It also symbolized Jesus' experience of being forsaken by God.

Attempts have been made to ascertain whether the darkness was caused by some natural phenomenon, for example, a total eclipse of the sun. The only total eclipse on record during the general period occurred on November 24, A.D. 29, in Byzantium and parts of Asia Minor and Syria. It lasted for one-and-a-half minutes at about 11:15 A.M. However, each of the Synoptics notes that the total darkness during the crucifixion lasted for around three hours.[53] It has also been suggested that a sirocco, a heavy dust storm blowing off the desert, might have been the cause, but such a phenomenon results in nothing more than semidarkness.[54]

At about the ninth hour, that is, around three in the afternoon, Jesus cried out in agony, "My God, my God, why have
you forsaken me!" This cry is a quotation of Psalm 22:1. As the
obedient Suffering Servant who was to atone for the sins of the
world, Jesus had to experience being utterly forsaken by God.
His agonized cry is graphic evidence that he was conscious of
being abandoned by God.

The words *Ēli, Ēli,* which Matthew translates "my God, my
God," are a Greek transliteration of the Hebrew (Mark has
Elōi, Elōi, which is Aramaic, as are the words *lema
sabachthani*). When the non-Jewish soldiers under the cross
heard the cry, they said, "This man calls Elijah." The difference
between *"Ēli"* and "Elijah" has caused people to ask why the
soldiers thought Jesus was calling the Old Testament prophet.
A study of the Dead Sea Scroll of Isaiah has shown that the old
Hebrew possessive suffix *-iya* was still in use in the time of
Christ.[55] Jesus most likely said, *"Ēliya, Ēliya"* ("my God, my
God").

Matthew 27:48 and Mark 15:36 tell us that immediately
thereafter one of the soldiers offered Jesus a drink. John 19:28
helps to clarify this action. Knowing that everything required
of him as the obedient Suffering Servant had been brought to
completion, Jesus cried out, "I am thirsty!" One of the effects of
crucifixion and the consequent agony was thirst. It is also possible that Jesus may not have been given anything to drink
since the Passover meal the preceding night. The Gospels do
not provide information on this matter. The soldier's action,
then, was a great kindness. The sour wine mixed with water,
sometimes mistakenly translated "vinegar," was actually a cher-
ished refreshing drink. This the soldier was willing to share
with Jesus.

Although Jesus had probably not been raised very far above
the ground, he was, according to John, sufficiently elevated
that the soldiers needed something on which to lift the sponge
soaked with the wine. They used the branches of a common
dwarflike shrub known as the Syrian hyssop. This is a stout,
hairy shrub that grows to about 30 inches. Its many stems
could easily hold the sponge so it could be raised up to Jesus'
mouth.[56] Some believe this event is foreshadowed in Psalm
69:21 ("They put gall in my food and gave me vinegar for my
thirst," NIV). It must be remembered, however, that the wine the

soldiers shared with Jesus in an act of kindness was a refreshing drink.

Matthew 27:49 and Mark 15:36 report that the soldiers then said, "Leave him alone now. Let us see if Elijah comes to rescue him." Apparently they were aware of the Jewish tradition that in time of need the faithful would be rescued by Elijah, whom God had taken bodily into heaven (2 Kings 2:11–12).[57] Whether the soldiers said this mockingly or innocently, we know that their final impression of Jesus was highly favorable (Matt. 27:54; Mark 15:39; Luke 23:47).

John's two uses of the verb *teleō* in connection with the offering of the sour wine are worth noting (19:28, 30). *Teleō* means "to bring to an end, finish, complete, carry out, accomplish, fulfill."[58] Jesus, knowing that except for his death everything that was necessary for his role as the obedient Suffering Servant "had been perfectly accomplished," spoke of his thirst. After receiving the drink, he cried out with a loud voice, "It is finished," to announce that his work as the Suffering Servant had been completed. This, his sixth word from the cross, was, then, a cry of victory.

Luke 23:46 records the seventh and final word on the cross, and this, like the sixth word, Jesus cried out with a loud voice. The refreshing drink given him by the soldiers had afforded him the strength to cry out, "Father, into your hands I commend my spirit," words that echo Psalm 31:5 (cf. Acts 7:59, where just before he dies, Stephen cries out, "Lord Jesus, receive my spirit"). Then, as John records, Jesus bowed his head. Matthew, Luke, and John note that he "gave up his spirit," which emphasizes that his death was a deliberate act of his own will.

The Cause of Jesus' Death

Jesus' death, which took place six to seven hours after his crucifixion, has been a subject of great interest to the medical world. Many specialists have expressed their views on the cause of death.[59] Pierre Barbet provides a summary of various suggestions.[60]

John Wilkinson, a theologian and medical missionary, surveys possible factors such as intense mental and spiritual agony, exposure, loss of blood, and shock. Wilkinson also analyzes four main theories which have been advanced: William

Stroud's theory of heart rupture, Vincent Taylor's of embolism, Barbet's theory of asphyxia (Barbet advanced the theory of Dr. LeBec, his predecessor at St. Joseph Hospital in Paris), and John Cameron's of acute dilation of the stomach.[61] In his article, which was followed up by responses from both a clergyman and a physician,[62] Wilkinson reiterated what he had emphasized in an earlier article about Jesus' seven words on the cross: the Gospel writers stress the fact that Jesus voluntarily gave up his life to fulfil his role as the obedient Suffering Servant.[63]

14

Jesus' Death and Burial

(Matt. 27:51–66; Mark 15:38–47; Luke 23:45, 47–56;
John 19:31–42)

Christ's Death

Accompanying Phenomena

All four Gospel accounts record that Jesus voluntarily gave
up his spirit and died. The Synoptics mention various phenomena that occurred at his death (Matt. 27:51–56; Mark 15:38–41;
Luke 23:45, 47–49), the first of which was the rending of the
curtain in the temple. Matthew, the most detailed of the
Synoptists, begins his account with the word *idou* ("see,
behold") to signal the importance of this event. All three
Synoptics use the same form of *schizō*, a strong verb meaning
"to rend or tear (apart)." Matthew and Mark tell us that the veil
"was torn in two from top to bottom"; Luke states that it "was
torn in the middle."

The word used for the temple curtain by all three Synoptics
is *katapetasma*. In the Septuagint this word is used for the curtain at the entrance to the sanctuary of the tabernacle, the
masak in Exodus 26:37; 38:18; and Numbers 3:26. This curtain
served the function of a door, and, as Carl Schneider notes, did
not have great worship significance.[1] Some hold that it was
this outer curtain that was torn at Christ's death.[2] A tearing of
this curtain in front of the holy building at the time of the
afternoon sacrifices would have been public and very dramatic
in its effect.[3] It would have been visible from the Mount of
Olives. For this reason some have conjectured that Golgotha

was located on the Mount of Olives in the area of the present-day Church of the Resurrection.[4]

But the term *katapetasma* is also used by the Septuagint for the inner curtain that separated the Holy Place from the Holy of Holies. Its function was to prevent the ordinary priest or Levite on duty in the Holy Place from looking into the Holy of Holies, where the ark of the covenant, which symbolized God's presence, stood until 587 B.C. *Yoma* 5:1 of the Mishnah notes that there was a cubit's space between two curtains that separated the temple into the Holy Place and the Holy of Holies. These curtains were so arranged that there was no direct opening, thereby preventing anyone from looking into the most sacred area of the Holy of Holies. Once a year, on the Day of Atonement, the high priest, dressed in simple white garments, entered through the inner curtain(s) to sprinkle blood on the mercy seat of the ark of the covenant (Lev. 16).

In the New Testament, *katapetasma* is used in Hebrews 6:19; 9:3; and 10:20 to refer to the inner veil. Stressing the certainty of Christ's once-and-for-all atonement for the sins of human-kind, Hebrews 6:19 and 10:20 speak of Christ as the great High Priest entering the inner sanctuary, the Holy of Holies, through the *katapetasma* to pour out his blood for our salvation.[5] Clearly, then, the term *katapetasma* in the Synoptics refers to the inner curtain, which was so significant in the worship of God's covenant people, and especially in the sacrificial rite on the Day of Atonement.

That the inner curtain was torn during the afternoon sacrifice when priests were on duty in the Holy Place means that they could now look into the most sacred part of the temple, an experience which otherwise they could and should never have had! What effect this had on the priests and the temple hierarchy can only be imagined. It should be noted that later many priests came to faith in the risen Christ (Acts 6:7). Perhaps these priests were the Christian community's source of information on this event.

The tearing of the beautiful veil symbolized the all-inclusiveness of Christ's atoning work. As the writer of Hebrews proclaims, the tearing of the curtain dramatically demonstrated that the sacrificial system of the temple no longer had any purpose. All the sacrifices through the centuries had pointed forward to Christ's perfect once-and-for-all sacrifice.

Matthew records other phenomena that followed Jesus' death: the earth was shaken and the rocks were split (27:51b). The verbs Matthew uses are notable. For the shaking of the earth, he uses *seiō*, from which the modern term "seismograph" is partially derived. For the splitting of the rocks (*petrai*, the crust of the earth),[6] he uses *schizō*, the very verb that describes the tearing of the curtain. All this was God's doing at the climactic hour. Scripture makes it clear that God as the Lord of the universe has such power (Exod. 19:16–18; 2 Sam. 22:8–16; 1 Kings 19:11; Pss. 68:8; 114:3–8; Isa. 29:6; Jer. 10:10; Ezek. 26:18; Hag. 2:6–7; Acts 16:26).

Extrabiblical sources likewise witness to a number of frightening phenomena that took place forty years before the destruction of the temple in A.D. 70. Josephus, for instance, tells us that "the priests on entering the inner court of the temple by night, as their custom was in the discharge of their ministrations, reported that they were conscious first of a quaking and a din, and after that of a voice as of a host, 'We are departing hence.'"[7] *Yoma* 39b recalls that "the doors of the temple opened of themselves until Rabbi Johanan ben Zakkai rebuked them, saying, 'O temple, temple! Why do you trouble yourself? I know that your end is near.'"

Matthew 27:52–53 records that the earthquake opened tombs in the immediate area of Jerusalem. The bodies of many of the saints buried in these tombs returned to life and after Jesus' resurrection were seen by many in the holy city.[8] Note the similarity between these verses and the prophecy of Ezekiel 37:12–13. One expectation of the Jewish messianic age was that the righteous dead would return to life to enjoy its blessings.[9]

Reaction of the Roman Soldiers

All three Synoptics record how the centurion in charge of the execution detail reacted to the death of Jesus (Matt. 27:54; Mark 15:39; Luke 23:47). Matthew notes that the centurion and the soldiers who were guarding the crosses became very much afraid as they experienced the earthquake and the other unusual phenomena. Mark mentions that the centurion was impressed by Jesus' cry ("It is finished") and his voluntarily giving up his life ("Father, into your hands I commend my spirit"). Luke also seems to indicate that the centurion was impressed by Jesus' behavior on the cross, which was so completely different from anything the career soldier had ever experienced before. Luke probably has in view Jesus' reaction to being crucified and mocked, his first three words as well as the three hours of unnatural darkness, and his awesome cry as recorded by Matthew and Mark, "My God, my God, why have you forsaken me!"

In Matthew the soldiers guarding the crosses join the centurion in saying, "Certainly the Son of God was this man!" (this translation follows the Greek word order). Mark records that the centurion said, "Certainly this man was the Son of God!" In both cases the predicate noun ("Son of God") precedes the verb; hence, according to E. C. Colwell's celebrated rule, the translator must supply the definite article even though it does not appear in the Greek.[10] The proper translation is, then, "the Son of God," not "a son of God."[11]

Just what did the centurion and his soldiers understand by the term "Son of God"? It has been suggested that they must have had in their view the Greek concept of *theios anēr* ("divine man")—certain heroes and miracle workers were believed to possess divine powers.[12] But while it cannot be said that the soldiers understood the term "Son of God" as fully as did Matthew and Mark, they clearly recognized that Jesus was far more than what the concept of *theios anēr* conveys. After all, they had observed Jesus' unique behavior from the crucifixion up to his unusual death. They had heard the mocking accusations that Jesus claimed to be the Son of God. They had also heard his seven words, experienced the startling hours of darkness, and shared their refreshing drink with him shortly before his death. These facts must be kept in mind.

In Luke the centurion's confession reads, "Certainly this man was righteous *(dikaios)*!" In view of the total context, *dikaios* is perhaps better translated "righteous" rather than "innocent."[13] Luke then notes that the crowd that had gathered to witness the sight beat their breasts (a Jewish custom of that age) and went their way. Luke, like Matthew and Mark, proceeds to tell us that women who had followed Jesus from Galilee were present to witness all these events.

Breaking the Legs

It was a tenet of Old Testament law that anyone who was executed had to be interred by sunset (Deut. 21:22–23; Josh.

8:29). This was particularly important if the following day was sacred. Now the Friday of Jesus' crucifixion happened to be the day after the Passover meal (Thursday), the first day of the seven-day Feast of Unleavened Bread, and also the day of preparation for the Sabbath, which officially began at sunset.[14] The Sabbath following the Passover was especially important, as John 19:31 carefully notes—"for great was the day of that Sabbath."[15] Mark 15:42 also states that it was the day of preparation for the Sabbath.

In an incident recorded only in John 19:31–37, members of the council ("the Jews" in v. 31) asked Pilate to order that the legs of the crucified be broken to hasten death and permit burial before sunset. Breaking the legs, a procedure known as *crurifragium*, interfered with breathing, since the victim could no longer lift himself up to exhale. Death followed in a few minutes.[16] It seems that the Roman government usually complied with requests for *crurifragium*. So Pilate gave the order, which was carried out by the soldiers under the cross. The legs of the two men crucified with Jesus were broken by iron bars. Archeological confirmation has been found in the fact that the leg bones of the crucified young man discovered at Giv'at ha-Mivtar in 1968 give evidence of having been broken to hasten death.[17]

Blood and Water

John records that after breaking the legs of the two men crucified with Jesus, the soldiers found that he was already dead. To verify this, one of them thrust the point of his weapon into Jesus' side. The word *lonchē* can mean either "spear" (Lat., *pilum*) or "lance" (Lat., *lancea*).[18] The spear, a heavy javelin used for hurling, was the basic weapon of the Roman legionnaires; it may be significant here that no Roman legions were stationed in Palestine at this time. The lance, on the other hand, was a lighter, longer-shafted javelin used for thrusting, and is likely the weapon the soldier used.[19]

John notes that when the soldier thrust his lance into Jesus' side, blood and water came out. This physical detail has generated much discussion. In 1953, for example, Pierre Barbet suggested that the lance must have pierced the heart cavity. Furthermore, what John calls "water" was probably a fluid originating in the pericardial sac.[20]

In 1957, A. F. Sava disputed Barbet's findings, which were based on the condition of bodies that had been dead for more than twenty-four hours. Sava, by contrast, had experimented with cadavers less than six hours after death. Sava's experiments showed that when a lance is thrust into the side of the chest, fluid from the pericardium and the heart "will flood the space around the lung rather than ooze its way slowly across the pierced lung" to the wound in the chest wall.[21] He suggested that in the case of Jesus "the blood and water were present just inside the rib cage between the pleura lining the chest and that lining the lung." Sava also suggested that Jesus' flogging a few hours before his crucifixion was enough to cause a bloody accumulation of fluid within the chest:

> Experience with severe chest injuries has demonstrated that nonpenetrating injuries of the chest are capable of producing an accumulation of a hemorrhagic fluid in the space between the ribs and the lung. This volume of bloody fluid varies with the severity of the injury and the degree of response to such an injury. . . . Such collections of blood in closed cavities do not clot. The red blood cells tend by their weight to gravitate toward the bottom of the containing cavity, thus dividing it into a dark red cellular component below, while the lighter clear serum accumulates in the upper half of the collection as a separate though contiguous layer. . . . From a purely anatomic-mechanical standpoint, therefore, the likelihood of hemorrhagic effusion between the lung and the ribs is far greater than a similar occurrence within the pericardial sac.[22]

In 1975, John Wilkinson, who is both theologian and medical missionary, analyzed and assessed various theories, including those of Barbet and Sava. Though it has been suggested that the lance was thrust into Jesus' right side,[23] Wilkinson argued that the term *pleura* ("side") in John 19:34 provides no specific information as to which side was pierced. He attributed the issue of blood and water to gravity and the vertical position of the body on the cross.[24] Noting that blood remains fluid for some time after death, Wilkinson concluded that the lance must have pierced the lower part of the heart cavity.[25] On the basis of his medical experience with severe injuries he agreed with Barbet that the "water" originated in the pericardial sac. This fluid "was thin, clear and colourless and quite distinct from the thick, opaque, red blood it accompanied."[26] The lance thrust released the fluid and, in penetrating the heart, also released the blood, which came out first. It is probable that more watery fluid flowed out than blood.[27]

In a recent discussion of the subject (1986), William Edwards, Wesley Gabel, and Floyd Hosmer theorize that the lance perforated "the distended and thin-walled right atrium or ventricle rather than the thick-walled and contracted left ventricle."[28] Figure 9 illustrates how the lance may have penetrated the sternum, parietal pericardium, and pericardial cavity. Edwards and his colleagues suggest that the water "probably represented serious pleural and pericardial fluid," and that the blood may have come "from the right atrium or ventricle . . . or perhaps from a hemopericardium."

After reporting the piercing of Jesus' side, John declares, "And he who saw has borne witness, and true is his witness, and that one knows that true is what he says, in order that you [emphatic] may believe" (19:35). Keep in mind that when John uses the term "witness" in either verb or noun form, it is always in the legal sense. His use of "true" or "truth" is always in the sense of what is genuinely, eternally sure.[29]

In concluding his account of the crucifixion, John notes that

Figure 9
The Piercing of Jesus' Side
(from Edwards et al., "Physical Death"; used by permission of the Mayo Foundation)

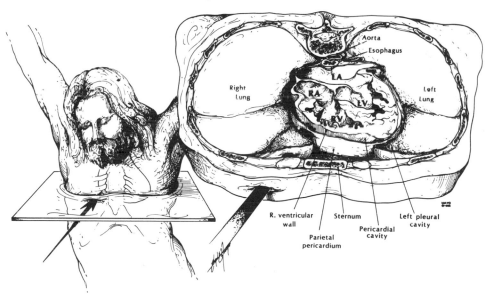

when the soldiers pierced Jesus' side instead of breaking his legs, the Scripture was fulfilled. Some suggest that in verse 36 John is alluding to Psalm 34:20: "He keeps all his bones; Not one of them is broken" (NASB). But in view of the context, it is more likely that John is quoting references to the Passover lamb, whose bones were not to be broken (Exod. 12:46; Num. 9:12). Indeed, in 1 Corinthians 5:7 the apostle Paul speaks of Christ as "our Passover lamb." First Peter 1:19 contains a similar reference.[30] In verse 37 John quotes the apocalyptic passage of Zechariah 12:10: "They will look on me, the one they have pierced" (NIV).

Jesus' Burial

The Role of Nicodemus and Joseph of Arimathea

The Gospels record Jesus' burial (Matt. 27:57–60; Mark 15:42–46; Luke 23:50–54; John 19:38–42). All four recount the role of Joseph of Arimathea; John also includes the participation of Nicodemus. Notably, both men were members of the council.

Nicodemus first appears in John 3:1–21, which tells of an event early in Jesus' ministry. Nicodemus had come to Jesus for instruction in the evening. Since many of Jerusalem's population would have gone to bed, night was considered an ideal time to study Scripture quietly or to converse about spiritual matters without interruption.[31] We next meet Nicodemus in John 7. During the Feast of Tabernacles the temple police were sent by the chief priests and Pharisees to arrest Jesus because of his teaching, but they failed to do so. When asked, "Why did you not bring him?" the officers replied, "No one ever spoke like this man!" (vv. 45–46). Nicodemus defended the police by asking, "Does our law condemn anyone without first hearing what he has to say and finding out what he is doing?" (v. 51). The Pharisees retorted: "Are you from Galilee, too? Search and see; the Prophet does not come from Galilee!" (v. 52).

Joseph, as the Gospels record, hailed from Arimathea. The location of this town is uncertain. Also called Rathamin (1 Macc. 11:34) and Ramatha,[32] it may be identical with Ramathaim-zophim (1 Sam. 1:1). Eusebius fixes the site at Rentis (Remphthis), 9 miles northeast of Lydda.[33] It may, then, have been around 20 miles northwest of Jerusalem. Some suggest that at the time of Jesus' death Joseph was living in Jerusalem.[34]

Luke and Mark note that Joseph was a member of the council. Luke further indicates that Joseph had not consented to the decision and action of the council in condemning Jesus. Since the accounts of the night meeting of the council and the early morning trial report that the council's verdict against Jesus was unopposed (Matt. 27:1; Mark 14:64), the question arises whether Joseph of Arimathea and Nicodemus had even been notified of these two meetings.[35]

In addition to his being a member of the council we know that Joseph of Arimathea was rich (Matthew), good and righteous (Luke), and honorable (Mark). Luke and Mark inform us that he was looking for the kingdom of God, that is, the fulfilment of the Jewish messianic hope. From Matthew and John we know that Joseph was a disciple of Jesus, though, as John notes, a secret disciple for fear of the council.

Joseph went to Pilate to ask for the body of Jesus. This was a most unusual request. First of all, it came from a member of the very group that had forced Pilate to condemn Jesus. Moreover, according to Roman law the body of someone executed on a charge of high treason could not be given to relatives or friends for burial; the idea was to prevent the burial site from becoming a shrine and focal point for any followers.[36] Pilate's ignoring the law was probably due to his considering Jesus innocent of the crime of treason, as he had professed several times during the trial.[37]

Pilate was amazed to hear that Jesus had already died. And so, as Mark states, before granting the request the governor checked with the captain of the execution detail to verify that the sentence of death had been carried out. When satisfied, Pilate gave the body to Joseph.

Since Golgotha was on a well-traveled road outside the walls of the city, it soon became public knowledge that Joseph of Arimathea and Nicodemus were the ones who took down Jesus' body and prepared it for burial. By handling Jesus' dead body, they would be ceremonially unclean for seven days and consequently unable to participate in the seven-day Feast of Unleavened Bread. Probably some servants helped them prepare the body since there was such a short period of time available before sunset, when the Sabbath would begin (Luke notes that the day of preparation for the Sabbath was about to end).

Each of the Synoptics records that Joseph had bought fine linen cloth *(sindōn)* in which to wrap the body of Jesus. Matthew notes that it was clean linen. John 19:40 uses the term *othonion*, which also means "linen cloth."[38] Since he uses the plural form, it has been suggested that the linen was torn into strips with which to wrap the body. John adds that Nicodemus brought a mixture of myrrh and aloes. Myrrh comes from a species of thorny-branched shrubs or trees that grow in Arabia, Ethiopia, and Somaliland on rocky ground. The stems and branches exude drops of oily resin. When they are cut, the resin flows freely, eventually solidifying.[39] Aloes is a perfumed oil that comes from the tall and somewhat broad leaves of a species known as *Aloe vera*. Probably cultivated in Jesus' time, *Aloe vera* is found today in Arab countries and in Palestine.[40] John tells us that Nicodemus brought about 100 *litrai* of the aloes and myrrh, which in our weight would be about 75 pounds.[41]

Although the exact details of the burial preparation are not given, it is probable that Jesus' body was carried from the site of execution to a private place, probably the antechamber of the tomb. Then, as we learn from Acts 9:37 and a passage in the Mishnah, the body was probably washed before being wrapped.[42] Seemingly the combination of myrrh and aloes was placed between the wrappings to counteract the odor of death.[43] A separate cloth was used to cover the head of Jesus (John 20:7).[44]

The Tomb

Where was the burial site of Jesus? Today two sites in particular lay claim to being the burial place of Jesus, but neither can be confirmed historically. Although some strongly favor the Garden Tomb, north of the Damascus Gate and near the Ecole Biblique, the evidence is very doubtful. The same is true for the Church of the Holy Sepulchre (see pp. 132–33).[45]

Having carefully studied the Gospel accounts of the burial of Jesus, Robert Houston Smith points to a tomb in the area of the traditional site of Akeldama, near the junction of the Hinnom and Kidron valleys (see pp. 98–99). This tomb, which was cut from rock in the early Roman period, has some interesting parallels to the description of Jesus' tomb. The Gospel accounts record that the tomb of Joseph of Arimathea, in

Figure 10
A Reconstruction of Jesus' Tomb

(as proposed by L. H. Vincent in *Jérusalem nouvelle* [Paris: Gabalda, 1914], 96). The three drawings on the bottom represent north-south elevations: *b* of the innermost chamber; *c* through the approach; and *d* through the first inner chamber. From Robert Houston Smith, "The Tomb of Jesus," *Biblical Archaeologist* 30 (1967): 86. Reprinted by permission of The Johns Hopkins University Press.

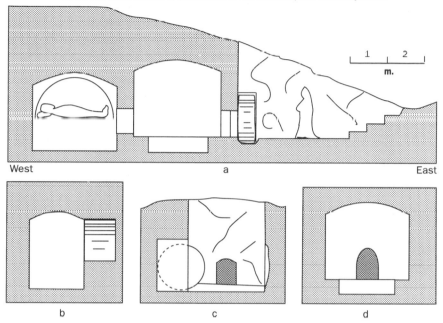

West   a   East

b   c   d

which no one had as yet been laid, was cut out of rock (the area of Jerusalem abounds in layered limestone). John 19:41 states that it lay in a garden, a detail reflecting the economic resources of Joseph, whom Matthew characterizes as a rich man. John 20:15 makes reference to a gardener. A stone was rolled in front of the entrance to the tomb. Smith notes that of the few tombs that give evidence of having been sealed by a stone, all date back to the time of Jesus. It should be noted that the Sanhedrin tombs that were constructed before the fall of Jerusalem in A.D. 70 also bear similarities to the Gospels' descriptions of Jesus' tomb.

The tomb probably had an antechamber in which the body of Jesus was prepared for burial. There may well have been a small doorway between this antechamber and the inner burial chamber. For a small doorway seems to be implied in the description of John and then Peter bending over, looking in, and seeing the linen cloths lying by themselves (Luke 24:12; John 20:5–7). John also records that while Mary Magdalene was weeping at the tomb, she bent over to look in and saw two angels sitting at the place where Jesus' body had been laid—one at the head and the other at the foot (John 20:11–12).[46]

We know from Mark 15:47 that Mary Magdalene and Mary, the mother of Joses, had earlier seen where Jesus was laid. This is confirmed by Matthew 27:61, who calls the companion simply "the other Mary." Luke 23:55 tells us that the women who had come with Jesus from Galilee followed Joseph to the tomb. Then they returned to where they were staying and prepared odor-counteracting spices and ointments with which to anoint Jesus' body after the Sabbath had ended.

The Guard at the Tomb

Matthew 27:62–66 records the reaction of the council to Jesus' death. They remembered that Jesus, whom they referred to as "that deceiver," had said he would rise on the third day. And so they came to Pilate to ask him to authorize a guard at the tomb in order to prevent Jesus' disciples from secretly removing the body and telling people that he had risen from the dead. In the council's thinking such an act would result in a worse deception than the first, namely, Jesus' claim and the disciples' belief that he was the Messiah.[47]

Pilate gave a curt, laconic reply: "You have a guard; go and make it as secure as you know how." David Hill suggests that the first clause may be translated, "Take a guard. . . ."[48]

Was Pilate giving the council permission to use members of the temple police or a guard of Roman soldiers? Pierre Benoit, who feels that the whole episode is a late (though not necessarily invented) tradition, suggests that it could be either.[49] D. A. Carson is of the opinion that Pilate gave the council permission to use the temple police.[50] R. T. France suggests that Roman soldiers are more likely.[51] It should be remembered that Jesus had been executed as "king of the Jews," a treasonous revolutionary. In view of the nature of this charge, reasons Alfred Plummer, Pilate would surely have given permission to use a detachment of Roman soldiers to seal the tomb and guard it until the third day. Plummer also suggests that the use of the term *koustōdia* ("guard"), which is a Latinism, implies a Roman presence at the tomb.[52]

15

Epilog: Jesus' Resurrection

(Matt. 28; Mark 16:1–8; Luke 24; John 20–21; Acts 1:3–11; 1 Cor. 15)

The closing chapters of the four Gospels record much important detail on Christ's resurrection. They affirm that Jesus rose from the dead on the third day and appeared to many: to the women, to Mary Magdalene, to the Emmaus disciples, to Peter, to ten disciples, to the eleven disciples a week later, to more than five hundred, to James his half brother, to seven disciples at the Sea of Galilee, then to the Eleven at his ascension, and later to the apostle Paul on the Damascus road. In 1 Corinthians 15:4–8 Paul lists some of these appearances in the manner of a legal brief admissible in a Roman or Jewish court.[1]

But what transpired between Christ's death and resurrection? According to the Apostles' Creed, he "was crucified, died, and was buried; he descended to hell." This last crucial clause, which reflects 1 Peter 3:18–20, has seen a variety of interpretations. Through ingenious thinking some link it to 1 Peter 4:6 and theorize that Jesus proclaimed the gospel to souls in hell in order to secure their release. Others look to Acts 2:27, 31 (cf. Ps. 16:10) and take the Greek word *hadēs* there to mean that Jesus went to the realm of the dead (the Hebrew "Sheol"); they forget that this term is also used in Scripture in a narrow sense to refer to the place of the damned and of the devil and his minions. Others interpret the descent to hell figuratively in the sense that Christ suffered God's wrath on the cross.[2]

A careful reading of 1 Peter 3:18–20 will help solve the prob-

153

lem. Christ once and for all died for the sins of humankind.
When he was made alive in the Spirit, he went to proclaim
kēryssō) his victory to the spirits in prison. In this context the
term "prison" refers to the "place where both the fallen angels
and the spirits of unbelievers are kept under guard (cf. Rev.
18:2; 20:7). This view is supported by the use of *abussos* in Rev.
9:1, 2, 11; 11:7; 17:8; 20:1, 3; and Luke 8:31, where *abussos* is
clearly the abode of the devils."[3] Christ's descent into hell was a
climactic proclamation of his victory and the fulfilment of
God's promise in Genesis 3:15.

Initial Evidences

Matthew 28:2–4 records that an angel came to roll away the
stone that sealed Jesus' tomb. From the description of the
angel and his garments Matthew's Jewish readers would have
understood that the angel reflected divine majesty and came as
a messenger from God. Matthew also notes the effect on the
soldiers guarding the tomb: they shook and became like dead
men.

From Mark 16:1 we learn that when the Sabbath ended at
sunset, the two Marys and Salome had purchased spices to
counteract the odor of death. The four Gospels record their
visit to the tomb (Matt. 28:1, 5–8; Mark 16:2–8; Luke 24:1–11;
John 20:1). As soon as the sun had risen, they hurried to the
tomb, wondering who would roll the stone away from the
entrance. But when they came near, they saw the stone had
been rolled away. The Synoptics record the women's reaction to
the two angels (Luke), who informed them that Jesus had risen
from the dead. "Go tell the disciples and Peter," they said (Mark
16:7). The astonished women ran to tell the disciples, as
Matthew and Luke record. But the disciples thought they were
talking nonsense (*lēros*—Luke 24:11).[4]

The Gospel of John centers attention on Mary Magdalene,
Peter, and John himself (20:1–18). When Mary Magdalene saw
that the stone had been rolled away, she ran and told John and
Peter, "They have taken the Lord out of the tomb; we know not
where they have laid him!" Peter and John at once ran to see
for themselves. Being younger, John outran Peter but stopped
at the entrance. When Peter arrived, he rushed in. He saw the
linen cloths lying there; the head covering was folded up by

itself. Luke 24:12 notes Peter's perplexed reaction: he wondered what had happened. John 20:9 tells us the two disciples failed to accept the witness of Scripture that Christ had to rise from the dead.

John goes on to record Jesus' appearance to Mary Magdalene. She mistook him for the gardener, but when he said, "Mary!" she exclaimed, "Rabboni!" Jesus replied, "Stop clinging to me . . . but go to my brothers and tell them, 'I am going up to my Father and your Father, to my God and to your God'" (v. 17). Matthew 28:9–10 records that Jesus appeared to other women (Mary the mother of James and probably Salome; cf. Mark 16:1) and told them to tell his brothers that he would see them in Galilee.

The Emmaus Disciples

Luke 24:13–35 describes Jesus' appearance to Cleopas and another of his followers on the road to Emmaus. The writer notes that Emmaus was 60 *stadia* from Jerusalem. A *stadion* is 607 feet, so the distance from Jerusalem to Emmaus was roughly 7 miles.

Several sites have been suggested through the centuries as being the Emmaus to which the two were walking on that first Easter day. A decisive factor in assessing these suggestions is the distance from Jerusalem. It must be remembered that the two disciples walked to Emmaus through the hills of Judea and rushed back at once to Jerusalem to share the glad news of Jesus' resurrection with the Eleven. Given the nature of the terrain, 20 miles was the maximum an average person could travel in a day. It is also important to keep in mind that the main meal of the day, to which the two invited Jesus, was normally eaten in the very late afternoon. Since dusk falls very quickly in Palestine, the two had to rush back to Jerusalem through the hills in the early evening.

Nicopolis is one of the sites suggested for Emmaus; today it is known as 'Amwas. Located 176 *stadia* west of Jerusalem, it is too far away to have been Luke's Emmaus. Other suggested sites are too close: Kaloniyeh, 30 *stadia* west of Jerusalem, and Mozah, a little north of Kaloniyeh. The site which best fits Luke's figure of 60 *stadia* is el-Qubeibeh, which lies 63 *stadia* northwest of Jerusalem in the beautiful valley of Beit Chanina.

Recent archeological investigation there has found a village dating back to the first century.[5]

Jesus' manner of dealing with the two disciples is notable. They had rejected the news of Jesus' resurrection brought by the women to whom he had appeared. Jesus permitted the two to vent their bitter disappointment that their earnest expectations of an earthly Messiah had been shattered by his crucifixion and death. Then, through a review of the Old Testament, he led them to see the true role of the Messiah as the obedient Suffering Servant and, only thereafter, as the Victorious Servant (Isa. 52:13–53:12).

In keeping with Near Eastern custom, the two disciples invited Jesus to stay with them since dusk was quickly approaching. Only after strong urging did he accept their invitation. Jesus, as their guest, assumed the role of the head of the house in speaking the usual blessing over the bread at the beginning of the simple meal. When they recognized their guest, Jesus disappeared. The two rushed back to Jerusalem to tell the disciples, but were greeted with the words, "Jesus has risen indeed, and has appeared to Simon."[6] Paul also notes this appearance to Simon Peter in 1 Corinthians 15:5.

Jesus' Appearances to His Disciples

Luke 24:36–43; John 20:19–31; and 1 Corinthians 15:5 record Jesus' appearance first to ten of his disciples and a week later to the Eleven. Luke characteristically stresses that Jesus appeared in his earthly body, pointing to his wounded hands and feet. Luke also notes that Jesus, in order to prove he was not a ghost, ate broiled fish as his disciples watched.[7]

Thomas totally rejected the witness of the ten disciples. Note how carefully he laid down the conditions that would be necessary for him to believe that Jesus had actually risen from the dead (John 20:25), and how specifically Jesus met those conditions in his words to Thomas a week later (v. 27). Thomas reacted with the firm confession, "My Lord and my God!"

Immediately after relating this episode John carefully notes why the Spirit led him to write his Gospel account, namely, to witness that Jesus truly is the Messiah and the Son of God promised in the prophecies of old. All who are led to believe this by the Holy Spirit on the basis of the firm witness of

Scripture will have eternal life in Jesus' name (vv. 30–31; see also 21:24).[8]

Scripture records several other appearances of the risen Christ, including one to seven disciples at the Sea of Galilee (John 21). Matthew 28:16–20 speaks of another appearance of the resurrected Christ to his disciples in Galilee. Paul mentions Jesus' appearance to more than five hundred believers and his appearance to James his half brother. Luke 24:44–53 and Acts 1:3–11 record the final meeting of Jesus with his disciples and his ascension into heaven. As they looked intently up, two angels appeared and promised that he would come again just as he had foretold (see, e.g., Matt. 25:31–46).

The most fitting postscript to the Gospel accounts of the marvelous events we have been examining is undoubtedly 1 Corinthians 15, the apostle Paul's glorious resurrection chapter in which he stresses both the certainty of Christ's resurrection and its implications for faith and life. Also included are the second coming of Christ and the role the Son of man will then play in keeping with the will of his heavenly Father. At the close of this chapter Paul stresses that the purpose of Christ's passion was climactically achieved at the moment of resurrection, namely, victory over Satan, sin, and death. The apostle concludes with a firm exhortation not only for the troubled church at Corinth, but for all believers until the end of time: "Therefore, my dear brothers, stand firm. Let nothing move you. Always give yourselves fully to the work of the Lord, because you know that your labor in the Lord is not in vain" (v. 58 NIV).

Appendix A

Deuteronomy 21:22–23 and Crucifixion

In Galatians 3:13 the apostle Paul wrote, "Christ redeemed us from the curse of the law, being made a curse for us, for it is written, 'Cursed is everyone who hangs on a tree.'" Paul is quoting from Deuteronomy 21:22–23, which reads, "If a man guilty of a capital offense is put to death and his body is hung on a tree, you must not leave his body on the tree overnight. Be sure to bury him that same day, because anyone who is hung on a tree is under God's curse" (NIV). Note that the guilty party was to be executed and then hung publicly. The question arises as to how Paul could apply this text to Jesus' crucifixion. A careful study of two of the Dead Sea Scrolls produced by the Qumran community—the Nahum pesher (4QpNah) and the Temple Scroll—provides the answer. These documents coupled with a knowledge of the intertestamental period have shed light on the Qumran community's interpretation of Deuteronomy 21, an interpretation that is reflected in Paul's inspired text.

The pertinent portion of the Nahum pesher (i.e., interpretation) is a commentary on Nahum 2:11–13. The prophet Nahum speaks of God's wrath against Assyria and its capital Nineveh because of their cold, wanton brutality, which was experienced by God's covenant people. He graphically depicts Nineveh as "the lions' den, the place . . . where the lion and lioness went. . . . The lion killed enough for his cubs and strangled the prey for his mate, filling his lairs with the kill and his dens with the prey" (NIV). Then come the words of judgment, "'I am against you,' declares the LORD Almighty." Verse 13 speaks of

159

God's wrath burning against Nineveh. This prophecy was fulfilled in 612 B.C., when Nineveh was taken by the Babylonians.

The Qumran community's interpretation of Nahum 2:11–13 is found in fragments 3 and 4, column 1, lines 1–11 of the Nahum pesher. The Qumran writer regards these verses as a foreshadowing of the encounter between Alexander Jannaeus, who served as high priest from 103 to 76 B.C., and Demetrius III Eucerus (95–88 B.C.).[1] Jannaeus's enemies in Jerusalem, in particular the Pharisees, had invited Demetrius, the Seleucid king of Syria, to assist them. After a fierce battle at Shechem Demetrius abandoned Palestine. Alexander then crucified eight hundred Pharisees in Jerusalem and had their families slaughtered.[2] Crucial for our purposes are lines 5–8 of the pesher (the words in brackets are suggested readings for lacunae):

5 [The interpretation of it] concerns the Lion of Wrath,
    who strikes by means of his nobles and his counselors,
6 [*and he fills with prey*] *his cave and his dens*
    with torn flesh.
    The interpretation of it concerns the Lion of Wrath
7 [who has found a crime punishable by] death
    in the Seekers-after-Smooth-Things,
    whom he hangs as live men
8 [on the tree, as it was thus done] in Israel of old,
    for of one hanged alive on the tree [Scripture reads].[3]

"The Seekers-after-Smooth-Things" is a reference to the Pharisees. Yigael Yadin suggests that the opening words of line 8 should read "[on the tree, as thus is in the law] in Israel as of old." The specific reference would be Deuteronomy 21:22–23.[4]

Yadin points out further that the words of column 64, lines 6–13, of the Temple Scroll shed light on this section of the Nahum pesher:

6 . . . If
7 a man has informed against his people and has delivered his people up to a foreign nation and has done evil to his people,
8 you shall hang him on the tree and he shall die. On the evidence of two witnesses and on the evidence of three witnesses,
9 he shall be put to death and they shall hang him on the tree. If a man has committed a crime punishable by death and has run away unto

10 the midst of the Gentiles, and has cursed his people and the children of Israel, you shall hang him also on the tree,

11 and he shall die, and you shall not leave their bodies upon the tree in the night, but you shall bury them the same day, for

12 the hanged upon the tree are accursed by God and men, and you shall not defile the land which I

13 give you for an inheritance. . . .[5]

The Pharisees, by seeking the assistance of the Gentile Demetrius and passing information on to him, had been guilty of treason. As a result of the failure of the revolt, eight thousand soldiers who had fought against Alexander fled and remained in exile, as Josephus informs us, until Alexander died.[6] According to the Temple Scroll, the Pharisees and their supporters would have been subject to execution on two counts: abetting the enemy and fleeing into exile among Gentiles. Consequently, as the Nahum pesher indicates, eight hundred Pharisees were crucified alive. In this instance they were not executed and then hung for all to see.[7]

These two Qumran texts, dating from the first century B.C. and the turn of the era, reflect a pre-Christian association between crucifixion and Deuteronomy 21:22–23. The Nahum pesher clearly demonstrates this expanded understanding of the Old Testament text. The Temple Scroll declares that one guilty of treason and flight to the Gentiles should be hanged and that one executed in this fashion came under the curse of God and men. The curse of men is reflected in the mockery of the crucified Christ by council members as well as by other passersby.[8]

Utilizing the expanded understanding of Deuteronomy, Paul in Galatians 3:13 states that by dying on the cross Christ experienced God's curse and atoned for the sins of all humankind. The atonement thus accomplished, Christ just before his death uttered those momentous words, "It is finished!" As various references in Acts and the Epistles emphasize, Christ's death and resurrection were the climax of his role as the Suffering and then Victorious Servant who fulfilled God's plan of salvation for sinners (Isa. 52:13–53:12).[9]

Appendix B

The Piercing of Jesus' Side

In his medical analysis of the piercing of Jesus' side, A. F. Sava drew the following conclusions, which are based on his own experiments with bodies that had been dead less than six hours:

1. The experience of thoracic surgeons confirms the occurrence of a massive bloody fluid accumulation between the rib cage and the lung following concussion of the chest.
2. Blood contained in body cavities does not clot either before or after death.
3. Experiments conducted by the author revealed the tendency of blood collected after death to settle into two layers, dark red below, with an overlying layer of clear pale yellow fluid above.
4. Experiments with reasonably fresh cadavers failed to reveal anything like a "gaping tunnel," formed by a penetrating instrument of some magnitude.
5. Study of the anatomical compartments of the chest supports the contention that blood from the heart cannot find its way across a perforated lung so as to be seen at a wound in the chest wall.
6. A stab wound through the chest directed to the heart, after the author had previously filled the pericardial sac with 1000 cc. of water, failed to produce any of the water at the chest wound. Rather, inside the chest and especially around the right lung, the water literally flooded the area.

7. The accumulation of a bloody fluid just within the rib
   cage, its separation into two layers and its subsequent
   evacuation through a wound in the chest wall, allowing
   first the heavier red component to precede the flow of
   clear fluid, fulfill most faithfully the conditions and the
   observations specifically described by the Gospel. [A. F.
   Sava, "The Wound in the Side of Christ," *Catholic Biblical
   Quarterly* 19 (1957): 346—used by permission]

Abbreviations

ABR	*Australian Biblical Review*
AJT	*American Journal of Theology*
ASTI	*Annual of the Swedish Theological Institute*
ATR	*Anglican Theological Review*
AUSS	*Andrews University Seminary Studies*
BA	*Biblical Archaeologist*
BAGD	Walter Bauer, *A Greek-English Lexicon of the New Testament and Other Early Christian Literature,* trans. and rev. William F. Arndt, F. Wilbur Gingrich, and Frederick W. Danker, 2d ed. (Chicago: University of Chicago Press, 1979)
BAR	*Biblical Archaeology Review*
Bib	*Biblica*
BibR	*Bible Review*
Bijdragen	*Bijdragen: Tijdschrift voor filosofie en theologie*
BJRL	*Bulletin of the John Rylands University Library*
BSac	*Bibliotheca Sacra*
BTB	*Biblical Theology Bulletin*
CBQ	*Catholic Biblical Quarterly*
CH	*Church History*
ChrH	*Christian Herald*
ChrT	*Christianity Today*
CJ	*Concordia Journal*
ConB	*Coniectanea biblica*
CTM	*Concordia Theological Monthly*
CTQ	*Concordia Theological Quarterly*
CurTM	*Currents in Theology and Mission*
EstBib	*Estudios biblicos*
EvQ	*Evangelical Quarterly*
Expos	*Expositor*
ExpTim	*Expository Times*
GR	*Gordon Review*

HibJ	Hibbert Journal
HTR	Harvard Theological Review
HUCA	Hebrew Union College Annual
IBS	Irish Biblical Studies
IEJ	Israel Exploration Journal
Int	Interpretation
JAAR	Journal of the American Academy of Religion
JAMA	Journal of the American Medical Association
JBL	Journal of Biblical Literature
JBTh	Journal of Bible and Theology
JETS	Journal of the Evangelical Theological Society
JJS	Journal of Jewish Studies
JQR	Jewish Quarterly Review
JR	Journal of Religion
JRS	Journal of Roman Studies
JSJ	Journal for the Study of Judaism
JSNT	Journal for the Study of the New Testament
JSR	Journal for the Study of Religion
JTS	Journal of Theological Studies
Jud	Judaism
LQ	Lutheran Quarterly
LW	Lutheran Witness
NIDNTT	Colin Brown, ed., *New International Dictionary of New Testament Theology*, 3 vols. (Grand Rapids: Zondervan, 1975–78)
NovT	Novum Testamentum
NTS	New Testament Studies
PEQ	Palestine Exploration Quarterly
PFlor	G. Vitelli and D. Comparetti, eds., *Papiri Fiorentini*, 3 vols. (Milan, 1906–15)
QDAP	Quarterly of the Department of Antiquities of Palestine
RB	Revue biblique
REJ	Revue des études juives
SBT	Studies in Biblical Theology (London: SCM)
Scr	Scripture
SE	Studia Evangelica
SJT	Scottish Journal of Theology
SZ	Stimmen der Zeit
TDNT	Gerhard Kittel and Gerhard Friedrich, eds., *Theological Dictionary of the New Testament*, trans. Geoffrey W. Bromiley, 10 vols. (Grand Rapids: Eerdmans, 1964–76)
Th	Theology

ThLit	*Theologische Literaturzeitung*
TS	*Theological Studies*
TT	*Theology Today*
TU	*Texte und Untersuchungen zur Geschichte der altchristlichen Literatur*
TynBul	*Tyndale Bulletin*
UTSR	*Union Theological Seminary Review*
VC	*Vigiliae Christianae*
Word World	*Word and World*
ZDPV	*Zeitschrift des Deutschen Palästina Vereins*
ZNW	*Zeitschrift für die neuetestamentliche Wissenschaft*

Notes

Chapter 1. Messianic Hopes and the Coming of Jesus

1. John J. Davis, ed., *Moses and the Gods of Egypt: Studies in Exodus*, 2d ed. (Winona Lake, Ind.: BMH, 1986), 133–36.

2. John Bright, *The Kingdom of God and Its Meaning for the Church* (Nashville: Abingdon, 1953), 67.

3. R. B. Wright, "Psalms of Solomon," in *Old Testament Pseudepigrapha*, ed. James H. Charlesworth (Garden City, N.Y.: Doubleday, 1985), vol. 2, pp. 639–70.

4. Frederick C. Grant, *The Economic Background of the Gospels* (New York: Oxford University Press, 1926), esp. 1–110.

5. Thomas W. Manson, *The Servant Messiah: A Study of the Public Ministry of Jesus* (New York: Cambridge University Press, 1961), 1–35.

6. Grant, *Economic Background*, 111–41; see also Isa. 29:18; 35:3–6; 42:6–7; 61:1–3.

7. A. E. Harvey, *Jesus on Trial: A Study in the Fourth Gospel* (Atlanta: John Knox, 1977), 18–122.

8. Martin H. Scharlemann, *Proclaiming the Parables* (St. Louis: Concordia, 1963), 1–46.

Chapter 2. Up to Jerusalem

1. C. K. Barrett, *The Gospel According to St. John*, 2d ed. (Philadelphia: Westminster, 1978), 405.

2. Josephus *Antiquities of the Jews* 17.10.10.

3. Leon Morris, *The Gospel According to John*, New International Commentary on the New Testament (Grand Rapids: Eerdmans, 1971), 566; Raymond E. Brown, *The Gospel According to John (I–XII)*, Anchor Bible 29 (Garden City, N.Y.: Doubleday, 1966), 439–40.

4. F. F. Bruce, *New Testament History* (New York: Thomas Nelson, 1969), 57–61.

5. George R. Beasley-Murray, *John* (Waco, Tex.: Word, 1987), 198.

6. Gustaf H. Dalman, *Sacred Sites and Ways: Studies in the Topography of the Gospels* (New York: Macmillan, 1935), 217–19; see also Brown, *John (I–XII)*, 447.

7. Bruce E. Schein, *Following the Way: The Setting of John's Gospel* (Minneapolis: Augsburg, 1980), 213–14.

8. Grant, *Economic Background*, 100–110.

Chapter 3. THE OPENING DAYS OF HOLY WEEK

1. Joachim Jeremias, *Jerusalem in the Time of Jesus: An Investigation into Economic and Social Conditions during the New Testament Period* (Philadelphia: Fortress, 1969).

2. Ibid., 77–84.

3. Ibid., 60–62.

4. Dalman, *Sacred Sites*, 264, 267.

5. Michael Avi-Yonah, "Roman Palestine Map," rev. ed. (Jaffa: Survey of Palestine, 1939).

6. Jack Finegan, *The Archaeology of the New Testament* (Princeton, N.J.: Princeton University Press, 1970), 88–91.

7. Dalman, *Sacred Sites*, 252–55; see also I. Loew, "Bethphage," *REJ* 62 (1911): 232–35.

8. *BAGD*, 570, 574; Heinz-Wolfgang Kuhn, "Das Reittier Jesu in der Einzugsgeschichte des Markusevangeliums," *ZNW* 50 (1959): 82–91.

9. Plutarch *Cato Minor* 7.

10. Harold N. and Alma L. Moldenke, *Plants of the Bible* (Waltham, Mass.: Chronica Botanica, 1952), 171.

11. William R. Farmer, "The Palm Branches in John 12, 13," *JTS*, n.s. 3 (1952–53): 62–66.

12. R. B. Wright, "Psalms of Solomon," in *Old Testament Pseudepigrapha*, ed. Charlesworth, vol. 2, p. 667.

13. Herbert C. Leupold, *Exposition of the Psalms* (Columbus: Wartburg, 1959), 819–20.

14. Frederick C. Grant, *Ancient Judaism and the New Testament* (Edinburgh: Oliver and Boyd, 1968), 47–48.

15. *BAGD*, 746.

16. Josephus *Antiquities of the Jews* 17.10.10.

17. *BAGD*, 604–5.

18. In *The Gospel According to Luke (I–IX)*, Anchor Bible 28 (Garden City, N.Y.: Doubleday, 1981), 440–41, Joseph A. Fitzmyer comments on Jesus' presence in Jerusalem at the age of twelve. A tractate of the Mishnah notes regulations that a Jewish boy had to observe the Torah at age thirteen and hence had to attend the festivals in Jerusalem (*Niddah* 5:6). It is thought that in pious families boys younger than thirteen went along to the great festivals in Jerusalem in order to become accustomed to their future obligations.

19. Moldenke, *Plants*, 104–6; Alfred Edersheim, *The Life and Times of Jesus the Messiah* (Grand Rapids: Eerdmans, 1936), vol. 2, pp. 374–75; H. B. Tristram, *Natural History of the Bible* (London: SPCK, 1867), 352.

20. For a discussion of the various approaches see Brown, *John (I–XII)*, 116–25. See also Joseph A. Fitzmyer, *The Gospel According to Luke (X–XXIV)*, Anchor Bible 28A (Garden City, N.Y.: Doubleday, 1985), 1260–68.

21. Josephus *Antiquities* 15.11.5.

22. Gaalyah Cornfeld, ed., *The Historical Jesus: A Scholarly View of the Man and His World* (New York: Macmillan, 1982), 142–57; Victor Eppstein, "The Historicity of the Gospel Account of the Cleansing of the Temple," *ZNW* 55 (1964): 42–58.

23. Emil Schürer, *A History of the Jewish People in the Time of Jesus Christ (175 B.C.–A.D. 135)*, rev. and trans. Geza Vermes et al., 4 vols., 2d rev. ed. (Edinburgh: T. and T. Clark, 1973–87), vol. 2, pp. 270–74; Shemuel Safrai and M. Stern, eds., *Compendia rerum Iudaicarum ad Novum Testamentum: The Literature of the Jewish People in the Period of the Second Temple and the*

Talmud (Philadelphia: Fortress, 1976), vol. 2, pp. 879–81; Keith F. Nickle, *The Collection: A Study in Paul's Strategy*, SBT 48 (Naperville, Ill.: Allenson, 1966), esp. chap. 3.

24. Neill Q. Hamilton, "Temple Cleansing and Temple Bank," *JBL* 83 (1964): 365–72; Cecil Roth, "The Cleansing of the Temple and Zechariah xiv 21," *NovT* 4 (1960): 174–81.

25. Cornfeld, *Historical Jesus*, 147–48; Nahman Avigad, *Discovering Jerusalem* (Nashville: Thomas Nelson, 1983), 129–31; Craig A. Evans, "Jesus' Action in the Temple: Cleansing or Portent of Destruction?" *CBQ* 51 (1989): 237–70, esp. 259–70 on the house of Annas.

Chapter 4. JESUS' FINAL DAY OF PUBLIC MINISTRY

1. Safrai and Stern, eds., *Compendia rerum Iudaicarum*, vol. 2, pp. 379–92; Schürer, *History of the Jewish People*, vol. 2, pp. 210–18.

2. For details on the nature and crushing burden of these taxes see Grant, *Economic Background*, 87–110; Bruce, *New Testament History*, 36–38.

3. In "The Nature of Biblical 'Leprosy' and the Use of Alternative Medical Terms in Modern Translations of the Bible," *PEQ* 107 (1975): 87–105, E. V. Hulse stresses that biblical leprosy was not the disease known today as leprosy. Although modern leprosy was known and recognized in New Testament times, it was not called *lepra*. Aside from other points he makes, Hulse suggests that *lepra* and the equivalent Hebrew term *ṣāra'at* would best be translated by a phrase such as "a repulsive scaly skin disease." The theologian and medical missionary John Wilkinson, among others, agrees with Hulse; see Wilkinson's "Leprosy and Leviticus: The Problem of Description and Identification," *SJT* 30 (1977): 153–69.

4. *BAGD*, 475.

5. Pliny the Elder *Natural History* 3.3.19.

6. *BAGD*, 529–30.

7. Michael Zohary, *Plants of the Bible* (New York: Cambridge University Press, 1982), 205.

8. *BAGD*, 662.

9. J. F. Coakley, "The Anointing at Bethany and the Priority of John," *JBL* 107 (1988): 246–49, documents six classical and two Judaic references to anointing the feet of guests. Normally this was done before a meal.

10. Ibid., 250–51, n. 51. For a married woman to expose her hair publicly was grounds for divorce. One *baraita* (*Nedarim* 30b) seems to suggest that the hair of women was always to be covered. A comment in the Mishnah indicates, however, that a woman about to be wed could go to her marriage with her hair unbound (*Ketubot* 2:1). Since the Mishnah was written down ca. A.D. 220, it is not certain whether this reflects the first-century-A.D. view.

11. *BAGD*, 104 5.

Chapter 5. THE PASSOVER: VARIOUS HYPOTHESES

1. Annie Jaubert, *The Date of the Last Supper* (Staten Island, N.Y.: Alba, 1965); idem, "Jésus et le Calendrier de Qumrân," *NTS* 7.1 (1960): 1–30.

2. See Barrett, *John*, 410; Morris, *John*, 574–75; and Brown, *John (I–XII)*, 447.

3. Jaubert, *Date* and "Jésus"; K. Holl, "Ein Bruchstück aus einem bisher unbekannten Brief des Epiphanius," in *Gesammelte Aufsätze zur Kirchengeschichte* 2 (Tübingen: J. C. B. Mohr, 1928), 204–24.

4. Jaubert, *Date* and "Jésus"; Schürer, *History of the Jewish People*, vol. 1, pp. 599–601; Josef Blinzler, *Der Prozess Jesu*, 4th rev. ed. (Regensburg: Friedrich Pustet, 1969), 109–26.

5. Following are a few of the many titles which could be cited: Joachim Jeremias, *The Eucharistic Words of Jesus* (London: SCM, 1964), 24–26; Eugen Ruckstuhl, *Chronology of the Last Days of Jesus: A Critical Study* (New York: Desclee, 1965); M. Black, "The Arrest and Trial of Jesus and the Date of the Last Supper," in *New Testament Essays*, ed. A. J. B. Higgins (Manchester: Manchester University Press, 1959), 19–33; I. Howard Marshall, *Last Supper and Lord's Supper* (Grand Rapids: Eerdmans, 1980), 73–75; George Ogg, "The Chronology of the Last Supper," in *Historicity and Chronology in the New Testament*, ed. Dennis E. Nineham et al. (London: SPCK, 1965), 75–96.

6. G. H. Box, "The Jewish Antecedents of the Eucharist," *JTS* 3 (1901–02): 357–69.

7. Jeremias, *Eucharistic Words*, 26–29; A. J. B. Higgins, "The Origins of the Eucharist," *NTS* 1.3 (1955): 200–209; Harold W. Hoehner, "Chronological Aspects of the Life of Christ. Part IV. The Day of Christ's Crucifixion," *BSac* 131 (July/Sept. 1974): 253–54.

8. Jeremias, *Eucharistic Words*, 29–31; Hoehner, "Life of Christ," 253–54.

9. Judah Benzion Segal, *The Hebrew Passover from the Earliest Times to* A.D. *70*, London Oriental Series 13 (London: Oxford University Press, 1963), 117.

10. Hans Kosmala, "J. B. Segal, *The Hebrew Passover from the Earliest Times to* A.D. *70*. London Oriental Series vol. 13 (Oxford University Press, 1963, xvii, 294 pp.): A Review," in *Studies, Essays and Reviews* (Leiden: Brill, 1978), vol. 1, pp. 67–72.

11. Josephus *Antiquities of the Jews* 2.14.6; 5.1.4; 18.2.2; *Jewish War* 6.9.3.

12. See also Josephus *Antiquities* 3.10.5; 9.13.2–3; 10.4.5; 11.4.8.

13. Ibid., 3.10.5.

14. Charles C. Torrey, "In the Fourth Gospel the Last Supper Was the Paschal Meal," *JQR* 42 (1951–52): 243–44. See also P. J. Heawood, "The Time of the Last Supper," *JQR* 42 (1951–52): 37–44.

15. Jeremias, *Eucharistic Words*, 20–21.

16. Josephus uses the word "Passover" in the wide sense in *Antiquities* 10.4.5; 20.5.1.

17. Frank J. Matera, *Passion Narratives and Gospel Theologies: Interpreting the Synoptics Through Their Passion Stories* (Mahwah, N.J.: Paulist, 1986), 13.

Chapter 6. THE PASSOVER MEAL

1. Jeremias, *Jerusalem*, 84; idem, *Eucharistic Words*, 42–43.

2. Alfred Plummer, *A Critical and Exegetical Commentary on the Gospel According to St. Luke*, International Critical Commentary, 5th ed. (Edinburgh: T. and T. Clark, 1969), 492; William Hendriksen, *The Gospel According to Luke* (Grand Rapids: Baker, 1978), 957.

3. Fitzmyer, *Luke (X–XXIV)*, 1383.

4. Jeremias, *Eucharistic Words*, 42–43.

5. Josephus *Antiquities of the Jews* 2.14.6; *Jewish War* 6.9.3; see also Cornfeld, ed., *Historical Jesus*, 142.

6. Jeremias, *Jerusalem*, 79.

7. Edersheim, *Jesus the Messiah*, vol. 2, 487–88; Plummer, *Luke*, 492.

8. Edersheim, *Jesus the Messiah*, vol. 2, p. 488.

9. Dalman, *Sacred Sites*, 315–20; Jerome Murphy-O'Connor, *The Holy Land: An Archaeological Guide from Earliest Times to 1700*, 2d ed. (New York: Oxford University Press, 1986), 93–94. See also Hans Kosmala, "Der Ort des letzten Mahles Jesu und das heutige Coenaculum," in *Studies, Essays and Reviews*, vol. 2, *New Testament* (Leiden: Brill, 1978), 48–52.

10. Benjamin Mazar, "Herodian Jerusalem in the Light of the Excavations South and South-West of the Temple Mount," *IEJ* 28 (1978): 230–37; idem, "Excavations near Temple Mount Reveal Splendors of Herodian Jerusalem," *BAR* 6.4 (July/Aug. 1980): 44–55. See also Edersheim, *Jesus the Messiah*, vol. 2, p. 490.

11. Dalman, *Sacred Sites*, 117, 319.

12. Edersheim, *Jesus the Messiah*, vol. 2, pp. 494–95.

13. Jeremias, *Eucharistic Words*, esp. 84–88. Among a variety of other resources, see George J. Bahr, "The Seder of Passover and the Eucharistic Words," *NovT* 12 (1970): 181–202; D. W. B. Robinson, "The Date and Significance of the Last Supper," *EvQ* 23 (1951): 126–33.

14. Jeremias, *Eucharistic Words*, 48–53, 86; see also Bahr, "The Seder of Passover," 192.

15. Jeremias, *Eucharistic Words*, 68–70, 207–18; Marshall, *Last Supper*, 80–82.

16. Mekilta on Exod. 21:12.

17. Jeremias, *Eucharistic Words*, 85; see also Bahr, "The Seder of Passover," 181–90.

18. Joachim Jeremias, "This Is My Body . . . ," *ExpTim* 83 (1971–72): 196–98.

19. Edersheim, *Jesus the Messiah*, vol. 2, pp. 494–95.

20. F. F. Bruce, *The Gospel of John* (Grand Rapids: Eerdmans, 1983), 290.

21. Barrett, *John*, 447.

22. Ibid., 446–47.

23. Bruce, *John*, 290–91.

24. Jeremias, *Eucharistic Words*, 85; see also Bahr, "The Seder of Passover," 191–94.

25. Jeremias, *Eucharistic Words*, 86.

26. See Jeremias, *Eucharistic Words*, 62–75; Fitzmyer, *Luke X–XXIV*, 1399, for a discussion of the meaning of the Greek word *artos*, which is used for both leavened and unleavened bread.

27. Jeremias, *Eucharistic Words*, 84.

28. Erwin Nestle and Kurt Aland, *Novum Testamentum Graece*, 25th ed. (London: United Bible Societies, 1971); Kurt Aland et al., *The Greek New Testament*, 2d ed. (London: United Bible Societies, 1968).

29. Kurt Aland et al., *Nestle-Aland Novum Testamentum Graece*, 26th ed. (Stuttgart: Deutsche Bibelstiftung, 1979); Kurt Aland et al., *The Greek New Testament*, 3d corrected ed. (New York: United Bible Societies, 1975).

30. On the problems of this particular text see, e.g., Pierre Benoit, "Le récit de la cène dans Lc XXII, 15–20: Etude de critique textuelle et littéraire," *RB* 48 (1939): 362–93; John C. Cooper, "The Problem of the Text in Luke 22:19–20," *LQ* 14 (1962): 39–48; Joseph A. Fitzmyer, "Papyrus Bodmer XIV: Some Features of Our Oldest Text of Luke," *CBQ* 24 (1962): 170–79; Jeremias, "This Is My Body," 196–203; Burton H. Throckmorton, Jr., "The Longer Reading of Luke 22:19b–20," *ATR* 30 (1948): 55–56. See also Bruce M. Metzger, *A Textual Commentary on the Greek New Testament* (New York: United Bible Societies, 1971), 173–77; William F. Arndt, *Bible Commentary: The Gospel According to St. Luke* (St. Louis: Concordia, 1956), 439–40.

31. *Berakot* 6:1.
32. Fitzmyer, *Luke X–XXIV,* 1399–1400; Jeremias, *Eucharistic Words,* 198–201. See also Matera, *Passion Narratives,* 21, who stresses, as do others, that in Semitic thought "body" refers to the whole person.
33. Marjorie H. Sykes, "The Eucharist as 'Anamnesis,'" *ExpTim* 71 (1959–60): 115–18; see also David W. A. Gregg, "Hebraic Antecedents to the Eucharistic ANAMNĒSIS Formula," *TynBul* 30 (1979): 165–68.
34. F. F. Bruce, *1–2 Corinthians,* New Century Bible (London: Oliphants, 1971), 111–12; Jeremias, *Eucharistic Words,* 244–55; Hermann Sasse, *This Is My Body,* rev. ed. (Adelaide: Lutheran, 1977), esp. 367–82.
35. *BAGD,* 182; see also Johannes Behm and Gottfried Quell, *"diathēkē,"* in *TDNT,* vol. 2, pp. 106–34.
36. R. T. France, "The Servant of the Lord in the Teaching of Jesus," *TynBul* 19 (1968): 26–52; Martin Hengel, "The Expiatory Sacrifice of Christ," *BJRL* 62 (1980): 454–75; Sydney H. T. Page, "The Suffering Servant Between the Testaments," *NTS* 31.4 (1985): 481–97.
37. Jeremias, *Eucharistic Words,* 179–82, 220–31; Julius D. Schniewind, *Das Evangelium nach Matthäus,* Neue Testament Deutsch 2, 11th ed. (Göttingen: Vandenhoeck and Ruprecht, 1964), 258; Hermann Strathmann, *Das Evangelium nach Markus,* Neue Testament Deutsch 1, 10th ed. (Göttingen: Vandenhoeck and Ruprecht, 1963), 185.
38. Jeremias, *Eucharistic Words,* 58–59.
39. Morris, *John,* 351–87.
40. Johannes Behm, *"paraklētos,"* in *TDNT,* vol. 5, pp. 800–14; see also Morris, *John,* 662–66.
41. Jeremias, *Eucharistic Words,* 255–62; William L. Lane, *The Gospel According to Mark,* New International Commentary on the New Testament (Grand Rapids: Eerdmans, 1974), 509.
42. Raymond E. Brown, *The Gospel According to John (XIII–XXI),* Anchor Bible 29A (Garden City, N.Y.: Doubleday, 1970), 652, 656–57; Barrett, *John,* 454–55, 469–70; Brooke Foss Westcott, *The Gospel According to St. John* (Grand Rapids: Baker, 1980 reprint), 211, 216.
43. C. H. Dodd, *The Interpretation of the Fourth Gospel* (New York: Cambridge University Press, 1953), 408–9; see also R. H. Lightfoot, *St. John's Gospel: A Commentary* (New York: Oxford University Press, 1972 reprint), 277–78; Alfred Plummer, *The Gospel According to St. John* (New York: Cambridge University Press, 1902), 285, 306–7.
44. Morris, *John,* 661.
45. Josephus *Antiquities* 18.2.2.

Chapter 7. Jesus in Gethsemane

1. Dalman, *Sacred Sites,* 321–22.
2. Josephus *Jewish Wars* 6.1.1.
3. Dalman, *Sacred Sites,* 322–23.
4. Ibid., 324–26; see also John Wilkinson, *Jerusalem as Jesus Knew It: Archaeology as Evidence* (London: Thames and Hudson, 1978), 127–31.
5. C. E. B. Cranfield, *The Gospel According to Saint Mark,* Cambridge Greek Testament Commentary (New York: Cambridge University Press, 1959), 431.
6. Pierre Benoit, *The Passion and Resurrection of Jesus Christ* (New York: Herder and Herder, 1969), 10.

7. Craig A. Blaising, "Gethsemane: A Prayer of Faith," *JETS* 22 (1979): 335.

8. J. Warren Holleran, *The Synoptic Gethsemane: A Critical Study* (Rome: Gregorian University Press, 1973), 14–15.

9. Vincent Taylor, *The Gospel According to St. Mark*, 2d ed. (New York: Macmillan, 1966), 553.

10. Lane, 516–17.

11. David Daube, "A Prayer Pattern in Judaism," *SE* 1 (1959): 539–45.

12. Joachim Jeremias, *The Prayers of Jesus*, SBT, n.s. 6 (London: SCM, 1974), 29, 57, 111; see also his *New Testament Theology: The Proclamation of Jesus* (New York: Scribner, 1971), 63–68.

13. Walther Zimmerli and Joachim Jeremias, *The Servant of God*, SBT 20 (London: SCM, 1957), 79–104; see also R. T. France, *Jesus and the Old Testament* (London: Tyndale, 1971), 110–35.

14. Blaising, "Gethsemane," 338–43. See also C. E. B. Cranfield, "The Cup Metaphor in Mark xiv.36 and Parallels," *ExpTim* 59 (1947–48): 137–38; Page, "Suffering Servant," 481–97.

15. C. J. Armbruster, "The Messianic Significance of the Agony in the Garden," *Scr* 16 (1964): 111–19.

16. Fitzmyer, *Luke (X–XXIV)*, 1443–44.

17. Bart D. Ehrman and Mark A. Plunkett, "The Angel and the Agony: The Textual Problem of Luke 22:43–44," *CBQ* 45 (1983): 401–16.

18. Holleran, *Synoptic Gethsemane*, 94–95.

19. William J. Larkin, "The Old Testament Background of Luke XXII.43–44," *NTS* 25.2 (1979): 250–54.

20. I. Howard Marshall, *The Gospel of Luke: A Commentary on the Greek Text*, New International Greek Testament Commentary (Grand Rapids: Eerdmans, 1978), 829. See also Larkin, "Old Testament Background"; R. S. Barbour, "Gethsemane in the Tradition of the Passion," *NTS* 16.3 (1970): 231–51; Benoit, *Passion*, 17–18.

21. Plummer, *Luke*, 509–10.

22. Ibid., 510–11.

23. William K. Hobart, *The Medical Language of St. Luke* (Grand Rapids: Baker, 1954), 81–83.

24. W. W. Keen, "The Bloody Sweat of Our Lord," *Baptist Quarterly Review* 14 (1892): 169–75; idem, "Further Studies on the Bloody Sweat of Our Lord," *BSac* 54 (1897): 469–83.

25. Benoit, *Passion*, 18.

26. William D. Edwards, Wesley J. Gabel, and Floyd E. Hosmer, "On the Physical Death of Jesus Christ," *JAMA* 255.11 (March 21, 1986): 1456; Howard A. Matzke, "An Anatomist Looks at the Physical Sufferings of Our Lord," *LW* 80 (Feb. 21, 1961): 6; J. Ryland Whitaker, "The Physical Cause of the Death of Our Lord," *Catholic Medical Guardian* 13 (1935): 83–85.

27. Cranfield lists various possibilities and opts for "Enough of this"; Lane feels "It is settled" is best (Cranfield, *Mark*, 435–36; Lane, *Mark*, 522). The statements in Mark that follow the word *apechei* explain its meaning. Holleran discusses and evaluates the various translations (*Synoptic Gethsemane*, 52–58).

Chapter 8. JESUS' ARREST

1. Jeremias, *Jerusalem*, 210–11.

2. Ibid., 160–63.

3. Blinzler, *Der Prozess Jesu,* 126–28.

4. Ibid., 90–98; Barrett, *John,* 518–19; Benoit, *Passion,* 45–48; David R. Catchpole, *The Trial of Jesus: A Study in the Gospels and Jewish Historiography from 1770 to the Present Day* (Leiden: Brill, 1971), 148–51.

5. Brown, *John (XIII–XXI),* 807–8; F. F. Bruce, *John,* 340; idem, "The Trial of Jesus in the Fourth Gospel," in *Gospel Perspectives: Studies of History and Tradition in the Four Gospels,* ed. R. T. France and David Wenham (Sheffield: JSOT, 1980), vol. 1, pp. 8–10; Morris, *John,* 741–42; John A. T. Robinson, *The Priority of John,* ed. J. F. Coakley (London: SCM, 1985), 240–43; David Rensberger, "The Politics of John: The Trial of Jesus in the Fourth Gospel," *JBL* 103 (1984): 399–401; D. A. Carson, *Matthew,* Expositor's Bible Commentary 8 (Grand Rapids: Zondervan, 1984), 546.

6. Josephus *Antiquities of the Jews* 15.11.1; 18.4.3; Robinson, *Priority of John,* 241–43.

7. Josephus *Jewish War* 5.5.8.

8. Ibid., 2.12.1; 5.5.8; *Antiquities* 20.5.3; 20.8.11.

9. Brown, *John (XIII–XXI),* 807–9.

10. Carson, *Matthew,* 569.

11. Barrett, *John,* 519; Morris, *John,* 742; Robert Houston Smith, "The Household Lamps of Palestine in New Testament Times," *BA* 29.1 (1966): 2–27.

12. Barrett, *John,* 521; Brown, *John (XIII–XXI),* 812.

13. Ethelbert Stauffer, *"egō,"* in *TDNT,* vol. 2, pp. 343–54; Friedrich Büchsel, *"eimi, ho ōn,"* in *TDNT,* vol. 2, pp. 398–400; see also Bruce, *John,* 341; Donald Guthrie, *New Testament Theology* (Downers Grove, Ill.: InterVarsity, 1981), 330–33.

14. Cranfield, *Mark,* 438–39; C. S. Mann, *Mark,* Anchor Bible 27 (Garden City, N.Y.: Doubleday, 1986), 598–99; Harry Fleddermann, "The Flight of a Naked Young Man (Mark 14:51–52)," *CBQ* 41 (1978): 412–18.

15. Pierre Barbet, *A Doctor at Calvary: The Passion of Our Lord Jesus Christ as Described by a Surgeon* (New York: Kennedy, 1953), 63.

Chapter 9. JESUS' TRIAL BEFORE THE COUNCIL

1. David R. Catchpole, *The Trial of Jesus: A Study in the Gospels and Jewish Historiography from 1770 to the Present Day* (Leiden: Brill, 1971).

2. Josef Blinzler, *Der Prozess Jesu,* 129–244; idem, "The Trial of Jesus in the Light of History," *Jud* 20 (1971): 49–55; A. N. Sherwin-White, *Roman Society and Roman Law in the New Testament* (New York: Oxford University Press, 1963), 1–47; idem, "The Trial of Christ," in *Historicity and Chronology in the New Testament,* ed. Dennis E. Nineham et al. (London: SPCK, 1965), 97–116; Pierre Benoit, *Passion,* 73–114; idem, *Jesus and the Gospel* (London: Darton, Longman and Todd, 1973), vol. 1, pp. 133–66; David R. Catchpole, "The Problem of the Historicity of the Sanhedrin Trial," in *The Trial of Jesus,* ed. Ernst Bammel (London: SCM, 1970), 47–65; Robert Gordis et al., "The Trial of Jesus in the Light of History," *Jud* 20 (1971): 6–74; Haim Cohn, "Reflections on the Trial of Jesus," *Jud* 20 (1971): 10–23; S. G. F. Brandon, "The Trial of Jesus," *Jud* 20 (1971): 43–48; T. A. Burkill, "The Competence of the Sanhedrin," *VC* 10 (1956): 80–96; idem, "The Trial of Jesus," *VC* 12 (1958): 1–18; Paul Winter, *On the Trial of Jesus* (Berlin: Walter de Gruyter, 1961); idem, "The Trial of Jesus and the Competence of the Sanhedrin," *NTS* 10.4 (1964): 494–99; Fitzmyer, *Luke (X–XXIV),* 1453–59; Joseph Klausner, *Jesus of*

Nazareth: His Life, Times, and Teaching (New York: Macmillan, 1945), 339–48; E. Dabrowski, "The Trial of Jesus in Recent Research," *SE* 4 (1968): 21–27.

3. For a summary see Carson, *Matthew*, 549–52.

4. Herbert Danby, "The Bearing of the Rabbinical Criminal Code on the Jewish Trial Narratives in the Gospels," *JTS* 21 (1919–20): 60.

5. Blinzler, *Der Prozess Jesu*, 207–9, 219, 227–29.

6. George F. Moore, *Judaism in the First Centuries of the Christian Era* (Cambridge, Mass.: Harvard University Press, 1958), vol. 2, p. 187, n. 5.

7. Danby, "Rabbinical Criminal Code," 51–76.

8. Jeremias, *Jerusalem*, 377–78; Schürer, *History of the Jewish People*, vol. 2, 229–35; E. Mary Smallwood, "High Priests and Politics in Roman Palestine," *JTS*, n.s. 13 (1962): 14–34.

9. Jeremias, *Jerusalem*, 96–99, 147–98; Schürer, *History of the Jewish People*, vol. 2, 200–238, 250; Smallwood, "High Priests," 14–34.

10. Jeremias, *Jerusalem*, 147–60; Josephus *Antiquities of the Jews* 13.13.5; 15.3.3; *Jewish War* 5.5.8.

11. Jeremias, *Jerusalem*, 160–63.

12. Ibid., 163–81.

13. Josephus *Jewish War* 2.17.6.

14. Avigad, *Discovering Jerusalem*, 85.

15. Ibid., 95–120.

16. Babylonian Talmud, *Pesaḥim* 57:1 = Tosefta, *Menaḥot* 13:21. See also Nahman Avigad, *Discovering Jerusalem*, 129–31; idem, "Excavations in the Jewish Quarter of the Old City of Jerusalem, 1969/70 (Preliminary Report)," *IEJ* 20 (1970): 1–8. In the second line of the folksong, Jeremias translates "woe unto me for their lances [or evil-speaking]" instead of "because of their slaves" (*Jerusalem*, 195).

17. Brown, *John (XIII–XXI)*, 820; Evans, "Jesus' Action," 259–70.

18. Benoit, *Passion*, 81, n. 1.

19. Jeremias, *Jerusalem*, 377–78.

20. Israel Abrahams, *Studies in Pharisaism and the Gospels*, 2d series (New York: Ktav, 1967), 132–33; see also William Barclay, *Crucified and Crowned* (London: SCM, 1961), 58.

21. Jeremias, *Jerusalem*, 223–32; Josephus *Vita* 2; *Jewish War* 2.14.8; 2.15.2; 2.17.2–3.

22. Jeremias, *Jerusalem*, 233–45; Josephus *Vita* 1–2, 38–39; *Jewish War* 2.17.3; *Antiquities* 18.1.4; 19.7.4.

23. Schürer, *History of the Jewish People*, vol. 2, pp. 225–26; Lane, *Mark*, 531–32.

24. Lane, *Mark*, 533.

25. Josephus *Antiquities* 4.8.115.

26. Philo *Legatio ad Gaium* 31, 39; Josephus *Jewish War* 5.5.2; 6.2.4; *Antiquities* 17.11.5; Blinzler, "Trial of Jesus," 51; Sherwin-White, *Roman Society*, 24–47 (on "sacrilege" see p. 38).

27. James A. Kleist, "Two False Witnesses (Mk 14:55ff.)," *CBQ* 9 (1947): 321–23.

28. Abrahams, *Studies in Pharisaism*, 1–3.

29. Manson, *Servant Messiah*, 1–35.

30. Nigel Turner, *Grammatical Insights into the New Testament* (Edinburgh: T. and T. Clark, 1966), 72–75.

31. Morris, *John*, 172–73. For more-detailed information see Guthrie, *New Testament Theology*, 270–91; also Otto Michel, "*ho huios tou anthrōpou*," in *NIDNTT*, vol. 3, pp. 612–34.

32. David R. Catchpole, "The Answer of Jesus to Caiaphas (Matt. XXVI. 64)," *NTS* 17.2 (1971): 213–26; Terrance Callan, "Psalm 110:1 and the Origin of the Expectation That Jesus Will Come Again," *CBQ* 44 (1982): 622–36; Olof Linton, "The Trial of Jesus and the Interpretation of Psalm CX," *NTS* 7.3 (1961): 258–62; H. K. McArthur, "Mark XIV.62," *NTS* 4.2 (1958): 156–58; Jane Schaberg, "Daniel 7, 12 and the New Testament Passion-Resurrection Predictions," *NTS* 31.2 (1985): 208–22; W. C. van Unnik, "Jesus the Christ," *NTS* 8.2 (1962): 101–16.

33. Herbert Danby, trans., *The Mishnah* (New York: Oxford University Press, 1956), 392.

34. Blinzler, *Der Prozess Jesu,* 137–62, esp. 152–56; see also David R. Catchpole, "You Have Heard His Blasphemy," *TynBul* 16 (April 1965): 10–18.

35. Morris, *John,* 293–96; see also Harvey, *Jesus on Trial,* 46–122.

36. Edwards et al., "Physical Death," 1456–58; Matzke, "Anatomist," 6–7.

37. Blinzler, *Der Prozess Jesu,* 162–66, 188, 194–95; John D. M. Derrett, *An Oriental Lawyer Looks at the Trial of Jesus and the Doctrine of Redemption* (London: University of London, 1966), 20; Lane, *Mark,* 539–40; Michael Grant, *The Jews in the Roman World* (New York: Dorset, 1984), 248–57; Otto Betz, "Die Verspottung des Messias: Markus 14, 65," in *Aufstieg und Niedergang der Römischen Welt,* ed. Hildegard Temporini and Wolfgang Haase (New York: Walter de Gruyter, 1982), vol. 2, pp. 637–39; Edward J. Young, *The Book of Isaiah* (Grand Rapids: Eerdmans, 1965), vol. 1, p. 383.

38. Westcott, *John,* 255.

39. Morris, *John,* 752; Donald Guthrie, *New Testament Introduction,* 3d ed. (Downers Grove, Ill.: Inter-Varsity, 1975), 241–71; Alfred Wikenhauser, *New Testament Introduction* (New York: Herder, 1963), 283–91. Even though the author of the fourth Gospel does not explicitly identify himself, he uses several circumlocutions for himself, such as "the other disciple" and "the disciple whom Jesus loved." In critical scholarship, it is more or less commonly agreed that this Gospel comes from the "Johannine circle." The interpretation of this phrase varies from one scholar to the other; however, historically the church has viewed the apostle John as the author of the fourth Gospel. A careful reading of the Johannine account of the trial of Jesus before the council suggests that John may well have been an eyewitness to this event as well as to the trial before Pilate.

40. Morris, *John,* 753; Brown, *John (XIII–XXI),* 824.

41. H. C. Kee, "Testaments of the Twelve Patriarchs," in *Old Testament Pseudepigrapha,* ed. Charlesworth, vol. 1, p. 822.

42. Cranfield, *Mark,* 447; see also David Brady, "The Alarm to Peter in Mark's Gospel," *JSNT* 4 (1979): 42–57.

43. J. Neville Birdsall, "*To rēma hōs eipen autō ho 'Iēsous:* Mk xiv. 72," *NovT* 2 (1958): 272–75.

44. Hans Kosmala, "The Time of Cockcrow," in *Studies, Essays and Reviews,* vol. 2, *New Testament* (Leiden: Brill, 1978), 76–81.

45. Cranfield, *Mark,* 448; G. M. Lee, "Mark 14, 72: *epibalōn eklaien,*" *Bib* 53 (1972): 411–12.

46. Plummer, *Luke,* 517.

47. Josephus *Antiquities* 12.3.3; 14.9.3–4; 20.9.1.

48. Fitzmyer, *Luke (X–XXIV),* 1468; Abrahams, *Studies in Pharisaism,* 1–3.

Chapter 10. THE DEATH OF JUDAS

1. *BAGD,* 511.

2. Friedrich Blass and A. Debrunner, *A Greek Grammar of the New*

Testament and Other Early Christian Literature, trans. and rev. Robert W. Funk (Chicago: University of Chicago Press, 1961), par. 127 (3); 299 (3).

3. Otto Michel, *"naos,"* in *TDNT,* vol. 4, p. 884.

4. Carson, *Matthew,* 566.

5. Jeremias, *Jerusalem,* 138–40.

6. Giuseppe Ricciotti, *The Acts of the Apostles* (Milwaukee: Bruce, 1958), 54; see also I. Howard Marshall, *The Acts of the Apostles,* Tyndale New Testament Commentaries (Grand Rapids: Eerdmans, 1980), 64–65.

7. F. F. Bruce, *The Acts of the Apostles: The Greek Text with Introduction and Commentary* (London: Tyndale, 1956), 77; see also "The Fragments of Papias," in J. B. Lightfoot, ed., *The Apostolic Fathers* (Grand Rapids: Baker, 1978), 270–71.

8. Kirsopp Lake, "The Death of Judas," in F. J. Foakes-Jackson and Kirsopp Lake, *The Beginnings of Christianity: The Acts of the Apostles,* 5 vols. (Grand Rapids: Baker, 1965–66 reprint), vol. 5, pp. 22–30.

9. F. F. Bruce, *The Book of Acts,* New International Commentary on the New Testament, rev. ed. (Grand Rapids: Eerdmans, 1988), 45.

10. Marshall, *Acts,* 65; F. F. Bruce, *Commentary on the Book of Acts,* New International Commentary on the New Testament (Grand Rapids: Eerdmans, 1973), 49–50.

11. Douglas J. Moo, "Tradition and Old Testament in Matt. 27:3–10," in *Gospel Perspectives,* vol. 3, *Studies in Midrash and Historiography,* ed. R. T. France and David Wenham (Sheffield: JSOT, 1983), 157–75; John A. Upton, "The Potter's Field and the Death of Judas," *CJ* 8.6 (1982): 213–19; Robert H. Gundry, *Matthew: A Commentary on His Literary and Theological Art* (Grand Rapids: Eerdmans, 1982), 554–58; R. T. France, *Jesus and the Old Testament,* 205–7; Benoit, *Jesus and the Gospel,* vol. 1, pp. 189–207.

12. Charles C. Torrey, "The Foundry of the Second Temple at Jerusalem," *JBL* 60 (1936): 247–60.

13. F. F. Bruce, *This and That: The New Testament Development of Some Old Testament Themes* (Exeter: Paternoster, 1968), 108–10.

14. Benoit, *Jesus and the Gospel,* vol. 1, pp. 189–207.

15. Dalman, *Sacred Sites,* 331–34.

Chapter 11. JESUS BEFORE PILATE AND HEROD

1. Sherwin-White, *Roman Society,* 1–12; E. Mary Smallwood, *The Jews under Roman Rule: From Pompey to Diocletian* (Leiden: Brill, 1976), 149–50; A. H. M. Jones, "The *Imperium* of Augustus," *JRS* 41 (1951): 111–19.

2. Seneca *On Anger* 2.7.3.

3. Sherwin-White, *Roman Society,* 45; Jerome Carcopino, *Daily Life in Ancient Rome* (New Haven: Yale University Press, 1940), 184–86.

4. Jerry Vardaman, "A New Inscription Which Mentions Pilate as 'Prefect,'" *JBL* 81 (1962): 70–71.

5. Josephus *Jewish War* 2.9.2; Tacitus *Annals* 15.44.

6. Smallwood, *Jews,* 145–46.

7. Ibid., 147.

8. Richard M. Mackowski, *Jerusalem, City of Jesus* (Grand Rapids: Eerdmans, 1980), 104–5; C. H. Johns, "Recent Excavations at the Citadel," *PEQ* 72 (1940): 53; idem, "The Citadel, Jerusalem," *QDAP* 14 (1950): 121–90; R. Amiran and A. Eitan, "Excavations in the Jerusalem Citadel," in Yigael

Yadin, ed., *Jerusalem Revealed: Archaeology in the Holy City, 1968–1974* (Jerusalem: Israel Exploration Society, 1975), 52–54; D. Bahat and M. Broshi, "Excavations in the Armenian Garden," in Yadin, ed., *Jerusalem Revealed*, 55–56.

9. Josephus *Jewish War* 5.4.4.

10. Mackowski, *Jerusalem*, 102–6; Bahat and Broshi, "Armenian Garden," 55–56.

11. Philo *Legatio ad Gaium* 38–39.

12. Josephus *Jewish War* 2.12.1; 2.14.8–15; *Antiquities of the Jews* 20.5.3.

13. Benoit, *Jesus and the Gospel*, vol. 1, pp. 168–82; see also Mackowski, *Jerusalem*, 104; Lane, *Mark*, 548; Brown, *John (XIII–XXI)*, 845; Blinzler, *Der Prozess Jesu*, 256–59.

14. A. Buechler, "The Levitical Impurity of the Gentile in Palestine before the Year 70," *JQR* 17 (1926–27): 1–81.

15. Sherwin-White, *Roman Society*, 17–45.

16. Ethelbert Stauffer, *Die Botschaft Jesu: Damals und Heute* (Bern: Francke, 1959), 95–112.

17. Morris, *John*, 293–96.

18. Harvey, *Jesus on Trial*, esp. 18–102, carefully notes the importance and implications of the terms "witness" and "certified agent" in John's Gospel.

19. Karl Heinrich Rengstorf, *Das Evangelium nach Lukas*, Das Neue Testament Deutsch 3 (Göttingen: Vandenhoeck and Ruprecht, 1962), 262; Fitzmyer, *Luke (I–IX)*, 322; *Luke (X–XXIV)*, 1476.

20. Sherwin-White, *Roman Society*, 28–32; see also Marshall, *Luke*, 854–55; Benoit, *Passion*, 144.

21. Smallwood, *Jews*, 146.

22. Josephus *Jewish War* 2.6.3.

23. Fitzmyer, *Luke (X–XXIV)*, 1482.

Chapter 12. JESUS' FINAL TRIAL BEFORE PILATE

1. Livy *History of Rome* 5.13.5–8.

2. Blinzler, *Der Prozess Jesu*, 301–5; Richard W. Husband, "The Pardoning of Prisoners by Pilate," *AJT* 21 (1917): 110–16.

3. *PFlor* 1.61.59.

4. Blinzler, *Der Prozess Jesu*, 301–5; Benoit, *Jesus and the Gospel*, vol. 1, pp. 137–38.

5. S. Langdon, "The Release of a Prisoner at the Passover," *ExpTim* 29 (1917–18): 328–30; Robert L. Merritt, "Jesus Barabbas and the Paschal Pardon," *JBL* 104 (1985): 57–68.

6. Ernst Bammel, "The Trial before Pilate," in *Jesus and the Politics of His Day*, ed. Ernst Bammel and C. F. D. Moule (New York: Cambridge University Press, 1984), 426–28.

7. Charles B. Chavel, "The Releasing of a Prisoner on the Eve of Passover in Ancient Jerusalem," *JBL* 60 (1941): 273–78; Blinzler, *Der Prozess Jesu*, 317–20; Robinson, *Priority of John*, 261.

8. Karl H. Rengstorf, "*lēstēs*," in *TDNT*, vol. 4, pp. 257–62.

9. Husband, "Pardoning of Prisoners," 112–16; Blinzler, *Der Prozess Jesu*, 308–9.

10. Fitzmyer, *Luke (X–XXIV)*, 1490; Brown, *John (XIII–XXI)*, 856–57.

11. Stevan L. Davies, "Who Is Called Bar Abbas?" *NTS* 27.2 (1981):

260–62; H. Z. Maccoby, "Jesus and Barabbas," *NTS* 16.1 (1969): 55–60; Horace A. Rigg, Jr., "Barabbas," *JBL* 64 (1945): 417–56. Benoit, *Passion,* 140, and Plummer, *Exegetical Commentary on the Gospel According to S. Matthew* (London: Elliot Stock, 1909), 389, reject the insertion of "Jesus" before "Barabbas"; see also Mann, *Mark,* 638–39.

12. Benoit, *Jesus and the Gospel,* vol. 1, 143–46; Blinzler, *Der Prozess Jesu,* 309–10.

13. Blinzler, *Der Prozess Jesu,* 309–14; Mann, *Mark,* 639; R. T. France, *The Gospel According to Matthew,* Tyndale New Testament Commentaries (Grand Rapids: Eerdmans, 1987), 391; Jeremias, *Jerusalem,* 111–19.

14. Tacitus *Annals* 3.33–35; Blinzler, *Der Prozess Jesu,* 313–17; Carson, *Matthew,* 569.

15. *BAGD,* 603–4; D. Fürst, "*paideuō,*" in *NIDNTT,* vol. 3, p. 778.

16. Benoit, *Jesus and the Gospel,* vol. 1, pp. 150–51.

17. Robinson, *Priority of John,* 261–66.

18. Blinzler, *Der Prozess Jesu,* 321–25, 334–36; F. F. Bruce, "Trial of Jesus," in *Gospel Perspectives,* ed. France and Wenham, vol. 1, p. 15.

19. Sherwin-White, *Roman Society,* 26–29; Blinzler, *Der Prozess Jesu,* 321–25.

20. James Hope Moulton and George Milligan, *The Vocabulary of the Greek New Testament* (Grand Rapids: Eerdmans, 1976 reprint), 390.

21. *BAGD,* 495.

22. Ibid., 865.

23. Barbet, *Doctor at Calvary,* 54.

24. Edwards et al., "Physical Death," 1458.

25. *BAGD,* 440; see also Blinzler, *Der Prozess Jesu,* 325–26.

26. *BAGD,* 29.

27. Zohary, *Plants,* 153–60.

28. See especially H. StJ. Hart, "The Crown of Thorns in John 19,2–5," *JTS,* n.s. 3 (1952–53): 66–75; Campbell Bonner, "The Crown of Thorns," *HTR* 46 (1953): 47–48.

29. Zohary, *Plants,* 134.

30. Edwards et al., "Physical Death," 1456, 1458; Matzke, "Anatomist," 7.

31. Blinzler, *Der Prozess Jesu,* 328–30; Brown, *John (XIII–XXI),* 875–76; Morris, *John,* 792–93; Bruce, *John,* 359; Barrett, *John,* 540.

32. Harvey, *Jesus on Trial,* 18–102.

33. David W. Wead, "We Have a Law," *NovT* 11 (1969): 185–89.

34. Morris, *John,* 797; Bruce, *John,* 362; Brown, *John (XIII–XXI),* 878–79.

35. John Henry Bernard, *A Critical and Exegetical Commentary on the Gospel According to St. John* (Edinburgh: T. and T. Clark, 1928), vol. 2, p. 621.

36. Ernst Bammel, "Φίλος τοῦ Καίσαρος," *ThLit* 4 (1952): 205–10.

37. Jerome O. Nriagu, "Occasional Notes: Saturnine Gout among Roman Aristocrats: Did Lead Poisoning Contribute to the Fall of the Empire?" *New England Journal of Medicine* 308.11 (March 17, 1983): 660–63.

38. C. W. Chilton, "The Roman Law of Treason under the Early Principate," *JRS* 45 (1955): 73–81. For a disagreement with Chilton on some aspects of Roman law, see Robert Samuel Rogers, "Treason in the Early Empire," *JRS* 49 (1959): 90–94.

39. Josephus *Antiquities of the Jews* 18.3.1; *Jewish War* 2.9.2–3.

40. Josephus *Antiquities* 18.3.2; *Jewish War* 2.9.4.

41. Philo *Legatio ad Gaium* 38.

42. Schürer, *History of the Jewish People,* vol. 1, pp. 383–87; Henry

Wansbrough, "Suffered under Pontius Pilate," *Scr* 44 (1966): 84–96; Carl H. Kraeling, "The Episode of the Roman Standards at Jerusalem," *HTR* 35 (1942): 263–89; Paul L. Maier, "Notes and Observations: The Episode of the Golden Roman Shields at Jerusalem," *HTR* 62 (1969): 109–21; idem, "Sejanus, Pilate, and the Date of the Crucifixion," *CH* 37 (1968): 3–13.

43. Carson, *Matthew*, 570–71; Hans Kosmala, "His Blood Be on Us and on Our Children (The Background of Mat. 27, 24–25)," *ASTI* 7 (1970): 94–126.

44. Blinzler, *Der Prozess Jesu*, 337–56; Benoit, *Jesus and the Gospel*, vol. 1, pp. 182–88.

45. Morris, *John*, 774–86.

46. Norman Walker, "The Reckoning of Hours in the Fourth Gospel," *NovT* 4 (1960): 69–73.

47. Sherwin-White, *Roman Society*, 24–47.

Chapter 13. JESUS' CRUCIFIXION

1. Martin Hengel, *Crucifixion in the Ancient World and the Folly of the Message of the Cross* (Philadelphia: Fortress, 1977), 1–32.

2. James B. Pritchard, *The Ancient Near East in Pictures* (Princeton, N.J.: Princeton University Press, 1955), #362, 368, 372–73.

3. Herodotus *History* 3.125.3; 3.132.2; 4.43.2, 7; 6.30.1; 7.194.1ff.

4. Hengel, *Crucifixion*, 22–32; see also Blinzler, *Der Prozess Jesu*, 357–58.

5. Blinzler, *Der Prozess Jesu*, 359; Ethelbert Stauffer, *Jerusalem und Rom im Zeitalter Jesu Christi* (Bern: Francke, 1957), 123–25; Josephus *Jewish War* 1.4.6; *Antiquities of the Jews* 13.14.2. See also Appendix A, "Deuteronomy 21:22–23 and Crucifixion," pp. 159–61.

6. Appian *Bella Civilia* 1.120.

7. Tacitus *Annals* 2.32.2; Hengel, *Crucifixion*, 51–63; Barbet, *Doctor at Calvary*, 49.

8. Josephus *Antiquities* 17.10.10; *Jewish War* 2.4.2; Smallwood, *Jews*, 110–13.

9. Josephus *Jewish War* 2.13.2; *Antiquities* 20.8.5.

10. Josephus *Jewish War* 2.14.9; Tessa Rajak, *Josephus: The Historian and His Society* (Philadelphia: Fortress, 1984), 72–75.

11. Josephus *Jewish War* 5.11.1; Hengel, *Crucifixion*, 25–26; Blinzler, *Der Prozess Jesu*, 358–59.

12. Suetonius *Galba* 9.2; Hengel, *Crucifixion*, 39–45.

13. Firsthand information on this exciting yet puzzling find has been provided by a number of those directly involved in the excavation: Nico Haas, "Anthropological Observations on the Skeletal Remains from Giv'at ha-Mivtar," *IEJ* 20 (1970): 38–59, and plates 19–24; Vassilios A. Tzaferis, "Crucifixion: The Archaeological Evidence," *BAR* 11.1 (Jan./Feb. 1985): 44–53; idem, "Jewish Tombs at and near Giv'at ha-Mivtar, Jerusalem," *IEJ* 20 (1970): 18–32; Joseph Naveh, "The Ossuary Inscriptions from Giv'at ha-Mivtar," *IEJ* 20 (1970): 33–37; Yigael Yadin, "Epigraphy and Crucifixion," *IEJ* 23 (1973): 18–22; Vilhelm Möller-Christensen, "Skeletal Remains from Giv'at ha-Mivtar," *IEJ* 26 (1976): 35–38; James H. Charlesworth, "Jesus and Jehohanan: An Archaeological Note on Crucifixion," *ExpTim* 84 (1972–73): 147–50; Joseph Zias and Eliezer Sekeles, "The Crucified Man from Giv'at ha-Mivtar: A Reappraisal," *IEJ* 35 (1985): 22–27.

14. Hengel, *Crucifixion*, 25; Seneca *Dialogue* 6.

15. Josephus *Jewish War* 5.11.1.

16. Barbet, *Doctor at Calvary*, 43, 45; John J. Collins, "The Archaeology of the Crucifixion," *CBQ* 1 (1939): 154–55.

17. Brown, *John (XIII–XXI)*, 901.

18. Blinzler, *Der Prozess Jesu*, 362; Collins, "Archaeology," 156.

19. Blinzler, *Der Prozess Jesu*, 367.

20. Edwards et al., "Physical Death," 1459–61; Barbet, *Doctor at Calvary*, 45–46, 100; Collins, "Archaeology," 155.

21. Barbet, *Doctor at Calvary*, 46–47, 65–66; Collins, "Archaeology," 157; Edwards et al., "Physical Death," 1459. See figure 6 (p. 129) for an illustration of how the spike was nailed through the wrist.

22. Barbet, *Doctor at Calvary*, 44–45.

23. Barbet, *Doctor at Calvary*; William Stroud, *The Physical Cause of the Death of Christ, and Its Relation to the Principles and Practice of Christianity* (New York: Appleton, 1871); Edward R. Bloomquist, "A Doctor Looks at the Crucifixion," *ChrH* 87 (March 1964): 35, 46–48; Jacques Brehant, "What Was the Medical Cause of Christ's Death?" *Medical World News*, 27 October 1966, 154–55, 159; C. T. Davis, "The Crucifixion of Jesus: The Passion of Christ from a Medical Point of View," *Arizona Medicine* 22 (1965): 183–87; Kenneth Leese, "The Physical Cause of the Death of Jesus: A Medical Opinion," *ExpTim* 83 (1971–72): 248; Matzke, "Anatomist," 6–7; Hermann Mödder, "Die Todesursache bei der Kreuzigung," *SZ* 144 (1949): 50–59; W. B. Primrose, "A Surgeon Looks at the Crucifixion," *HibJ* 47 (1948–49): 382–88; A. F. Sava, "The Wound in the Side of Christ," *CBQ* 19 (1957): 343–46; Engelbert Sons, "Die Todesursache bei der Kreuzigung," *SZ* 146 (1950): 60–64; John Wilkinson, "The Physical Cause of the Death of Christ," *ExpTim* 83 (1971–72): 104–7; Whitaker, "Physical Cause," 83–107.

24. Deut. 25:2–3 specifies not more than forty lashes, while 2 Cor. 11:24 mentions the limit of thirty-nine.

25. Barbet, *Doctor at Calvary*, 48, 83–84; Edwards et al., "Physical Death," 1457.

26. Barbet, *Doctor at Calvary*, 92–105; Edwards et al., "Physical Death," 1459–60; Bloomquist, "Doctor Looks," 48; Davis, "Crucifixion of Jesus," 183–87.

27. Edwards et al., "Physical Death," 1460–61; Barbet, *Doctor at Calvary*, 100.

28. Bloomquist, "Doctor Looks," 48; Barbet, *Doctor at Calvary*, 106–12; Brehant, "Medical Cause," 155, 159.

29. Edwards et al., "Physical Death," 1461; Matzke, "Anatomist," 7; Bloomquist, "Doctor Looks," 48.

30. *BAGD*, 14.

31. Nahman Avigad, "A Depository of Inscribed Ossuaries in the Kidron Valley," *IEJ* 12 (1962): 1–12; Carson, *Matthew*, 574–75; Mann, *Mark*, 645; Lane, *Mark*, 562–63; Cranfield, *Mark*, 454; Benoit, *Passion*, 163–65.

32. Josephus *Against Apion* 2.4.

33. Josephus *Antiquities* 16.6.1–5.

34. Bruce, *New Testament History*, 129.

35. For critical theories on the source of Luke 23:27–31 see Fitzmyer, *Luke (X–XXIV)*, 1494–96.

36. Matt. 26:65–66 and Mark 14:63–64 note that Jesus was condemned for blasphemy. Lev. 24:14 and Num. 15:35–36 stipulate that blasphemers were to be executed outside the camp. After the conquest of Canaan, these executions took place outside city walls.

37. Brown, *John (XIII–XXI)*, 899–900; Benoit, *Passion*, 168–69; Dalman, *Sacred Sites*, 346–49.

38. Charles Gordon, "Eden and Golgotha," *Palestine Exploration Fund Quarterly Statement* 10 (1885): 78–81; see also Murphy-O'Connor, *Holy Land*, 124–25. For a more complete account see Wilkinson, *Jerusalem*, 148, 198–200.

39. Dalman, *Sacred Sites*, 346–81; Blinzler, *Der Prozess Jesu*, 362–63; André Parrot, *Golgotha and the Church of the Holy Sepulchre*, Studies in Biblical Archaeology 6 (London: SCM, 1957); Charles Couasnon, *The Church of the Holy Sepulchre in Jerusalem*, Schweich Lectures of the British Academy (London: Oxford University Press, 1974), 12–13 on Golgotha; Wilkinson, *Jerusalem*, 144–51; Jerome Murphy-O'Connor, *Holy Land*, 43–53; idem, "The Garden Tomb and the Misfortune of an Inscription," *BAR* 12.2 (March/April 1986): 54–55; Dan Bahat, "Does the Holy Sepulchre Church Mark the Burial of Jesus?" *BAR* 12.3 (May/June 1986): 26–45; Gabriel Barkay, "The Garden Tomb: Was Jesus Buried Here?" *BAR* 12.2 (March/April 1986): 40–57; L. E. Cox Evans, "The Holy Sepulchre," *PEQ* 100 (1968): 112–36; a series of articles by L. Y. Rahmani, "Ancient Jerusalem's Funerary Customs and Tombs," *BA* 44 (1981): 171–77, 229–35; 45 (1982): 43–53, 109–19; J.-P. B. Ross, "The Evolution of a Church—Jerusalem's Holy Sepulchre," *BAR* 2.3 (Sept./Oct. 1976): 3–8, 11.

40. *Sanhedrin* 43a.

41. Dioscorides Pedanius *Materia medica* 1.64.3; Lane, *Mark*, 564.

42. Pliny *Natural History* 14.13 (15); Blinzler, *Der Prozess Jesu*, 365–66.

43. Marshall, *Luke*, 867–68.

44. Benoit, *Passion*, 173.

45. Arndt, *Luke*, 468–69.

46. David Daube, "'For they know not what they do': Luke 23,34," *TU* 79 (1961): 58–70.

47. Barrett, *John*, 549; Blinzler, *Der Prozess Jesu*, 367–68; Ernst Bammel, "The *Titulus*," in *Jesus and the Politics of His Day*, ed. Ernst Bammel and C. F. D. Moule (New York: Cambridge University Press, 1984), 353–54.

48. Plummer, *Luke*, 534.

49. Joachim Jeremias, "*Paradeisos*," in *TDNT*, vol. 5, p. 770. For further evaluation of the textual variant see Marshall, *Luke*, 872–73; Metzger, *Textual Commentary*, 181.

50. Jeremias, "*Paradeisos*," 765–73.

51. Brown, *John (XIII–XXI)*, 904–6; Morris, *John*, 810–11. Scholars disagree as to whether three or four women were present, for it is unclear whether "his mother's sister" and "Mary the wife of Clopas" refer to one or two people. It seems unlikely, of course, that Mary had a sister named Mary. The problem arises in part because the Greek in this instance does not use the term for wife *(gynē)*. In addition, it must be remembered that early Greek manuscripts had neither word breaks nor punctuation.

52. Ekrem Akurgal, *Ancient Civilizations and Ruins of Turkey: From Prehistoric Times until the End of the Roman Empire*, 3d ed. (Istanbul: Haset Kitabevi, 1973), esp. 144, 156–57, 170.

53. John F. A. Sawyer, "Why Is a Solar Eclipse Mentioned in the Passion Narrative (Luke XXIII.44–5)?" *JTS*, n.s. 23 (1972): 124–28. J. K. Fotheringham, "The Evidence of Astronomy and Technical Chronology for the Date of the Crucifixion," *JTS* 35 (1934): 146–62.

54. Mann, *Mark*, 650; Denis Baly, *The Geography of the Bible: A Study in Historical Geography* (New York: Harper, 1957), 67–70; *Basic Biblical Geography* (Philadelphia: Fortress, 1987), 26.

55. A. Guillaume, "Mt. xxvii, 46, in the Light of the Dead Sea Scroll of Isaiah," *PEQ* 83 (1951): 78–80.

56. Zohary, *Plants*, 96–97; John Wilkinson, "The Seven Words from the Cross," *SJT* 17 (1964): 76–78.

57. Joachim Jeremias, *"Ēl(e)ias,"* in *TDNT*, vol. 2, pp. 928–35; Dale C. Allison, Jr., "Elijah Must Come First," *JBL* 103 (1984): 256–58; Morris M. Faierstein, "Why Do the Scribes Say That Elijah Must Come First?" *JBL* 100 (1981): 75–86; Joseph A. Fitzmyer, "More about Elijah Coming First," *JBL* 104 (1985): 295–96.

58. *BAGD*, 810–11.

59. See n. 23.

60. Barbet, *Doctor at Calvary*, 68–80.

61. Wilkinson, "Physical Cause," 104–7.

62. R. O. Ball, "Physical Cause of the Death of Jesus: A Theological Comment," *ExpTim* 83 (1971–72): 248; Leese, "Physical Cause," 248.

63. Wilkinson, "Seven Words," *SJT* 17 (1964): 69–82.

Chapter 14. Jesus' Death and Burial

1. Carl Schneider, *"katapetasma,"* in *TDNT*, vol. 3, pp. 628–30.

2. For various views see Fitzmyer, *Luke (X XXIV)*, 1518 19; Lane, *Mark*, 574–75; Mann, *Mark*, 653–54; Harry L. Chronis, "The Torn Veil: Cultus and Christology in Mark 15:37–39," *JBL* 101 (1982): 97–114; Dennis D. Sylva, "The Temple Curtain and Jesus' Death in the Gospel of Luke," *JBL* 105 (1986): 239–50; S. Motyer, "The Rending of the Veil: A Markan Pentecost?" *NTS* 33.1 (1987): 155–57; Eta Linnemann, *Studien zur Passionsgeschichte* (Göttingen: Vandenhoeck and Ruprecht, 1978), 160–61.

3. Lane, *Mark*, 575; Samuel T. Lachs, *A Rabbinic Commentary on the New Testament: The Gospel of Matthew, Mark, and Luke* (Hoboken, N.J.: Ktav, 1987), 434.

4. Ernest L. Martin, *Secrets of Golgotha: The Forgotten History of Christ's Crucifixion* (Alhambra, Calif.: ASK, 1988), is the most recent proponent of this view. See also Howard M. Jackson, "The Death of Jesus in Mark and the Miracle from the Cross," *NTS* 33.1 (1987): 24–25.

5. Schneider, *"katapetasma,"* in *TDNT*, vol. 3, pp. 628–30.

6. *BAGD*, 654.

7. Josephus *Jewish War* 6.5.3–4, where various other unnatural phenomena are also recorded.

8. Carson, *Matthew*, 581–82.

9. See Psalms of Solomon 2–3, and 14–15, esp. 2:31; 3:12; 14:10; and 15:10, in R. B. Wright, "Psalms of Solomon," in *Old Testament Pseudepigrapha*, ed. Charlesworth, vol. 2, pp. 652–55, 664.

10. E. C. Colwell, "A Definite Rule for the Use of the Article in the Greek New Testament," *JBL* 52 (1933): 12–21; see also C. F. D. Moule, *An Idiom Book of New Testament Greek* (New York: Cambridge University Press, 1953), 115–17.

11. Lane, *Mark*, 571, 576; Carson, *Matthew*, 582–83; Cranfield, *Mark*, 460; Philip H. Bligh, "A Note on *Huios Theou* in Mark 15:39," *ExpTim* 80 (1968–69): 51–53; Robert G. Bratcher, "A Note on *huios theou* (Mark xv. 39)," *ExpTim* 68 (1956–57): 27–28.

12. Carl R. Holladay, *Theios Aner in Hellenistic Judaism: A Critique of the Use of This Category in New Testament Christology*, Society of Biblical Literature Dissertation Series 40 (Missoula, Mont.: Scholars, 1977).

13. Adolf von Schlatter, *Das Evangelium nach Markus und Lukas* (Stutt-

gart: Calwer, 1954), 394; Robert J. Karris, "Luke 23:47 and the Lucan View of Jesus' Death," *JBL* 105 (1986): 65–74.

14. For further details see chap. 5.

15. Brown, *John (XIII–XXI)*, 933–34; Morris, *John*, 816–18.

16. Edwards et al., "Physical Death," 1461; Matzke, "Anatomist," 7.

17. Haas, "Anthropological Observations," 57–59; Tzaferis, "Crucifixion," 50–53. For more information on Deut. 21:22–23 and crucifixion see Appendix A, pp. 159–61.

18. *BAGD*, 479.

19. Brown, *John (XIII–XXI)*, 935; Morris, *John*, 818–20; John Wilkinson, "The Incident of the Blood and Water in John 19.34," *SJT* 28 (1975): 150–51.

20. Barbet, *Doctor at Calvary*, chap. 7; William Stroud, *The Physical Cause of the Death of Christ, and Its Relation to the Principles and Practices of Christianity* (New York: Appleton, 1871).

21. Sava, "Wound," 344.

22. Ibid., 345–46. See Appendix B (p. 163) for a summary of Sava's conclusions.

23. Bloomquist, "Doctor Looks," 48.

24. Wilkinson, "Incident," 152–53.

25. Ibid., 159–62.

26. Ibid., 162.

27. Ibid., 166–69.

28. Edwards et al., "Physical Death," 1462–63; see also Matzke, "Anatomist," 7; Brehant, "Medical Cause," 159. For a critical discussion of a variety of views on this event and its significance see Brown, *John (XIII–XXI)*, 946–52.

29. Morris, *John*, 89–91, 293–96.

30. Brown, *John (XIII–XXI)*, 937–38; Bruce, *John*, 377; Barrett, *John*, 558, believes this Johannine reference to be primarily to the Passover lamb.

31. Barrett, *John*, 204; Morris, *John*, 210–11.

32. Josephus *Antiquities* 13.4.9.

33. Eusebius *Onomasticon* 32.

34. Blinzler, *Der Prozess Jesu*, 391–92; Brown, *John (XIII–XXI)*, 938; Dalman, *Sacred Sites*, 225–26.

35. Leon Morris, *The Gospel According to St. Luke*, Tyndale New Testament Commentaries (Grand Rapids: Eerdmans, 1974), 331; Arndt, *Luke*, 476, 478.

36. Ulpian *On the Duties of Proconsul* 9.

37. Blinzler, *Der Prozess Jesu*, 386–87, 393–94.

38. *BAGD*, 555.

39. Zohary, *Plants*, 200.

40. Ibid., 204.

41. *BAGD*, 475.

42. *Šabbat* 23:5; Lane, *Mark*, 580.

43. Morris, *John*, 826; Brown, *John (XIII–XXI)*, 940–42; Barrett, *John*, 558–60; Bruce, *John*, 379; Th. C. De Kruijf, "'More Than Half a Hundredweight' of Spices (John 19, 39 NEB): Abundance and Symbolism in the Gospel of John," *Bijdragen* 43 (1982): 234–39.

44. Scientific tests have now firmly established that the Shroud of Turin was not the gravecloth of Jesus. Cardinal Anastasio Ballestrero of Turin has stated that the cloth was made between 1260 and 1390. The first records of the shroud trace it back to Lirey, France, in 1354. Among others, see "Shroud's Age Ruled Medieval," *St. Louis Post-Dispatch*, 14 Oct. 1988, p. 1; also a Vatican news release "Respect for Shroud Reaffirmed," in *St. Louis Review* 37.42 (21 Oct. 1988): 2.

45. See especially Robert Houston Smith, "The Tomb of Jesus," *BA* 30.3 (1967): 74–90; also, Gabriel Barkay, "Garden Tomb," 40–57; Bahat, "Holy

Sepulchre Church," 26–45; Ross, "Evolution of a Church," 3–11; Cornfeld, ed., *Historical Jesus*, 199–217; Murphy-O'Connor, *Holy Land*, 43–53; Dalman, *Sacred Sites*, 346–81; Evans, "Holy Sepulchre," 112–36; Jeffrey Chadwick, "To the Editor: In Defense of the Garden Tomb," *BAR* 12.4 (July/Aug. 1986): 16–17; Pierre Benoit, "To the Editor: The Inscription Allegedly Relating to the Garden Tomb," *BAR* 12.4 (July/Aug. 1986): 58; Wilkinson, *Jerusalem*, 146–50, 180–97; W. Harold Mare, *The Archaeology of the Jerusalem Area* (Grand Rapids: Baker, 1987), 185–90.

46. Smith, "Tomb of Jesus," 85–89. Barkay states, "Burial caves of the Second Temple period usually have two rooms aligned one behind the other" ("Garden Tomb," 52).

47. David Hill, *The Gospel of Matthew*, New Century Bible Commentary (Grand Rapids: Eerdmans, 1972), 357–58; Plummer, *Matthew*, 408–11.

48. Hill, *Matthew*, 358.

49. Benoit, *Passion*, 226–27.

50. Carson, *Matthew*, 586; see also G. M. Lee, "The Guard at the Tomb," *Th* 72, no. 586 (April 1969): 167–75; William Lane Craig, "The Guard at the Tomb," *NTS* 30.2 (1984): 273–81.

51. France, *Matthew*, 405.

52. Plummer, *Matthew*, 410.

Chapter 15. EPILOG: JESUS' RESURRECTION

1. Bruce, *1–2 Corinthians*, 140. Among recent articles on Jesus' resurrection are the following: Samuel O. Abogunrin, "The Language and Nature of the Resurrection of Jesus Christ in the New Testament," *JETS* 24 (1981): 55–65; William Lane Craig, "Guard," 273–81; idem, "The Historicity of the Empty Tomb of Jesus," *NTS* 31.1 (1985): 39–67; Thomas R. W. Longstaff, "The Women at the Tomb: Matthew 28:1 Re-examined," *NTS* 27.2 (1981): 277–82; Joseph Plevnik, "The Eyewitnesses of the Risen Christ in Luke 24," *CBQ* 49 (1986): 90–103; Hugo Staudinger, "The Resurrection of Jesus Christ as Saving Event and as 'Object' of Historical Research," *SJT* 36 (1983): 309–26.

2. Joachim Jeremias, *"Hadēs,"* in *TDNT*, vol. 1, pp. 148–49; Martin H. Scharlemann, "'He Descended into Hell'—An Interpretation of 1 Peter 3:18–20," *CTM* 27 (1956): 81–94.

3. Scharlemann, "He Descended into Hell," 92.

4. Longstaff, "Women at the Tomb"; Plevnik, "Eyewitnesses," 90–94.

5. Dalman, *Sacred Sites*, 226–31; Fitzmyer, *Luke (X–XXIV)*, 1561–62; Marshall, *Luke*, 892–93; Murphy-O'Connor, *Holy Land*, 320; Plummer, *Luke*, 551–52.

6. Plevnik, "Eyewitnesses," 94–98.

7. Ibid., 98–101.

8. In his book *Jesus on Trial*, A. E. Harvey stresses that John's Gospel account must be read in the light of the importance that the Jewish legal system placed on the roles of witness and the certified agent. See also Morris, *John*, 115–26, 293–96, and 335–37.

Appendix A. DEUTERONOMY 21:22–23 AND CRUCIFIXION

1. Josephus *Jewish War* 1.4.5–6; *Antiquities* 13.14.2.

2. Joseph A. Fitzmyer, "Crucifixion in Ancient Palestine, Qumran Literature, and the New Testament," *CBQ* 40 (1978): 493–513; Yigael Yadin,

"Pesher Nahum (4QpNahum) Reconsidered," *IEJ* 21 (1971): 1–12; David J. Halperin, "Crucifixion, the Nahum Pesher, and the Rabbinic Penalty of Strangulation," *JJS* 32 (1981): 32–46; J. Massyngberde Ford, "'Crucify him, crucify him' and the Temple Scroll," *ExpTim* 87 (1975–76): 275–78.

3. Fitzmyer, "Crucifixion in Ancient Palestine," 500; see also the "Commentary on Nahum," in Geza Vermes, *The Dead Sea Scrolls in English* (Baltimore: Penguin, 1970 reprint), 231–32.

4. Yadin, "Pesher Nahum," 12.

5. Ibid., 8; see also Johann Maier, *The Temple Scroll: An Introduction, Translation and Commentary*, Journal for the Study of the Old Testament Supplemental Series 34 (Sheffield: JSOT, 1985), 55.

6. Josephus *Antiquities* 13.14.2; *Jewish War* 1.4.6.

7. Yadin, "Pesher Nahum," 8–12; Fitzmyer, "Crucifixion in Ancient Palestine," 502–7; Halperin, "Crucifixion," 32–43. Joseph M. Baumgarten, "Does *TLH* in the Temple Scroll Refer to Crucifixion?" *JBL* 91 (1972): 472–81, argues that the Temple Scroll is not referring to crucifixion. But Ford, "'Crucify him,'" 276, points out that Baumgarten like Yadin fails to consider New Testament texts, which are also primary sources.

8. Fitzmyer, "Crucifixion in Ancient Palestine," 507–13; Ford, "'Crucify him,'" 276.

9. Richard Zehnle, "The Salvific Character of Jesus' Death in Lucan Soteriology," *TS* 30 (1969): 420–44; Page, "Suffering Servant," 481–97; I. Howard Marshall, "The Death of Jesus in Recent New Testament Study," *Word World* 3 (1983): 12–21.

Bibliography

Abogunrin, Samuel O. "The Language and Nature of the Resurrection of Jesus Christ in the New Testament." *JETS* 24 (1981): 55–65.

Abrahams, Israel. *Studies in Pharisaism and the Gospels*. 2d series. New York: Ktav, 1967.

Abramowski, Luise, and A. E. Goodman. "Luke XXIII. 46. ΠΑΡΑΤΙΘΕΜΑΙ in a Rare Syriac Setting." *NTS* 13.3 (1967): 290–91.

Akurgal, Ekrem. *Ancient Civilizations and Ruins of Turkey: From Prehistoric Times until the End of the Roman Empire*. 3d ed. Istanbul: Haset Kitabevi, 1973.

Allison, Dale C., Jr. "Elijah Must Come First." *JBL* 103 (1984): 256–58.

Anderson, Norman. *A Lawyer among the Theologians*. Grand Rapids: Eerdmans, 1973.

Armbruster, C. J. "The Messianic Significance of the Agony in the Garden." *Scr* 16 (1964): 111–19.

Arndt, William F. *Bible Commentary: The Gospel According to St. Luke*. St. Louis: Concordia, 1956.

Avigad, Nahman. "A Depository of Inscribed Ossuaries in the Kidron Valley." *IEJ* 12 (1962): 1–12.

_____. *Discovering Jerusalem*. Nashville: Thomas Nelson, 1983.

_____. "Excavations in the Jewish Quarter of the Old City of Jerusalem, 1969/70 (Preliminary Report)." *IEJ* 20 (1979): 1–8.

Avi-Yonah, Michael. "Roman Palestine Map." Rev. ed. Jaffa: Survey of Palestine, 1939.

_____, ed. *Encyclopedia of Archaeological Excavations in the Holy Land*. Vol. 2. Jerusalem: Israel Exploration Society and Masada Press, 1976.

Bacchiocchi, Samuele. *The Time of the Crucifixion and the Resurrection*. Berrien Springs, Mich.: Biblical Perspectives, 1985.

Bahat, Dan. "Does the Holy Sepulchre Church Mark the Burial of Jesus?" *BAR* 12.3 (May/June 1986): 26–45.

Bahr, George J. "The Seder of Passover and the Eucharistic Words." *NovT* 12 (1970): 181–202.

Bajsić, Alois. "Pilatus, Jesus und Barabbas." *Bib* 48 (1967): 7–28.

Ball, R. O. "Physical Cause of the Death of Jesus: A Theological Comment." *ExpTim* 83 (1971–72): 248.

Baly, Denis. *Basic Biblical Geography*. Philadelphia: Fortress, 1987.

_____. *The Geography of the Bible: A Study in Historical Geography*. New York: Harper, 1957.

Bammel, Ernst. "Crucifixion as a Punishment in Palestine." In *The Trial of Jesus*, ed. Ernst Bammel, 162–65. London: SCM, 1970.

_____. "*Ex illa itaque die consilium fecerunt. . . .*" In *The Trial of Jesus*, ed. Ernst Bammel, 11–40. London: SCM, 1970.

_____. "Φίλος τοῦ Καίσαρος." *ThLit* 4 (1952): 205–10.

_____. "The *Titulus*." In *Jesus and the Politics of His Day*, ed. Ernst Bammel and C. F. D. Moule, 353–64. New York: Cambridge University Press, 1984.

_____. "The Trial before Pilate." In *Jesus and the Politics of His Day*, ed. Ernst Bammel and C. F. D. Moule, 415–51. New York: Cambridge University Press, 1984.

_____, ed. *The Trial of Jesus: Cambridge Studies in Honour of C. F. D. Moule*. SBT, n.s. 13. London: SCM, 1970.

_____, and C. F. D. Moule, eds. *Jesus and the Politics of His Day*. New York: Cambridge University Press, 1984.

Bampfylde, G. "John xix 28: A Case for a Different Translation." *NovT* 11 (1969): 247–60.

Barbet, Pierre. *A Doctor at Calvary: The Passion of Our Lord Jesus Christ as Described by a Surgeon*. New York: Kennedy, 1953.

Barbour, R. S. "Gethsemane in the Tradition of the Passion." *NTS* 16.3 (1970): 231–51.

Barclay, William. *Crucified and Crowned*. London: SCM, 1961.

Barkay, Gabriel. "The Garden Tomb: Was Jesus Buried Here?" *BAR* 12.2 (March/April 1986): 40–57.

_____. "Jerusalem Tombs from the Days of the First Temple." *BAR* 12.2 (March/April 1986): 22–39.

_____, and Amos Koner. "Burial Caves North of the Damascus Gate, Jerusalem." *IEJ* 26 (1976): 53–57.

Barrett, C. K. *The Gospel According to St. John*. 2d ed. Philadelphia: Westminster, 1978.

_____. *Jesus and the Gospel Tradition*. London: SPCK, 1967.

_____. "The Lamb of God." *NTS* 1.3 (1955): 210–18.

Barton, George A. "'A Bone of Him Shall Not Be Broken,' John 19:36." *JBL* 49 (1930): 13–19.

Bauer, Walter. *A Greek-English Lexicon of the New Testament and Other Early Christian Literature*. Translated and revised by William F. Arndt, F. Wilbur Gingrich, and Frederick W. Danker. 2d ed. Chicago: University of Chicago Press, 1979.

Baumgarten, Joseph M. "Does *TLH* in the Temple Scroll Refer to Crucifixion?" *JBL* 91 (1972): 472–81.

_____. "On the Testimony of Women in 1QSa." *JBL* 76 (1957): 266–69.

Beasley-Murray, George R. *John.* Waco, Tex.: Word, 1987.

Beavis, Mary Ann. "The Trial before the Sanhedrin (Mark 14:53–65): Reader Response and Greco-Roman Readers." *CBQ* 49 (1987): 581–96.

Benoit, Pierre. *Jesus and the Gospel.* Vol. 1. London: Darton, Longman and Todd, 1973.

_____. *The Passion and Resurrection of Jesus Christ.* New York: Herder and Herder, 1969.

_____. "Le récit de la cène dans Lc XXII, 15–20: Etude de critique textuelle et littéraire." *RB* 48 (1939): 362–93.

_____. "To the Editor: The Inscription Allegedly Relating to the Garden Tomb." *BAR* 12.4 (July/Aug. 1986): 58.

Bernard, John Henry. *A Critical and Exegetical Commentary on the Gospel According to St. John.* Vol. 2. Edinburgh: T. and T. Clark, 1928.

Betz, Otto. "Die Verspottung des Messias: Markus 14, 65." In *Aufstieg und Niedergang der Römischen Welt,* ed. Hildegard Temporini and Wolfgang Haase (New York: Walter de Gruyter, 1982), vol. 2, pp. 637–39.

Birdsall, J. Neville. *"To rēma hōs eipen autō ho 'Iēsous:* Mk xiv. 72." *NovT* 2 (1958): 272–75.

Black, M. "The Arrest and Trial of Jesus and the Date of the Last Supper." In *New Testament Essays,* ed. A. J. B. Higgins, 19–33. Manchester: Manchester University Press, 1959.

Blaising, Craig A. "Gethsemane: A Prayer of Faith." *JETS* 22 (1979): 333–43.

Blass, Friedrich, and A. Debrunner. *A Greek Grammar of the New Testament and Other Early Christian Literature.* Translated and revised by Robert W. Funk. Chicago: University of Chicago Press, 1961.

Bligh, Philip H. "A Note on *Huios Theou* in Mark 15:39." *ExpTim* 80 (1968–69): 51–53.

Blinzler, Josef. "Die Grablegung Christi in historischer Sicht." In *Resurrexit: Actes du symposium international sur la resurrection de Jesus (Rome 1970),* ed. Edouard Dhanis, 56–107. Rome: Editrice vaticana, 1974.

_____. "The Jewish Punishment of Stoning in the New Testament Period." In *The Trial of Jesus,* ed. Ernst Bammel, 147–61. London: SCM, 1970.

_____. *Der Prozess Jesu.* 4th rev. ed. Regensburg: Friedrich Pustet, 1969.

_____. "The Trial of Jesus in the Light of History." *Jud* 20 (1971): 49–55.

Bloomquist, Edward R. "A Doctor Looks at the Crucifixion." *ChrH* 87 (March 1964): 35, 46–48.

Bokser, Baruch M. *The Origins of the Seder: The Passover Rite and Early Rabbinic Judaism.* Berkeley: University of California Press, 1984.

_____. "Was the Last Supper a Passover Seder?" *BibR* 3.2 (1987): 24–33.

Bonner, Campbell. "The Crown of Thorns." *HTR* 46 (1953): 47–48.

Borgen, Peder. "John and the Synoptics in the Passion Narrative." *NTS* 5.4 (1959): 246–59.

Box, G. H. "The Jewish Antecedents of the Eucharist." *JTS* 3 (1901–02): 357–69.

Brady, David. "The Alarm to Peter in Mark's Gospel." *JSNT* 4 (1979): 42–57.

Brandon, S. G. F. "The Trial of Jesus." *Jud* 20 (1971): 43–48.

Bratcher, Robert G. "A Note on *huios theou* (Mark xv. 39)." *ExpTim* 68 (1956–57): 27–28.

Brehant, Jacques. "What Was the Medical Cause of Christ's Death?" *Medical World News*, 27 October 1966, 154–55, 159.

Bright, John. *The Kingdom of God and Its Meaning for the Church*. Nashville: Abingdon, 1953.

Brown, Colin. *That You May Believe: Miracles of Faith—Then and Now*. Grand Rapids: Eerdmans, 1985.

_____, ed. *New International Dictionary of New Testament Theology*. 3 vols. Grand Rapids: Zondervan, 1975–78.

Brown, Raymond E. "The Burial of Jesus (Mark 15:42–47)." *CBQ* 50 (1988): 233–45.

_____. *The Gospel According to John (I–XII)*. Anchor Bible 29. Garden City, N.Y.: Doubleday, 1966.

_____. *The Gospel According to John (XIII–XXI)*. Anchor Bible 29A. Garden City, N.Y.: Doubleday, 1970.

Bruce, F. F. *The Acts of the Apostles: The Greek Text with Introduction and Commentary*. London: Tyndale, 1956.

_____. *The Book of Acts*. New International Commentary on the New Testament. Rev. ed. Grand Rapids: Eerdmans, 1988.

_____. *Commentary on the Book of Acts*. New International Commentary on the New Testament. Grand Rapids: Eerdmans, 1973.

_____. *1–2 Corinthians*. New Century Bible. London: Oliphants, 1971.

_____. *The Gospel of John*. Grand Rapids: Eerdmans, 1983.

_____. *New Testament History*. New York: Thomas Nelson, 1969.

_____. *This and That: The New Testament Development of Some Old Testament Themes*. Exeter: Paternoster, 1968.

_____. "The Trial of Jesus in the Fourth Gospel." In *Gospel Perspectives: Studies of History and Tradition in the Four Gospels*, ed. R. T. France and David Wenham, vol. 1, pp. 7–20. Sheffield: JSOT, 1980.

Buechler, A. "The Levitical Impurity of the Gentile in Palestine before the Year 70." *JQR* 17 (1926–27): 1–81.

Burkill, T. A. "The Competence of the Sanhedrin." *VC* 10 (1956): 80–96.

_____. "The Trial of Jesus." *VC* 12 (1958): 1–18.

Burkitt, F. C. "The Last Supper and the Paschal Meal." *JTS* 17 (1915–16): 291–97.

Callan, Terrance. "Psalm 110:1 and the Origin of the Expectation That Jesus Will Come Again." *CBQ* 44 (1982): 622–36.

Carcopino, Jerome. *Daily Life in Ancient Rome*. New Haven: Yale University Press, 1940.

Carson, D. A. "Christological Ambiguities in the Gospel of Matthew." In *Christ the Lord*, ed. Harold H. Rowdon, 97–114. Downers Grove, Ill.: InterVarsity, 1982.

_____. *Matthew.* Expositor's Bible Commentary 8. Grand Rapids: Zondervan, 1984.

Catchpole, David R. "The Answer of Jesus to Caiaphas (Matt. XXVI. 64)." *NTS* 17.2 (1971): 213–26.

_____. "The Problem of the Historicity of the Sanhedrin Trial." In *The Trial of Jesus,* ed. Ernst Bammel, 47–65. London: SCM, 1970.

_____. *The Trial of Jesus: A Study in the Gospels and Jewish Historiography from 1770 to the Present Day.* Leiden: Brill, 1971.

_____. "The 'Triumphal' Entry." In *Jesus and the Politics of His Day,* ed. Ernst Bammel and C. F. D. Moule, 319–34. New York: Cambridge University Press, 1984.

_____. "You Have Heard His Blasphemy." *TynBul* 16 (April 1965): 10–18.

Cerfaux, Lucien. *The Church in the Theology of Saint Paul.* New York: Herder and Herder, 1959.

Chadwick, Jeffrey. "To the Editor: In Defense of the Garden Tomb." *BAR* 12.4 (July/Aug. 1986): 16–17.

Chandler, Walter M. *The Trial of Jesus from a Lawyer's Standpoint.* 2 vols. New York: Federal Book, 1925.

Charlesworth, James H. "Jesus and Jehohanan: An Archaeological Note on Crucifixion." *ExpTim* 84 (1972–73): 147–50.

_____, ed. *Old Testament Pseudepigrapha.* 2 vols. Garden City, N.Y.: Doubleday, 1983, 1985.

Chavel, Charles B. "The Releasing of a Prisoner on the Eve of Passover in Ancient Jerusalem." *JBL* 60 (1941): 273–78.

Chenderlin, Fritz. "Distributed Observance of the Passover—A Hypothesis." *Bib* 56 (1975): 369–93.

Chilton, C. W. "The Roman Law of Treason under the Early Principate." *JRS* 45 (1955): 73–81.

Chronis, Harry L. "The Torn Veil: Cultus and Christology in Mark 15:37–39." *JBL* 101 (1982): 97–114.

Chwolson, Daniel. *Das letzte Passamahl Christi und der Tag seines Todes.* Rev. ed. Amsterdam: APA-Philo Press, 1979.

Coakley, J. F. "The Anointing at Bethany and the Priority of John." *JBL* 107 (1988): 241–56.

Cohn, Haim. "Reflections on the Trial of Jesus." *Jud* 20 (1971): 10–23.

Cohn Sherbok, Dan. "A Jewish Note on TO POTĒRION TĒS EULOGIAS." *NTS* 27.5 (1981): 704–9.

Collins, John J. "The Archaeology of the Crucifixion." *CBQ* 1 (1939): 154–59.

Colwell, E. C. "A Definite Rule for the Use of the Article in the Greek New Testament." *JBL* 52 (1933): 12–21.

Conzelmann, Hans. "History and Theology in the Passion Narratives of the Synoptic Gospels." *Int* 24.2 (1970): 178–97.

Cooper, John C. "The Problem of the Text in Luke 22:19–20." *LQ* 14 (1962): 39–48.

Cornfeld, Gaalyah, ed. *The Historical Jesus: A Scholarly View of the Man and His World.* New York: Macmillan, 1982.

Couasnon, Charles. *The Church of the Holy Sepulchre in Jerusalem.* Schweich Lectures of the British Academy. London: Oxford University Press, 1974.

Craig, William Lane. "The Guard at the Tomb." *NTS* 30.2 (1984): 273–81.

_____. "The Historicity of the Empty Tomb of Jesus." *NTS* 31.1 (1985): 39–67.

Cranfield, C. E. B. "The Cup Metaphor in Mark xiv.36 and Parallels." *ExpTim* 59 (1947–48): 137–38.

_____. *The Gospel According to Saint Mark.* Cambridge Greek Testament Commentary. New York: Cambridge University Press, 1959.

Cullmann, Oscar. *The Christology of the New Testament.* Rev. ed. Philadelphia: Westminster, 1963.

_____. *The State in the New Testament.* Rev. ed. London: SCM, 1963.

Dabrowski, E. "The Trial of Jesus in Recent Research." *SE* 4 (1968): 21–27.

Dahl, Nils A. *The Crucified Messiah and Other Essays.* Minneapolis: Augsburg, 1974.

Dalman, Gustaf H. *Jesus—Jeshua: Studies in the Gospels.* New York: Macmillan, 1929.

_____. *Sacred Sites and Ways: Studies in the Topography of the Gospels.* New York: Macmillan, 1935.

Danby, Herbert. "The Bearing of the Rabbinical Criminal Code on the Jewish Trial Narratives in the Gospels." *JTS* 21 (1919–20): 51–76.

_____, trans. *The Mishnah.* New York: Oxford University Press, 1956.

Danker, Frederick W. *Jesus and the New Age, According to St. Luke.* St. Louis: Clayton, 1972.

Daube, David. "The Anointing at Bethany and Jesus' Burial." *ATR* 32 (1950): 186–99.

_____. "'For they know not what they do': Luke 23, 34." *TU* 79 (1961): 58–70.

_____. *The New Testament and Rabbinic Judaism.* London: Athlone, 1956.

_____. "A Prayer Pattern in Judaism." *SE* 1 (1959): 539–45.

Davies, Philip R. "Calendrical Change and Qumran Origins: An Assessment of Vanderkam's Theory." *CBQ* 45 (1983): 80–89.

Davies, P. S. "The Meaning of Philo's Text about the Gilded Shields." *JTS*, n.s. 37 (1986): 109–14.

Davies, Stevan L. "Who Is Called Bar Abbas?" *NTS* 27.2 (1981): 260–62.

Davies, William D. *The Gospel and the Land.* Berkeley: University of California Press, 1974.

_____. "Unsolved New Testament Problems: The Jewish Background of the Teaching of Jesus: Apocalyptic or Pharisaism?" *ExpTim* 59 (1947–48): 233–37.

Davis, C. T. "The Crucifixion of Jesus: The Passion of Christ from a Medical Point of View." *Arizona Medicine* 22 (1965): 183–87.

Davis, John J., ed. *Moses and the Gods of Egypt: Studies in Exodus.* 2d ed. Winona Lake, Ind.: BMH, 1986.

De Kruijf, Th. C. "'More than Half a Hundredweight' of Spices (John 19, 39 NEB): Abundance and Symbolism in the Gospel of John." *Bijdragen* 43 (1982): 234–39.

Demsky, Aaron. "When the Priests Trumpeted the Onset of the Sabbath." *BAR* 12.6 (Nov./Dec. 1986): 50–52, 72.

Derrett, John D. M. *An Oriental Lawyer Looks at the Trial of Jesus and the Doctrine of Redemption.* London: University of London, 1966.

Dodd, C. H. *The Interpretation of the Fourth Gospel.* New York: Cambridge University Press, 1953.

Doyle, A. D. "Pilate's Career and the Date of the Crucifixion." *JTS* 42 (1941): 190–93.

Eckhardt, E. "Das Praetorium des Pilatus." *ZDPV* 34 (1911): 39–48.

Edersheim, Alfred. *The Life and Times of Jesus the Messiah.* 2 vols. Grand Rapids: Eerdmans, 1936.

Edgar, S. L. "New Testament and Rabbinic Messianic Interpretation." *NTS* 5.1 (1958): 47–54.

Edwards, William D., Wesley J. Gabel, and Floyd E. Hosmer. "On the Physical Death of Jesus Christ." *JAMA* 255.11 (March 21, 1986): 1455–63.

Ehrman, Albert. "Judas Iscariot and Abba Saqqara." *JBL* 97 (1978): 572–73.

Ehrman, Bart D. "Jesus' Trial before Pilate: John 18:28–19:16." *BTB* 13 (1983): 124–31.

_____, and Mark A. Plunkett. "The Angel and the Agony: The Textual Problem of Luke 22:43–44." *CBQ* 45 (1983): 401–16.

Elert, Werner. *Eucharist and Church Fellowship in the First Four Centuries.* St. Louis: Concordia, 1966.

Elliott, J. K. "The Anointing of Jesus." *ExpTim* 85 (1973–74): 105–7.

Ellis, E. Earle. *The Gospel of Luke.* New Century Bible. Grand Rapids: Eerdmans, 1966.

Enslin, Morton S. "The Temple and the Cross." *Jud* 20 (1971): 24–31.

Eppstein, Victor. "The Historicity of the Gospel Account of the Cleansing of the Temple." *ZNW* 55 (1964): 42–58.

Evans, Craig A. "Jesus' Action in the Temple: Cleansing or Portent of Destruction?" *CBQ* 51 (1989): 237–70.

_____. "'Peter Warming Himself': The Problem of an Editorial 'Seam.'" *JBL* 101 (1982): 245–49.

Evans, L. E. Cox. "The Holy Sepulchre." *PEQ* 100 (1968): 112–36.

Faierstein, Morris M. "Why Do the Scribes Say That Elijah Must Come First?" *JBL* 100 (1981): 75–86.

Farmer, William R. "The Palm Branches in John 12, 13." *JTS*, n.s. 3 (1952–53): 62–66.

Filson, Floyd V. *A Commentary on the Gospel According to St. Matthew.* London: Adam and Charles Black, 1960.

Finegan, Jack. *The Archaeology of the New Testament.* Princeton, N.J.: Princeton University Press, 1970.

_____. "A Quest for the History behind the Passion." *JBTh* 16 (1962): 102–4.

Fitzmyer, Joseph A. "Anti-Semitism and the Cry of 'All the People' (Mt 27:25)." *TS* 26 (1965): 667–71.

_____. "Crucifixion in Ancient Palestine, Qumran Literature, and the New Testament." *CBQ* 40 (1978): 493–513.

_____. *The Gospel According to Luke (I–IX).* Anchor Bible 28. Garden City, N.Y.: Doubleday, 1981.

_____. *The Gospel According to Luke (X–XXIV).* Anchor Bible 28A. Garden City, N.Y.: Doubleday, 1985.

_____. "More about Elijah Coming First." *JBL* 104 (1985): 295–96.

_____. "Papyrus Bodmer XIV: Some Features of Our Oldest Text of Luke." *CBQ* 24 (1962): 170–79.

Fleddermann, Harry. "The Flight of a Naked Young Man (Mark 14:51–52)." *CBQ* 41 (1978): 412–18.

Flusser, David G. *Jesus.* New York: Herder and Herder, 1969.

_____. "The Passover Supper and the Essene Meal." In *The Historical Jesus,* ed. Gaalyah Cornfeld, 123–25. New York: Macmillan, 1982.

Foakes-Jackson, F. J., and Kirsopp Lake. *The Beginnings of Christianity: The Acts of the Apostles.* 5 vols. Grand Rapids: Baker, 1965–66 reprint.

Ford, J. Massyngberde. "'Crucify him, crucify him' and the Temple Scroll." *ExpTim* 87 (1975–76): 275–78.

_____. "'Mingled Blood' from the Side of Christ (John XIX.34)." *NTS* 15.3 (1969): 337–38.

Fortna, Robert T. "Jesus and Peter at the High Priest's House: A Test Case for the Question of the Relation Between Mark's and John's Gospels." *NTS* 24.3 (1978): 371–83.

Fotheringham, J. K. "The Evidence of Astronomy and Technical Chronology for the Date of the Crucifixion." *JTS* 35 (1934): 146–62.

France, R. T. *The Evidence for Jesus.* Downers Grove, Ill.: Inter-Varsity, 1986.

_____. *The Gospel According to Matthew.* Tyndale New Testament Commentaries. Grand Rapids: Eerdmans, 1987.

_____. *Jesus and the Old Testament.* London: Tyndale, 1971.

_____. "The Servant of the Lord in the Teaching of Jesus." *TynBul* 19 (1968): 26–52.

_____, and David Wenham, eds. *Gospel Perspectives.* Vols. 1–2, *Studies of History and Tradition in the Four Gospels.* Sheffield: JSOT, 1980–81.

_____, and David Wenham, eds. *Gospel Perspectives.* Vol. 3, *Studies in Midrash and Historiography.* Sheffield: JSOT, 1983.

Fuller, R. C. "The Drink Offered to Christ at Calvary." *Scr* 2 (1947): 114–15.

Galvin, John P. "Jesus' Approach to Death: An Examination of Some Recent Studies." *TS* 41 (1980): 713–44.

Garnsey, Peter. "The Criminal Jurisdiction of Governors." *JRS* 58 (1968): 51–59.

_____. "The *Lex Iulia* and the Appeal under the Empire." *JRS* 56 (1966): 167–89.

Gartner, Bertil E. *Iscariot.* Facet Books Biblical Series 29. Philadelphia: Fortress, 1971.

Giblin, Charles H. "John's Narration of the Hearing before Pilate (John 18,28–19,16a)." *Bib* 67 (1986): 221–39.

Gordis, Robert, et al. "The Trial of Jesus in the Light of History." *Jud* 20 (1971): 6–74.

Gordon, Charles. "Eden and Golgotha." *Palestine Exploration Fund Quarterly Statement* 10 (1885): 78–81.

Grant, Frederick C. *Ancient Judaism and the New Testament.* Edinburgh: Oliver and Boyd, 1968.

_____. *The Economic Background of the Gospels.* New York: Oxford University Press, 1926.

_____. "*On the Trial of Jesus:* A Review Article." *JR* 44 (1964): 230–37.

Grant, Michael. *The Jews in the Roman World.* New York: Dorset, 1984.

Green, H. Benedict. *The Gospel According to Matthew in the Revised Standard Version.* New Clarendon Bible. New York: Oxford University Press, 1975.

Gregg, David W. A. "Hebraic Antecedents to the Eucharistic ANAMNĒSIS Formula." *TynBul* 30 (1979): 165–68.

Grundmann, Walter. *Das Evangelium nach Matthäus.* Theologischer Handkommentar zum Neuen Testament. Berlin: Evangelische, 1968.

Guillaume, A. "Mt xxvii, 46, in the Light of the Dead Sea Scroll of Isaiah." *PEQ* 83 (1951): 78–80.

Gundry, Robert H. *Matthew: A Commentary on His Literary and Theological Art.* Grand Rapids: Eerdmans, 1982.

Guthrie, Donald. *New Testament Introduction.* 3d ed. Downers Grove, Ill.: Inter-Varsity, 1975.

_____. *New Testament Theology.* Downers Grove, Ill.: Inter-Varsity, 1981.

Haas, Nico. "Anthropological Observations on the Skeletal Remains from Giv'at ha-Mivtar." *IEJ* 20 (1970): 38–59.

Habermas, Gary R. *Ancient Evidence for the Life of Jesus: Historical Records of His Death and Resurrection.* Nashville: Thomas Nelson, 1984.

Hachlili, Rachel, and Ann Killebrew. "Jewish Funerary Customs during the Second Temple Period, in the Light of the Excavations at the Jericho Necropolis." *PEQ* 115 (1983): 109–39.

Halperin, David J. "Crucifixion, the Nahum Pesher, and the Rabbinic Penalty of Strangulation." *JJS* 32 (1981): 32–46.

Hamilton, Neill Q. "Temple Cleansing and Temple Bank." *JBL* 83 (1964): 365–72.

Hart, H. StJ. "The Coin of 'Render unto Caesar . . .' (A Note on Some Aspects of Mark 12:13–17; Matt. 20:15–22; Luke 20:20–26)." In *Jesus and the Politics of His Day,* ed. Ernst Bammel and C. F. D. Moule, 241–48. New York: Cambridge University Press, 1984.

_____. "The Crown of Thorns in John 19, 2–5." *JTS,* n.s. 3 (1952–53): 66–75.

Harvey, A. E. *Jesus and the Constraints of History*. Bampton Lectures. Philadelphia: Westminster, 1982.

_____. *Jesus on Trial: A Study in the Fourth Gospel*. Atlanta: John Knox, 1977.

_____. "Melito and Jerusalem." *JTS*, n.s. 17 (1960): 401–4.

Heawood, P. J. "The Time of the Last Supper." *JQR* 42 (1951–52): 37–44.

Hendriksen, William. *The Gospel According to John*. Grand Rapids: Baker, 1953.

_____. *The Gospel According to Luke*. Grand Rapids: Baker, 1978.

Hengel, Martin. *The Atonement: The Origins of the Doctrine in the New Testament*. Philadelphia: Fortress, 1981.

_____. *Crucifixion in the Ancient World and the Folly of the Message of the Cross*. Philadelphia: Fortress, 1977.

_____. "The Expiatory Sacrifice of Christ." *BJRL* 62 (1980): 454–75.

_____. *Was Jesus a Revolutionist?* Facet Books Biblical Series 28. Philadelphia: Fortress, 1971.

Higgins, A. J. B. "The Origins of the Eucharist." *NTS* 1.3 (1955): 200–209.

_____, ed. *New Testament Essays: Studies in Memory of Thomas Walter Manson, 1893–1958*. Manchester: University of Manchester Press, 1959.

Hilhorst, A. "The Wounds of the Risen Christ." *EstBib* 41 (1983): 165–67.

Hill, D. "Jesus before the Sanhedrin—On What Charge?" *IBS* 7 (1985): 174–86.

Hill, David. *The Gospel of Matthew*. New Century Bible Commentary. Grand Rapids: Eerdmans, 1972.

Hitchcock, F. R. Montgomery. "The Use of *graphein*." *JTS* 31 (1929–30): 271–75.

Hobart, William K. *The Medical Language of St. Luke*. Grand Rapids: Baker, 1954.

Hoehner, Harold W. "Chronological Aspects of the Life of Christ. Part IV. The Day of Christ's Crucifixion." *BSac* 131 (July/Sept. 1974): 241–64.

_____. "Why Did Pilate Hand Jesus over to Antipas?" In *Jesus on Trial*, ed. Ernst Bammel, 84–90. London: SCM, 1970.

Holl, K. "Ein Bruchstück aus einem bisher unbekannten Brief des Epiphanius." In *Gesammelte Aufsätze zur Kirchengeschichte* 2, pp. 204–24. Tübingen: J. C. B. Mohr, 1928.

Holladay, Carl R. *Theios Aner in Hellenistic Judaism: A Critique of the Use of This Category in New Testament Christology*. Society of Biblical Literature Dissertation Series 40. Missoula, Mont.: Scholars, 1977.

Holleran, J. Warren. *The Synoptic Gethsemane: A Critical Study*. Rome: Gregorian University Press, 1973.

Hopkins, Ian W. J. "The City Region in Roman Palestine." *PEQ* 112 (1980): 19–32.

Horbury, William. "The Passion Narratives and Historical Criticism." *Th* 75, no. 620 (Feb. 1972): 58–71.

_____. "The Trial of Jesus in Jewish Tradition." In *The Trial of Jesus*, ed. Ernst Bammel, 103–21. London: SCM, 1970.

Horsley, Richard A. *Jesus and the Spiral of Violence: Popular Jewish Resistance in Roman Palestine*. San Francisco: Harper and Row, 1987.

_____. "Popular Messianic Movements around the Time of Jesus." *CBQ* 46 (1984): 471–95.

_____. "The Zealots: Their Origin, Relationships and Importance in the Jewish Revolt." *NovT* 28 (1986): 159–92.

Horvath, Tibor. "Why Was Jesus Brought to Pilate?" *NovT* 11 (1969): 174–84.

Howard, J. K. "Passover and Eucharist in the Fourth Gospel." *SJT* 20 (1967): 329–37.

Huber, Wolfgang. *Passa und Ostern: Untersuchungen zur Osterfeier der alten Kirche*. Berlin: Töpelmann, 1969.

Hulse, E. V. "The Nature of Biblical 'Leprosy' and the Use of Alternative Medical Terms in Modern Translations of the Bible." *PEQ* 107 (1975): 87–105.

Husband, Richard W. "The Pardoning of Prisoners by Pilate." *AJT* 21 (1917): 110–16.

Jackson, Howard M. "The Death of Jesus in Mark and the Miracle from the Cross." *NTS* 33.1 (1987): 16–37.

Jaubert, Annie. *The Date of the Last Supper*. Staten Island, N.Y.: Alba, 1965.

_____. "Jésus et le Calendrier de Qumrân." *NTS* 7.1 (1960): 1–30.

Jeremias, Joachim. *The Eucharistic Words of Jesus*. London: SCM, 1964.

_____. *Golgotha*. Leipzig: Pfeiffer, 1926.

_____. *Jerusalem in the Time of Jesus: An Investigation into Economic and Social Conditions during the New Testament Period*. Philadelphia: Fortress, 1969.

_____. *New Testament Theology: The Proclamation of Jesus*. New York: Scribner, 1971.

_____. *Die Passahfeier der Samaritaner und ihre Bedeutung für das Verständnis der Alttestamentlichen Passahüberlieferung*. Giessen: Töpelmann, 1932.

_____. *The Prayers of Jesus*. SBT, n.s. 6. London: SCM, 1974.

_____. "This Is My Body . . . ." *ExpTim* 83 (1971–72): 196–203.

_____. "Zur Geschichtlichkeit des Verhörs Jesu vor dem Hohen Rat." In *Abba: Studien zur neutestamentlichen Theologie und Zeitgeschichte*, 139–44. Göttingen: Vandenhoeck and Ruprecht, 1966.

Johns, C. H. "The Citadel, Jerusalem." *QDAP* 14 (1950): 121–90.

_____. "Recent Excavations at the Citadel." *PEQ* 72 (1940): 36–58.

Jones, A. H. M. "The *Imperium* of Augustus." *JRS* 41 (1951): 111–19.

Juel, Donald. *Messiah and Temple: The Trial of Jesus in the Gospel of Mark*. Missoula, Mont.: Scholars, 1977.

Karris, Robert J. "Luke 23:47 and the Lucan View of Jesus' Death." *JBL* 105 (1986): 65–74.

Keen, W. W. "The Bloody Sweat of Our Lord." *Baptist Quarterly Review* 14 (1892): 169–75.

_____. "Further Studies on the Bloody Sweat of Our Lord." *BSac* 54 (1897): 469–83.

Kempthorne, Renatus. "The Marcan Text of Jesus' Answer to the High Priest (Mark XIV 62)." *NovT* 19 (1977): 197–208.

Kiley, Mark. "'Lord, Save My Life' (Ps. 116:4) as Generative Text for Jesus' Gethsemane Prayer (Mark 14:36a)." *CBQ* 48 (1986): 655–59.

Kilpatrick, G. D. "A Theme of the Lucan Passion Story and Luke xxiii.47." *JTS* 43 (1942): 34–36.

Kingdon, H. Paul. "The Origins of the Zealots." *NTS* 19.1 (1972): 74–81.

Kittel, Gerhard, and Gerhard Friedrich, eds. *Theological Dictionary of the New Testament.* Translated by Geoffrey W. Bromiley. 10 vols. Grand Rapids: Eerdmans, 1964–76.

Klausner, Joseph. *Jesus of Nazareth: His Life, Times, and Teaching.* New York: Macmillan, 1945.

Kleist, James A. "Two False Witnesses (Mk 14:55ff.)." *CBQ* 9 (1947): 321–23.

Kodell, Jerome. "Luke's Use of *Laos*, 'People,' Especially in the Jerusalem Narrative (Lk. 19, 28–24, 53)." *CBQ* 31 (1969): 327–43.

Kohlbeck, J., and Eugenia Litowski. "New Evidence May Explain Image on Shroud of Turin." *BAR* 12 (1986): 18–29.

Kosmala, Hans. "His Blood Be on Us and on Our Children (The Background of Mat. 27, 24–25)." *ASTI* 7 (1970): 94–126.

_____. "J. B. Segal, *The Hebrew Passover from the Earliest Times to A.D. 70.* London Oriental Series vol. 13 (Oxford University Press, 1963, xvii, 294 pp.): A Review." In *Studies, Essays and Reviews*, vol. 1, *Old Testament*, pp. 67–72. Leiden: Brill, 1978.

——. "Der Ort des letzten Mahles Jesu und das heutige Coenaculum." In *Studies, Essays and Reviews*, vol. 2, *New Testament*, pp. 48–52. Leiden: Brill, 1978.

_____. "The Time of Cockcrow." In *Studies, Essays and Reviews*, vol. 2, *New Testament*, pp. 76–81. Leiden: Brill, 1978.

Kraeling, Carl H. "The Episode of the Roman Standards at Jerusalem." *HTR* 35 (1942): 263–89.

Kuhn, Heinz–Wolfgang. "Das Reittier Jesu in der Einzugsgeschichte des Markusevangeliums." *ZNW* 50 (1959): 82–91.

Kurz, William S. "Luke 22:14–38 and Greco-Roman and Biblical Farewell Addresses." *JBL* 104 (1985): 251–68.

Lachs, Samuel T. *A Rabbinic Commentary on the New Testament: The Gospels of Matthew, Mark, and Luke.* Hoboken, N.J.: Ktav, 1987.

Lambert, John C. "The Passover and the Lord's Supper." *JTS* 4 (1902–03): 184–93.

Lane, William L. *The Gospel According to Mark.* New International Commentary on the New Testament. Grand Rapids: Eerdmans, 1974.

Langdon, S. "The Release of a Prisoner at the Passover." *ExpTim* 29 (1917–18): 328–30.

Larkin, William J. "The Old Testament Background of Luke XXII.43–44." *NTS* 25.2 (1979): 250–54.

Lee, G. M. "The Guard at the Tomb." *Th* 72, no. 586 (April 1969): 169–75.

_____. "Mark 14, 72: *epibalōn eklaien*." *Bib* 53 (1972): 411–12.

Leese, Kenneth. "The Physical Cause of the Death of Jesus: A Medical Opinion." *ExpTim* 83 (1971–72): 248.

Lenski, R. C. H. *The Interpretation of St. John's Gospel*. Minneapolis: Augsburg, 1963 reprint.

_____. *The Interpretation of St. Luke's Gospel*. Minneapolis: Augsburg, 1964 reprint.

_____. *The Interpretation of St. Mark's Gospel*. Minneapolis: Augsburg, 1964 reprint.

_____. *The Interpretation of St. Matthew's Gospel*. Minneapolis: Augsburg, 1964 reprint.

Leupold, Herbert C. *Exposition of the Psalms*. Columbus: Wartburg, 1959.

Lightfoot, J. B., ed. *The Apostolic Fathers*. Grand Rapids: Baker, 1978 reprint.

Lightfoot, R. H. *St. John's Gospel: A Commentary*. New York: Oxford University Press, 1972 reprint.

Lindars, Barnabas. *The Gospel of John*. New Century Bible. Grand Rapids: Eerdmans, 1972.

Lindeskog, Gösta. "The Veil of the Temple." *Coniectanea Neotestamentica* 11 (1947): 132–37.

Linnemann, Eta. *Studien zur Passionsgeschichte*. Göttingen: Vandenhoeck and Ruprecht, 1978.

Linton, Olof. "The Trial of Jesus and the Interpretation of Psalm CX." *NTS* 7.3 (1961): 258–62.

Litwak, Kenneth D. "The Use of Quotations from Isaiah 52:13–53:12 in the New Testament." *JETS* 26 (1983): 385–94.

Loew, I. "Bethphage." *REJ* 62 (1911): 232–35.

Lofthouse, W. F. "Fatherhood and Sonship in the Fourth Gospel." *ExpTim* 43 (1931–32): 442–48.

Longenecker, Richard N. *The Christology of Early Jewish Christianity*. SBT, n.s. 17. London: SCM, 1970.

Longstaff, Thomas R. W. "The Women at the Tomb: Matthew 28:1 Re-examined." *NTS* 27.2 (1981): 277–82.

Lowther Clarke, W. K. "St Luke and the Pseudepigrapha: Two Parallels." *JTS* 15 (1913–14): 597–99.

McArthur, H. K. "Mark XIV.62." *NTS* 4.2 (1958): 156–58.

Maccoby, H. Z. "Jesus and Barabbas." *NTS* 16.1 (1969): 55–60.

Mackowski, Richard M. *Jerusalem, City of Jesus*. Grand Rapids: Eerdmans, 1980.

M'Neile, A. H. *The Gospel According to St. Matthew*. New York: St. Martin's, 1961.

Mahoney, Aidan. "A New Look at an Old Problem (John 18, 12–14, 19–24)." *CBQ* 27 (1965): 137–44.

Maier, Johann. *The Temple Scroll: An Introduction, Translation and Commen-*

tary. Journal for the Study of the Old Testament Supplemental Series 34. Sheffield: JSOT, 1985.

Maier, Paul L. "Notes and Observations: The Episode of the Golden Roman Shields at Jerusalem." *HTR* 62 (1969): 109–21.

_____. "Sejanus, Pilate, and the Date of the Crucifixion." *CH* 37 (1968): 3–13.

Mann, C. S. *Mark*. Anchor Bible 27. Garden City, N.Y.: Doubleday, 1986.

Manson, Thomas W. *The Servant Messiah: A Study of the Public Ministry of Jesus*. New York: Cambridge University Press, 1961.

Mantel, Hugo. *Studies in the History of the Sanhedrin*. Cambridge, Mass.: Harvard University Press, 1962.

Mare, W. Harold. *The Archaeology of the Jerusalem Area*. Grand Rapids: Baker, 1987.

Marshall, I. Howard. *The Acts of the Apostles*. Tyndale New Testament Commentaries. Grand Rapids: Eerdmans, 1980.

_____. "The Death of Jesus in Recent New Testament Study." *Word World* 3 (1983): 12–21.

_____. *The Gospel of Luke: A Commentary on the Greek Text*. New International Greek Testament Commentary. Grand Rapids: Eerdmans, 1978.

_____. *Last Supper and Lord's Supper*. Grand Rapids: Eerdmans, 1980.

Martin, Ernest L. *Secrets of Golgotha: The Forgotten History of Christ's Crucifixion*. Alhambra, Calif.: ASK, 1988.

Martinez, E. R. *The Gospel Accounts of the Death of Jesus*. Rome: Gregorian University Press, 1970.

Mastin, B. A. "The Date of the Triumphal Entry." *NTS* 16.1 (1969): 76–82.

Matera, Frank J. "The Death of Jesus According to Luke: A Question of Sources." *CBQ* 47 (1984–85): 469–85.

_____. *Passion Narratives and Gospel Theologies: Interpreting the Synoptics Through Their Passion Stories*. Mahwah, N.J.: Paulist, 1986.

Matzke, Howard A. "An Anatomist Looks at the Physical Sufferings of Our Lord." *LW* 80 (Feb. 21, 1961): 6–7.

Mazar, Benjamin. "Excavations near Temple Mount Reveal Splendors of Herodian Jerusalem." *BAR* 6.4 (July/Aug. 1980): 44–59.

_____. "Herodian Jerusalem in the Light of the Excavations South and South-West of the Temple Mount." *IEJ* 28 (1978): 230–37.

_____. "Iron Age Burial Caves North of Damascus Gate in Jerusalem." *IEJ* 26 (1976): 1–8.

Merkel, Helmut. "Peter's Curse." In *The Trial of Jesus*, ed. Ernst Bammel, 66–71. London: SCM, 1970.

Merritt, Robert L. "Jesus Barabbas and the Paschal Pardon." *JBL* 104 (1985): 57–68.

Metzger, Bruce M. *A Textual Commentary on the Greek New Testament*. New York: United Bible Societies, 1971.

Michaels, J. Ramsey. "The Centurion's Confession and the Spear Thrust." *CBQ* 29 (1967): 102–9.

Miller, Johnny V. "The Time of the Crucifixion." *JETS* 26 (1983): 157–66.

Mödder, Hermann. "Die Todesursache bei der Kreuzigung." *SZ* 144 (1949): 50–59.

Moldenke, Harold N., and Alma L. Moldenke. *Plants of the Bible.* Waltham, Mass.: Chronica Botanica, 1952.

Möller-Christensen, Vilhelm. "Skeletal Remains from Giv'at ha-Mivtar." *IEJ* 26 (1976): 35–38.

Montefiore, Hugh. "When Did Jesus Die?" *ExpTim* 72 (1960–61): 53–54.

Montgomery, John Warwick. "Jesus Takes the Stand: An Argument to Support the Gospel Accounts." *ChrT* 26 (April 9, 1982): 26–27.

Moo, Douglas J. *The Old Testament in the Gospel Passion Narratives.* Sheffield: Almond, 1983.

_____. "Tradition and Old Testament in Matt. 27:3–10." In *Gospel Perspectives,* vol. 3, *Studies in Midrash and Historiography,* ed. R. T. France and David Wenham, 157–75. Sheffield: JSOT, 1983.

Moore, George F. *Judaism in the First Centuries of the Christian Era.* 3 vols. Cambridge, Mass.: Harvard University Press, 1958.

Morgan, Robert. "'Nothing More Negative . . .': A Concluding Unscientific Postscript to Historical Research on the Trial of Jesus." In *The Trial of Jesus,* ed. Ernst Bammel, 135–46. London: SCM, 1970.

Morris, Leon. *The Apostolic Preaching of the Cross.* 3d ed. London: Tyndale, 1965.

_____. *The Atonement: Its Meaning and Significance.* Downers Grove, Ill.: Inter-Varsity, 1983.

_____. *The Gospel According to John.* New International Commentary on the New Testament. Grand Rapids: Eerdmans, 1971.

_____. *The Gospel According to St. Luke.* Tyndale New Testament Commentaries. Grand Rapids: Eerdmans, 1974.

Mosley, A. W. "Historical Reporting in the Ancient World." *NTS* 12.1 (1965): 10–26.

Motyer, S. "The Rending of the Veil: A Markan Pentecost?" *NTS* 33.1 (1987): 155–57.

Moule, C. F. D. *An Idiom Book of New Testament Greek.* New York: Cambridge University Press, 1953.

Moulton, James Hope, and George Milligan. *The Vocabulary of the Greek New Testament.* Grand Rapids: Eerdmans, 1976 reprint.

Murphy-O'Connor, Jerome. "The Garden Tomb and the Misfortune of an Inscription." *BAR* 12.2 (March/April 1986): 54–55.

_____. *The Holy Land: An Archaeological Guide from Earliest Times to 1700.* 2d ed. New York: Oxford University Press, 1986.

Nations, Archie L. "Historical Criticism and the Current Methodological Crisis." *SJT* 36 (1983): 59–71.

Naveh, Joseph. "The Ossuary Inscriptions from Giv'at ha-Mivtar." *IEJ* 20 (1970): 33–37.

Neusner, Jacob. "Messianic Themes in Formative Judaism." *JAAR* 52 (1984): 357–74.

_____. "Pharisaic Law in New Testament Times." *UTSR* 26 (1970–71): 331–40.

_____. "The Use of the Mishnah for the History of Judaism prior to the Time of the Mishnah." *JSJ* 11 (1980): 177–85.

Nickle, Keith F. *The Collection: A Study in Paul's Strategy.* SBT 48. Naperville, Ill.: Allenson, 1966.

Nineham, Dennis E., et al. *Historicity and Chronology in the New Testament.* London: SPCK, 1965.

Nriagu, Jerome O. "Occasional Notes: Saturnine Gout among Roman Aristocrats: Did Lead Poisoning Contribute to the Fall of the Empire?" *New England Journal of Medicine* 308.11 (March 17, 1983): 660–63.

Ogg, George. "The Chronology of the Last Supper." In *Historicity and Chronology in the New Testament,* ed. Dennis E. Nineham et al., 75–96. London: SPCK, 1965.

O'Meara, Thomas F. "The Trial of Jesus in an Age of Trials." *TT* 28 (1972): 451–65.

O'Neill, J. C. "The Silence of Jesus." *NTS* 15.2 (1969): 153–67.

Osborne, Grant R. "John 21: Test Case for History and Redaction in the Resurrection Narratives." In *Gospel Perspectives,* vol. 2, *Studies of History and Tradition in the Four Gospels,* ed. R. T. France and David Wenham, 293–328. Sheffield: JSOT, 1981.

Overstreet, R. Larry. "Roman Law and the Trial of Christ." *BSac* 135 (1978): 323–32.

Page, Sydney H. T. "The Suffering Servant Between the Testaments." *NTS* 31.4 (1985): 481–97.

Parrot, André. *Golgotha and the Church of the Holy Sepulchre.* Studies in Biblical Archaeology 6. London: SCM, 1957.

Perry, John M. "The Three Days in the Synoptic Passion Predictions." *CBQ* 48 (1986): 637–54.

Plevnik, Joseph. "The Eyewitnesses of the Risen Christ in Luke 24." *CBQ* 49 (1986): 90–103.

Plummer, Alfred. *A Critical and Exegetical Commentary on the Gospel According to St. Luke.* International Critical Commentary. 5th ed. Edinburgh: T. and T. Clark, 1969.

_____. *Exegetical Commentary on the Gospel According to S. Matthew.* London: Elliot Stock, 1909.

_____. *The Gospel According to St. John.* New York: Cambridge University Press, 1902.

Pobee, John. "The Cry of the Centurion: A Cry of Defeat." In *The Trial of Jesus,* ed. Ernst Bammel, 91–102. London: SCM, 1970.

Primrose, W. B. "A Surgeon Looks at the Crucifixion." *HibJ* 47 (1948–49): 382–88.

Pritchard, James B. *The Ancient Near East in Pictures.* Princeton, N.J.: Princeton University Press, 1955.

Rahmani, L. Y. "Ancient Jerusalem's Funerary Customs and Tombs." *BA* 44 (1981): 171–77, 229–35; 45 (1982): 43–53, 109–19.

Rajak, Tessa. *Josephus: The Historian and His Society.* Philadelphia: Fortress, 1984.

Ramsay, William M. "About the Sixth Hour." *Expos,* 4th ser., vol. 7 (1893): 216–23.

Rengstorf, Karl Heinrich. *Das Evangelium nach Lukas.* Das Neue Testament Deutsch 3. Göttingen: Vandenhoeck and Ruprecht, 1962.

Rensberger, David. "The Politics of John: The Trial of Jesus in the Fourth Gospel." *JBL* 103 (1984): 395–411.

Reu, M. *Two Treatises on the Means of Grace.* Minneapolis: Augsburg, 1952.

Ricciotti, Giuseppe. *The Acts of the Apostles.* Milwaukee: Bruce, 1958.

Rice, George E. "The Role of the Populace in the Passion Narrative of Luke in Codex Bezae." *AUSS* 19 (1981): 147–53.

Richardson, Peter. "The Israel-Idea in the Passion Narratives." In *The Trial of Jesus,* ed. Ernst Bammel, 1–10. London: SCM, 1970.

Rigg, Horace A., Jr. "Barabbas." *JBL* 64 (1945): 417–56.

Rivkin, Ellis. "Beth Din, Boulé, Sanhedrin: A Tragedy of Errors." *HUCA* 46 (1975): 181–99.

———. *What Crucified Jesus? The Political Execution of a Heretic.* Nashville: Abingdon, 1984.

Robinson, D. W. B. "The Date and Significance of the Last Supper." *EvQ* 23 (1951): 126–33.

Robinson, John A. T. *The Priority of John.* Edited by J. F. Coakley. London: SCM, 1985.

Rogers, Robert Samuel. "Treason in the Early Empire." *JRS* 49 (1959): 90–94.

Rosenblatt, Samuel. "The Crucifixion of Jesus from the Standpoint of Pharisaic Law." *JBL* 75 (1956): 315–21.

Ross, J.-P. B. "The Evolution of a Church—Jerusalem's Holy Sepulchre." *BAR* 2.3 (Sept./Oct. 1976): 3–11.

Roth, Cecil. "The Cleansing of the Temple and Zechariah xiv 21." *NovT* 4 (1960): 174–81.

Rowdon, Harold H., ed. *Christ the Lord: Studies in Christology Presented to Donald Guthrie.* Downers Grove, Ill.: Inter-Varsity, 1982.

Rowe, Robert D. "Is Daniel's 'Son of Man' Messianic?" In *Christ the Lord,* ed. Harold H. Rowdon, 71–96. Downers Grove, Ill.: Inter-Varsity, 1982.

Ruckstuhl, Eugen. *Chronology of the Last Days of Jesus: A Critical Study.* New York: Desclee, 1965.

Rusk, Roger. "The Day He Died." *ChrT* 18 (March 29, 1974): 720–22.

Safrai, Shemuel. *Die Wallfahrt im Zeitalter des zweiten Temples.* Neukirchen-Vluyn: Neukirchener, 1981.

———, and M. Stern, eds. *Compendia rerum Iudaicarum ad Novum Testamentum: The Literature of the Jewish People in the Period of the Second Temple and the Talmud.* Vols. 1–2. Philadelphia: Fortress, 1974, 1976.

Saldarini, Anthony J. *Jesus and the Passover.* Ramsey, N.J.: Paulist, 1984.

Sandmel, Samuel. "The Trial of Jesus: Reservations." *Jud* 20 (1971): 69–74.

Sasse, Hermann. *This Is My Body.* Rev. ed. Adelaide: Lutheran, 1977.

Sava, A. F. "The Wound in the Side of Christ." *CBQ* 19 (1957): 343–46.

Sawyer, John F. A. "Why Is a Solar Eclipse Mentioned in the Passion Narrative (Luke XXIII.44–5)?" *JTS*, n.s. 23 (1972): 124–28.

Schaberg, Jane. "Daniel 7, 12 and the New Testament Passion-Resurrection Predictions." *NTS* 31.2 (1985): 208–22.

Scharlemann, Martin H. "'He Descended into Hell'—An Interpretation of 1 Peter 3:18–20." *CTM* 27 (1956): 81–94.

_____. *Proclaiming the Parables.* St. Louis: Concordia, 1963.

Schein, Bruce E. *Following the Way: The Setting of John's Gospel.* Minneapolis: Augsburg, 1980.

Schlatter, Adolf von. *Der Evangelist Matthäus: Seine Sprache, sein Ziel, seine Selbständigkeit.* 6th ed. Stuttgart: Calwer, 1963.

_____. *Das Evangelium nach Markus und Lukas.* Stuttgart: Calwer, 1954.

Schniewind, Julius D. *Das Evangelium nach Matthäus.* Neue Testament Deutsch 2. 11th ed. Göttingen: Vandenhoeck and Ruprecht, 1964.

Schürer, Emil. *A History of the Jewish People in the Time of Jesus Christ (175 B.C.–A.D. 135).* Revised and translated by Geza Vermes et al. 4 vols. 2d rev. ed. Edinburgh: T. and T. Clark, 1973–87.

Schwartz, Daniel R. "Two Pauline Allusions to the Redemptive Mechanism of the Crucifixion." *JBL* 102 (1983): 259–68.

Segal, Judah Benzion. *The Hebrew Passover from the Earliest Times to A.D. 70.* London Oriental Series 13. London: Oxford University Press, 1963.

Senior, Donald. "The Death of Jesus and the Resurrection of the Holy Ones (Mt 27:51–53)." *CBQ* 38 (1976): 312–29.

_____. *The Passion of Jesus in the Gospel of Mark.* Wilmington, Del.: Michael Glazier, 1984.

Shepherd, Massey H., Jr. "Are Both the Synoptics and John Correct about the Date of Jesus' Death?" *JBL* 80 (1961): 123–32.

Sherwin-White, A. N. *Roman Society and Roman Law in the New Testament.* New York: Oxford University Press, 1963.

_____. "The Trial of Christ." In *Historicity and Chronology in the New Testament,* ed. Dennis E. Nineham et al., 97–116. London: SPCK, 1965.

Sloyan, Gerard S. *Jesus on Trial: The Development of the Passion Narratives and Their Historical and Ecumenical Implications.* Philadelphia: Fortress, 1973.

_____. "The Last Days of Jesus." *Jud* 20 (1971): 56–68.

Smalley, Stephen S. "Review of *The Trial of Jesus: A Study in the Gospels and Jewish Historiography from 1770 to the Present Day* by David R. Catchpole (Leiden: Brill, 1971)." *EvQ* 45 (1973): 184–85.

Smallwood, E. Mary. "High Priests and Politics in Roman Palestine." *JTS*, n.s. 13 (1962): 14–34.

_____. *The Jews under Roman Rule: From Pompey to Diocletian.* Leiden: Brill, 1976.

Smith, D. Moody. "Mark 15:46: The Shroud of Turin as a Problem of History and Faith." *BA* 46.4 (1983): 251–54.

Smith, Robert H. "Paradise Today: Luke's Passion Narrative." *CurTM* 3 (1976): 323–36.

Smith, Robert Houston. "The Household Lamps of Palestine in New Testament Times." *BA* 29.1 (1966): 2–27.

_____. "The Tomb of Jesus." *BA* 30.3 (1967): 74–90.

Soards, Marion L. "The Silence of Jesus before Herod: An Interpretative Suggestion." *ABR* 33 (1985): 41–45.

Sons, Engelbert. "Die Todesursache bei der Kreuzigung." *SZ* 146 (1950): 60–64.

Staudinger, Hugo. "The Resurrection of Jesus Christ as Saving Event and as 'Object' of Historical Research." *SJT* 36 (1983): 309–26.

Stauffer, Ethelbert. *Die Botschaft Jesu: Damals und Heute.* Bern: Francke, 1959.

_____. *Jerusalem und Rom im Zeitalter Jesu Christi.* Bern: Francke, 1957.

Stott, John R. W. *The Cross of Christ.* Downers Grove, Ill.: Inter-Varsity, 1986.

Strathmann, Hermann. *Das Evangelium nach Johannes.* Neue Testament Deutsch 4. 10th ed. Göttingen: Vandenhoeck and Ruprecht, 1963.

_____. *Das Evangelium nach Markus.* Neue Testament Deutsch 1. 10th ed. Göttingen: Vandenhoeck and Ruprecht, 1963.

Stroud, William. *The Physical Cause of the Death of Christ, and Its Relation to the Principles and Practice of Christianity.* New York: Appleton, 1871.

Sweet, J. P. M. "The Zealots and Jesus." In *Jesus and the Politics of His Day,* ed. Ernst Bammel and C. F. D. Moule, 1–9. New York: Cambridge University Press, 1984.

Sykes, Marjorie H. "The Eucharist as 'Anamnesis.'" *ExpTim* 71 (1959–60): 115–18.

Sylva, Dennis D. "Nicodemus and His Spices (John 19.39)." *NTS* 34.1 (1988): 148–51.

_____. "The Temple Curtain and Jesus' Death in the Gospel of Luke." *JBL* 105 (1986): 239–50.

Tabory, J. "The Passover Eve Ceremony—An Historical Outline." *Immanuel* 12 (1981): 32–42.

Talmon, S. "Messianic Expectations at the Turn of the Era." *Face to Face* 10 (1983): 4–12.

Taylor, Vincent. *The Gospel According to St. Mark.* 2d ed. New York: Macmillan, 1966.

_____. *Jesus and His Sacrifice: A Study of the Passion-Sayings in the Gospels.* New York: Macmillan, 1965.

_____. "The Narrative of the Crucifixion." *NTS* 8.4 (1962): 333–34.

_____. *The Passion Narrative of St. Luke: A Critical and Historical Investigation.* New York: Cambridge University Press, 1972.

Tcherikover, Victor. *Hellenistic Civilization and the Jews.* New York: Atheneum, 1975.

_____. "Was Jerusalem a 'Polis'?" *IEJ* 14 (1964): 61–78.

Throckmorton, Burton H., Jr. "The Longer Reading of Luke 22:19b–20." *ATR* 30 (1948): 55–56.

Torrey, Charles C. "The Foundry of the Second Temple at Jerusalem." *JBL* 60 (1936): 247–60.

_____. "In the Fourth Gospel the Last Supper Was the Paschal Meal." *JQR* 42 (1951–52): 243–44.

Tristram, H. B. *Natural History of the Bible.* London: SPCK, 1867.

Trudinger, L. Paul. "'Eli, Eli, Lama Sabachthani': A Cry of Dereliction? or Victory?" *JETS* 17 (1974): 235–38.

Turner, Nigel. *Grammatical Insights into the New Testament.* Edinburgh: T. and T. Clark, 1966.

Tzaferis, Vassilios A. "Crucifixion: The Archaeological Evidence." *BAR* 11.1 (Jan./Feb. 1985): 44–53.

_____. "Jewish Tombs at and near Giv'at ha-Mivtar, Jerusalem." *IEJ* 20 (1970): 18–32.

Upton, John A. "The Potter's Field and the Death of Judas." *CJ* 8.6 (1982): 213–19.

Vanderkam, James C. "The Origin, Character, and Early History of the 364-Day Calendar: A Reassessment of Jaubert's Hypothesis." *CBQ* 41 (1979): 390–411.

van Unnik, W. C. "Jesus the Christ." *NTS* 8.2 (1962): 101–16.

Vardaman, Jerry. "A New Inscription Which Mentions Pilate as 'Prefect.'" *JBL* 81 (1962): 70–71.

Verdman, P. J. "Sanhedrin and Gabbatha." *ASTI* 2 (1963): 118–20; 6 (1967): 132–34.

Vermes, Geza. *The Dead Sea Scrolls in English.* Baltimore: Penguin, 1970 reprint.

_____. "The Jesus Notice of Josephus Re-examined." *JJS* 38 (1987): 1–10.

_____. *Jesus the Jew: A Historian's Reading of the Gospel.* New York: Macmillan, 1973.

Verrall, A. W. "Christ before Herod: Luke XXIII 1–16." *JTS* 10 (1908–09): 321–53.

Wacholder, Ben Zion. "Chronomessianism: The Timing of Messianic Movements and the Calendar of Sabbatical Cycles." *HUCA* 46 (1975): 201–18.

Walaskay, Paul W. "The Trial and Death of Jesus in the Gospel of Luke." *JBL* 94 (1975): 81–93.

Walker, Norman. "The Reckoning of Hours in the Fourth Gospel." *NovT* 4 (1960): 69–73.

Wallace, James E. "The Trial of Jesus: A Legal Response." *TT* 28 (1972): 466–69.

Wansbrough, Henry. "Suffered under Pontius Pilate." *Scr* 44 (1966): 84–96.

Wead, David W. "We Have a Law." *NovT* 11 (1969): 185–89.

Weber, Hans-Ruedi. *The Cross: Tradition and Interpretation of the Crucifixion of Jesus in the World of the New Testament.* Grand Rapids: Eerdmans, 1978.

Wenham, John W. *Easter Enigma: Are the Resurrection Accounts in Conflict?* Grand Rapids: Zondervan, 1984.

_____. "How Many Cock-Crowings? The Problem of Harmonistic Text-Variants." *NTS* 25.4 (1979): 523–25.

Westcott, Brooke Foss. *The Gospel According to St. John.* Grand Rapids: Baker, 1980 reprint.

Whitaker, J. Ryland. "The Physical Cause of the Death of Our Lord." *Catholic Medical Guardian* 13 (1935): 83–107.

Wikenhauser, Alfred. *New Testament Introduction.* New York: Herder, 1963.

Wilcox, Max. "The Denial-Sequence in Mark XIV. 26–31, 66–72." *NTS* 17.4 (1971): 426–36.

_____. "'Upon the Tree'—Deut. 21:22–23 in the New Testament." *JBL* 96 (1977): 85–99.

Wilkinson, John. "The Incident of the Blood and Water in John 19.34." *SJT* 28 (1975): 149–72.

_____. *Jerusalem as Jesus Knew It: Archaeology as Evidence.* London: Thames and Hudson, 1978.

_____. "Leprosy and Leviticus: The Problem of Description and Identification." *SJT* 30 (1977): 153–69.

_____. "The Physical Cause of the Death of Christ." *ExpTim* 83 (1971–72): 104–7.

_____. "The Seven Words from the Cross." *SJT* 17 (1964): 69–82.

Wilson, William Riley. *The Execution of Jesus: A Judicial, Literary, and Historical Investigation.* New York: Scribner, 1970.

Winter, Paul. *On the Trial of Jesus.* Berlin: Walter de Gruyter, 1961.

_____. "The Trial of Jesus and the Competence of the Sanhedrin." *NTS* 10.4 (1964): 494–99.

Wood, Bryant G. "Jerusalem Report: Israeli Scholars Date Garden Tomb to the Israelite Monarchy." *Bible and Spade* 11 (1982): 30–32.

Yadin, Yigael. "Epigraphy and Crucifixion." *IEJ* 23 (1973): 18–22.

_____. "Pesher Nahum (4QpNahum) Reconsidered." *IEJ* 21 (1971): 1–12.

_____. ed. *Jerusalem Revealed: Archaeology in the Holy City, 1968–1974.* Jerusalem: Israel Exploration Society, 1975.

Yamauchi, Edwin M. "The Crucifixion and Docetic Christology." *CTQ* 46 (1981): 1–20.

_____. "Historical Notes on the Trial and Crucifixion of Jesus Christ." *ChrT* 15 (April 9, 1971): 634–39.

_____. "Passover Plot or Easter Triumph? A Critical Review of H. Schonfield's Recent Theory." *GR* 10 (1967): 150–60.

_____. "Sociology, Scripture and the Supernatural." *JETS* 27 (1984): 169–92.

Young, Edward J. *The Book of Isaiah.* Vol. 1. Grand Rapids: Eerdmans, 1965.

Zahn, Theodor. *Grundriss der Geschichte des Lebens Jesu.* Leipzig: A. Deichert, 1928.

Zehnle, Richard. "The Salvific Character of Jesus' Death in Lucan Soteriology." *TS* 30 (1969): 420–44.

Zeitlin, Solomon. *Who Crucified Jesus?* New York: Harper, 1942.

Zias, Joseph, and Eliezer Sekeles. "The Crucified Man from Giv'at ha-Mivtar: A Reappraisal." *IEJ* 35 (1985): 22–27.

Zimmerli, Walther, and Joachim Jeremias. *The Servant of God.* SBT 20. London: SCM, 1957.

Zohary, Michael. *Plants of the Bible.* New York: Cambridge University Press, 1982.

Scripture Index

Genesis

2–3—135
3:15—11, 70, 154
9:27a—11
12—12
12:3—11
13:10—135
15:13–16—11
17:1–8—11
22:18—11
24:13—52

Exodus

1–12—58
2:24—11
10:21–23—136
12—51
12:1–11—52
12:1–20—47
12:6—53
12:6–8—47, 55
12:7—52
12:8—60
12:13—52
12:15–20—47
12:26–27—60
12:27—52
12:42—70
12:46—148
19:4—12
19:16–18—143
20:2—12
21:32—42
24:1–8—62

24:8—62
26:37—141
30:11–16—35
34:25—52
38:18—141

Leviticus

15:19–24—105
16—142
17:11—62
17:14—62
23:5–8—47
24:10–16—89, 101
24:14—183 n. 36
24:16—116
25:8–55—14

Numbers

3:26—141
9:7—52
9:12—148
9:13—52
12:3—29
12:14—90
15:35–36—183 n. 36
19:2—28
19:16—105
28:16–25—47
31:19—105
35:30—86

Deuteronomy

7:1–6—12
7:7—12

13—116, 135
16:1–8—47, 51
16:2—48
16:3—61
16:4—105
16:5–7—67
17:6—86
17:14–20—14, 88
18:15–18—29, 31
19:15—86
21:3—28
21:6–9—119
21:22–23—144, 159–61
23:18—97
25:2–3—183 n. 24
25:9—90

Joshua

8:29—144–45

Judges

16:16—70

1 Samuel

1:1—148
8:10–18—14
20:13—93

2 Samuel

3:9—93
7:12–16—14, 22, 30, 88, 96
7:14—88
15:24–37—80

Miscellaneous Ancient Writings

Subject Index